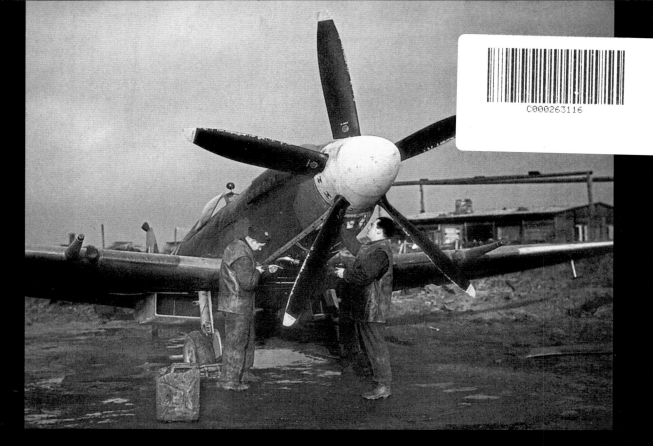

BEGINNING OF THE END

The Supermarine Spitfire was many things but it was never a successful long-range fighter. Therefore, just as the sight of short-range Messerschmitt Bf 109s flying right over London had symbolised the terrifying extent of Adolf Hitler's power in 1940, so too did the appearance of Spitfires over Berlin in 1945 herald the hour of his final defeat.

Spitfires Over Berlin: The Air War in Europe 1945 tells the story of the last four months of the Second World War through the experiences of airmen on both sides of the conflict. Many myths and half-truths have grown up around the events of those final months – like the 'final dogfight' of the war that supposedly took place between an L-4H Grasshopper and a Fi 156 Storch. In fact this was far from the war's last aerial combat.

From a starting point just beyond Germany's borders on January 1, the British and American air forces cut through the Luftwaffe's flagging strength from the west, while the Russians hammered it from the east, until both sides met and Spitfires encountered Yaks over the German capital. Yet even then, Bf 109s, Fw 190s and Me 262s continued to fly sorties until the bitter end on the evening of May 8.

Setting out to write the story of the closing chapter of the air war in Europe, I was surprised to discover that while some tales had been told before individually, and several overviews had been written, no one had previously brought a collection of stories together to illustrate all the diverse operations and activities taking place right across the warzone at roughly the same time.

In fact, in some cases, such as destruction of B-17G 42-31333 'Wee Willie', the operations of 350 Squadron's Spitfires over Berlin in 1945 and the callous murder of P-51 pilot Captain Chester E Coggeshall Jr, very little seemed to have been written before in any detail.

And one fact seems to have been entirely overlooked by history: who did score the very last aerial victory of the war in Europe? Different claims have been reported but can we now say conclusively who did the shooting and who was shot.

This publication is not a full history of the period – rather it seeks to give a flavour of the furious and destructive days of aerial combat that led to the Luftwaffe's, and Germany's, outright defeat on all fronts.

The actions of those who fought with bravery and determination at the end to bring the bloodiest air war the world has ever seen to its final conclusion should never be forgotten.

Dan Sharp

CONTENTS

FRONT COVER:
Spitfire over Berlin by Mark Postlethwaite. Pilot Officer Des Watkins flying Spitfire XIV RB155 of 350 Squadron shoots down a Focke-Wulf Fw 190 over the outskirts of Berlin on the evening of April 20, 1945. For the full story see page 98.

AUTHOR: Dan Sharp
CONTRIBUTORS: Andrew Arthy, Clive Rowley
DESIGN: atg-media.com
REPROGRAPHICS: Jonathan Schofield and Simon Duncan
PUBLISHER: Dan Savage
MARKETING MANAGER: Charlotte Park
COMMERCIAL DIRECTOR: Nigel Hole

PUBLISHED BY: Mortons Media Group Ltd, Media Centre, Morton Way, Horncastle, Lincolnshire LN9 6JR.
Tel. 01507 529529

THANKS TO: Serge Bonge, Greg Lance-Watkins, John Mooney, PATS, Mark Postlethwaite, Alexander Power, John Sharratt, J Kurt Spence, Mark Styling and Stephen Walton

PRINTED BY: William Gibbons and Sons, Wolverhampton

ISBN: 978-1-909128-69-9

ABOVE: A Focke-Wulf Fw 190F-8 of II./SG 1 fires rockets at Soviet tanks amid the ruins of Berlin during the last days of the Second World War. Based in Tutow, 110 miles to the north, the unit was heavily involved in the siege of the German capital. Painting by MARK POSTLETHWAITE

LUFTWAFFE REBORN

THE GERMAN AIR FORCE AT THE BEGINNING OF 1945

Intensive bombing had crippled the German aircraft industry by the summer of 1944 as the Third Reich crumbled on all fronts. But even as disaster threatened, the genius of Armaments and War Production Minister Albert Speer was bringing about a near miraculous revival of the Luftwaffe…

R ome fell to the Allies on June 4, 1944, and two days later the Normandy landings of D-Day heralded the beginning of the Second World War's end game.

Within months, the Western Allies had broken the deadlock around their landing sites on the French coast and were advancing rapidly inland, with the Soviets simultaneously driving in hard from the east.

V-1 flying bombs and then V-2 missiles began hitting targets in Britain, but Germany's air force was struggling to oppose those of the British, Americans and Soviets. In France, airfields held since the Blitzkrieg of 1940 were quickly swallowed up by the Allied advance.

Hundreds of aircraft that had been newly delivered to front line Luftwaffe units had to be abandoned during the summer of 1944 and units suffered casualties as pilots were shot down attempting to switch airfields.

Along the western fringes of Germany, surviving air and ground crew arrived at airstrips in a chaotic jumble of badly under-strength groups and squadrons. Tons of equipment had been destroyed or left behind – not just aircraft but also vehicles, spare parts, tools and a wide variety of other valuable gear.

It was a mess and it was made worse by the fact that the German aircraft manufacturers, concentrated at 27 easily identifiable and well known production centres such as Messerschmitt's Augsburg plant and Focke-Wulf's Bremen factory, had been repeatedly hit by the bombers

MAIN PICTURE: Smoke rises from the site of
Focke-Wulf's Marienburg aircraft factory during a USAAF raid
on October 9, 1943. As 1944 arrived, the raids grew in
frequency and intensity but plans were already being drawn
up to blunt their effectiveness and allow a renaissance of
wartime aircraft production in Germany.

RIGHT: At the beginning of 1944 the Luftwaffe was beginning to run out of aircraft as the Allied bombing campaign razed all the major German manufacturing facilities. It was Armaments and War Production Minister Albert Speer, formerly Adolf Hitler's architect, who came up with a way to thwart the Allies and dramatically increase production. He is pictured here on the right, walking with Hitler..

ABOVE RIGHT: With components being moved around Germany in a complex ballet of production, assembly lines for both the Fw 190, as pictured here, and the Bf 109 multiplied exponentially.

BELOW RIGHT: Rows of Messerschmitt Bf 109G-6 fighters are assembled. The G-6 was mass produced in numbers that dwarfed almost every other aircraft type in Germany.

BELOW: Dispersing aircraft production to small workshops such as this in backwater towns and villages gave the Luftwaffe all the Messerschmitt Bf 109s and Fw 190s it could handle and then some.

of both the USAAF and the RAF. From the autumn of 1943 onwards those 27 centres had been bombed again and again in a concentrated effort by the Allies to destroy Germany's aircraft manufacturing capability.

Seeing the catastrophic damage they had caused and given the number of German fighters that had been shot down, destroyed on the ground or captured, the British and Americans came to believe that the Luftwaffe was a spent force.

But they had reckoned without Albert Speer, the minister responsible for managing Germany's wartime economy, and his Ministry of War Production. He realised that there was a highly complex but also highly effective way to prevent the Allies from destroying aircraft factories – by dispersing them to large number of much smaller sites.

Most of the 27 centres remained but they were rapidly supplemented by more than 700 additional plants set up in tunnels and caves, forests and on the premises of

companies that ostensibly did something else – such as furniture makers and cigarette machine manufacturers.

By carefully orchestrating this vast web of smaller scale producers, Speer was able to not only restore production to pre-bombing levels but also to actually increase it. A total of 3821 new combat aircraft were delivered in September 1944, the highest monthly figure ever achieved by the German aircraft industry.

Not only had production capacity been increased, it had also been concentrated on the aircraft most urgently needed for Germany's defence – single-seat fighters. Four out of every five of the new machines were Messerschmitt Bf 109s and Focke-Wulf Fw 190s.

Types such as the Arado Ar 196 maritime reconnaissance aircraft, the DFS 230 and Gotha Go 242 gliders, troublesome Heinkel He 177 bomber, the reliable Junkers Ju 52 transport and the Ju 290 long-range transport were removed from production schedules. These were followed in September by even front line types such as the Henschel Hs 129 and Ju 87 Stuka ground attack aircraft, the Messerschmitt Me 410 heavy fighter and the venerable Heinkel He 111 bomber.

Narrowing production down to little more than two types had its drawbacks too however. With supply lines geared increasingly towards just Bf 109 and Fw 190 components, it was difficult to get advanced types into mass production.

Just 18 of the new Arado Ar 234 jet bomber/ reconnaissance aircraft were built in September 1944, along with 35 Messerschmitt Me 163 rocket-powered interceptors, 91 Messerschmitt Me 262 jet fighters and 28 Heinkel He 219 Uhu night fighters.

There were other problems that gave cause for concern too. Germany's petrochemical industry was another regular target for Allied bombing raids and although the Luftwaffe had accumulated significant reserves – it had 580,000 tons of fuel in May 1944 – these were quickly depleted by ongoing operations so that by September 1944 it had just 180,000 tons remaining.

One seemingly minor problem that was also becoming a major headache was the weakness of German aircraft tyres. Unable to receive imported rubber, Germany was forced to rely on low grade synthetic and reclaimed rubber tyres which were more prone to burst under the weight of a heavy aircraft. This problem was particularly acute with jet aircraft, which had a higher landing speed.

In spite of all this, however, Germany now had a formidable fighter force at its disposal once again.

THE GREAT BLOW

The sudden influx of Bf 109s and Fw 190s in the autumn of 1944 meant all of the Luftwaffe's depleted fighter units from France could be rebuilt with spare aircraft to hold in reserve. But this was just the beginning. By shortening the training courses of new pilots and drawing in pilots from dissolved bomber and heavy fighter units, the single-seat fighter Gruppen were expanded from three Staffeln to four.

In mid-November 1944, the Luftwaffe's units had 3300 serviceable fighters available, compared to just 1900 two months earlier.

Astonished by this rapid reversal in his fortunes, the Luftwaffe's General of Fighters, Generalmajor Adolf Galland, came up with a daring plan that he believed would put a stop to the ruinous USAAF daylight bombing raids that were steadily crippling Germany.

With a sufficiently overwhelming force of fighters deployed all at once in ideal conditions, he hoped to inflict devastating damage on the American bomber fleet. If enough bombers could be destroyed all in one go, he reasoned, the Americans might rethink their strategy and would certainly have to call a halt to operations for some time while replacements were brought over from the US.

He called this operation 'The Great Blow' and was somewhat surprised when the Luftwaffe's high command approved its implementation almost without question.

In his autobiography, The First and the Last, Galland wrote: "The Great Blow had been carefully planned and worked out in all details. All commodores and commanders were called together for a rehearsal at Treuenbrietzen, during which four or five different action and approach flights were practised with all variations.

"It was wholly agreed that in the frame of the planned action the following points had to be achieved. First, in the first action at least 2000 fighters in 11 combat formations were to be brought into contact with the approaching bomber formation.

"Second, during the fly-in and the return of the enemy about another 150 fighters of the Luftwaffe Command West were to be sent up. Third, in the second action another 500 fighters were to be brought into contact with the enemy.

"Fourth, about 100 night fighters were to screen the borders toward Sweden and Switzerland to catch damaged or straggling single bombers. Fifth, to shoot down an approximate total of 400-500 four-engined bombers against a loss of about 400 aircraft and about 100-150 pilots.

"This was going to be the largest and most decisive air battle of the war. On November 12, 1944, the entire fighter arm was ready for action: 18 fighter wings with 3700 aircraft and pilots. A fighting force such as the Luftwaffe

> *He called this operation 'The Great Blow' and was somewhat surprised when the Luftwaffe's high command approved its implementation almost without question.*

ABOVE: The Heinkel He 177, Germany's only heavy bomber, was axed to make more room on production lines for the Bf 109 and Fw 190.

BELOW: The sheer space on Germany's production lines occupied by the Bf 109 made it difficult for manufacturers to get new types brought into service – ultimately to the detriment of the Luftwaffe when it faced advanced Allied types. Very few developments were viewed as important enough to risk the disruption of 109 production.

ABOVE: The Luftwaffe's general of fighters, Generalmajor Adolf Galland, pictured right, was amazed by the huge numbers of aircraft suddenly being delivered to his units during the autumn of 1944 and quickly came up with a plan he believed would see his rebuilt forces strike a crippling blow against the USAAF Eighth Air Force bomber fleet. This would give German industry a chance to recover and might even force the Americans to stop daylight bomber raids.

RIGHT: Another of the many types retired as aircraft production was focused on just two main fighters was the Henschel Hs 129 ground-attack aircraft. It had earned a fearsome reputation as a tank-buster but Albert Speer believed it was simply no longer possible for Germany to have dozens of different machines in production at once.

BELOW: Generalmajor Adolf Galland was a skilled and flamboyant fighter pilot who was also a huge fan of Mickey Mouse and cultivated an image of cigar-chomping bravado which made him popular with his men. His Great Blow plan to destroy a large portion of the American bomber force resulted in huge reserves of fighters being built up – only for Hitler to find a different use for them.

had never possessed before. More than 3000 of these were expecting The Great Blow.

"Now it was a question of awaiting favourable weather. Good weather was one of the essentials for this mass action. It was a difficult decision to hold back the defensive fighters, which were standing by in the face of the air armadas dropping gigantic bomb loads daily. But contrary to my previous experience the leaders kept calm and did not insist on vain and costly forced action."

Galland believed that by this stage the Allies had an inkling of what The Great Blow entailed, particularly since large numbers of Luftwaffe fighters were now being sent up on a daily basis for training flights, but he held his nerve in readiness for the ideal moment to strike.

The events of November 2, 1944, proved to be his undoing however. That day 1174 bombers and 968 fighters from the USAAF's Eighth Air Force, split into five groups, attacked a selection of oil industry and rail targets across Germany. It was a fairly typical mission for the Americans.

The Luftwaffe put up a large fighter force to oppose them – 490 fighters from 10 Gruppen. The Germans initially had some success; armoured bomber-killer Fw 190 Sturmbocks of IV.(Sturm)/JG 3 shot down 11 bombers from the 91st Bomb Group and destroyed another two by ramming them. II./JG 4 downed another nine bombers, this time from the 457th Bomb Group.

In both instances, American escort fighters then showed up and inflicted heavy casualties on the unwieldy attackers. There had been 61 Sturmbock aircraft taking part in the defensive mission and 31 of them were shot down by P-51 Mustangs. In total, the Luftwaffe destroyed 40 of the 1174 bombers and 16 of the 968 fighters, for a loss of 120 of its own fighters.

The Führer himself reviewed these figures at length four days later, on November 6, and concluded that the outcome of the defensive action had been "thoroughly unsatisfactory". It seemed clear to him that repeating the exercise on a much greater scale by allowing Galland's Great Blow to proceed was likely to see much greater losses for a similarly ineffectual result.

Instead, he approved another plan drawn up by his generals which involved using Germany's similarly rebuilt

army to strike a decisive blow on the ground against the British and Americans in the west, with the fighter force providing aerial cover and support. Operation Wacht am Rhein or 'Watch on the Rhine' would involve seven Panzer divisions – some 200,000 men.

Its objectives were primarily to capture the strategically important harbour of Antwerp and to drive a wedge between the British and American ground forces.

When the tanks began to roll, the Luftwaffe's fighters would simultaneously launch an attack on the Allies' forward air bases to put them out of action. This was Operation Bodenplatte or 'Baseplate'. Next they would provide what amounted to an air exclusion zone over the battlefield to prevent Allied aircraft from harassing the advancing ground forces and give close air support when necessary during the operation.

When Galland was informed that The Great Blow had been cancelled in favour of Watch on the Rhine, he was horrified. What seemed, on paper, to be a sensible and reasonable use of his rebuilt fighter force

> *When Galland was informed that The Great Blow had been cancelled in favour of Watch on the Rhine, he was horrified.*

was, he knew, a recipe for disaster.

He wrote: "In the middle of November I received an alarming order, the whole impact of which I could not foresee. The fighter reserves were to be prepared for action on the front where a great land battle was expected in the west. This was incredible!

"The whole training had been aimed at action in the defence of the Reich. All new pilots should have had some training in the totally different conditions at the front, but petrol shortage prevented this. The experience and standard of the unit leaders and pilots could be regarded as just passable for the defence of the Reich, but for action at the front they were absolutely out of the question.

"Besides, the squadrons had now without exception a strength of 70 aircraft and were therefore much too large for the airfields at the front. On November 20 the transfer to the west was ordered regardless of my scruples and objections."

The beginning of the attack had been slated for November 27 but was delayed for more than two weeks while sufficient fuel reserves were gathered.

WATCH ON THE RHINE

In readiness for Operation Baseplate, the Luftwaffe units due to participate flew to their forward airfields at low altitude, under the Allies' radar, and maintained radio silence. The element of surprise was vital. Everything was ready by December 14 and on that day the unit commanders were gathered together at the headquarters of Jagdkorps II near Altenkirchen, western Germany, by Generalmajor Dietrich Peltz, the mission commander.

He outlined the plan in detail – to attack 16 airfields in Belgium, France and Holland at the same time with 1000 fighters, causing maximum damage before turning around and heading for home, hopefully with minimal casualties.

Watch on the Rhine was launched at 5.30am on December 16 with a thunderous 90 minute artillery bombardment from around 1600 guns across a front that stretched for some 80 miles. Then thousands of 6th Panzer Army troops moved forwards.

The code words that would have launched Operation Baseplate were not broadcast, however, and the Luftwaffe's simultaneous attack on 16 airfields did not take place. The airmen were stood down due to heavy banks

of low cloud and thick fog over the battlefield. Neither the Germans nor the Allies were able to mount any significant airborne operations.

An attempt by the Germans to mount an airborne assault using paratroopers dropping from Junkers Ju 52s was a disaster and the poor visibility extended into December 17 too. The Luftwaffe flew 600 sorties on the 17th but lost 55 pilots in various air combats. For the next six days, while battle raged on the ground, aircraft on both sides sat idle and every airfield was covered with snow.

The Watch on the Rhine assault ground to a halt on December 20, with the German advance having created a 40 mile deep 'bulge' in the front line, but the weather did not let up until December 24, Christmas Eve 1944, when it finally relented and a series of furious air battles began.

Again, the Luftwaffe suffered severe casualties – 85 pilots killed in a single day. The clear weather presented the Allied bomber forces with a golden opportunity too and 11 of the Luftwaffe's forward fighter bases were badly hit.

The Battle of the Bulge was now well under way and after two weeks of appalling weather and appalling casualties, the Luftwaffe's commanders had all but forgotten about the plan to attack Allied forward airfields. The huge fighter force assembled for Adolf Galland's Great Blow was being steadily worn away and the remainder was engaged in a fight to the death with a numerically far superior foe.

So it came as something of a surprise when the codes triggering the commencement of Operation Baseplate were broadcast on December 31, 1944. ●

ABOVE: Two Waffen-SS soldiers cross the road near the Belgian village of Poteau after ambushing an American armoured column. An M8 Greyhound armoured car is still burning in the background. This was early in the morning on December 18, 1944 – the third day of Operation Watch on the Rhine, also known as the Battle of the Bulge.

LEFT: Another photo from the ambush at Poteau. The weather was bitterly cold and soldiers on both sides were hampered by the weather during the first week of the battle.

BELOW: A German Panzerkampfwagen Tiger Ausf B heavy tank passes a column of captured American soldiers in Belgium in December 1944. By December 20, the German advance had ground to a halt and fierce fighting ensued. In attempting to support and cover ground units, the Luftwaffe's carefully husbanded reserves of pilots, aircraft and fuel were steadily depleted. Yet on the last day of 1944, the order was given to launch Operation Baseplate – what ought to be a decisive and devastating attack on the Allied fighter and fighter-bomber force.

A column of prisoners from the US Army's 99th Division are marched along the street in Merlscheid, Belgium, in December 1944. The Americans were captured by the German 3rd Parachute Division on the first day of the Battle of the Bulge – when the Luftwaffe was to have launched an opening attack on Allied advanced landing grounds.

ALL-OUT ATTACK

JANUARY 1, 1945: OPERATION BASEPLATE

It was nearly two weeks since the beginning of Operation Watch on the Rhine – the Battle of the Bulge – and the plan to begin it with a large scale assault on the Allies' forward air bases had been almost forgotten. Then the code words activating Operation Baseplate were transmitted at last…

L uftwaffe units on the front line in the west received two code words in the early afternoon of December 31, 1944: Varus and Teutonicus.

Varus was the signal indicating that Operation Baseplate would be called into effect within the next 24 hours and Teutonicus gave authority for senior officers to brief their pilots on the mission objectives and get all their fighters armed and ready for takeoff.

At 6.30pm the final code word was given: Hermann. This was accompanied by confirmation of the date of the attack, January 1, and the time that the aircraft would be expected to reach their targets: 9.20am.

The lineup of Luftwaffe units was formidable, despite losses already sustained while supporting the initial phase of Watch on the Rhine. It included most of JG 1, JG 2, JG 3, JG 4, JG 6, JG 11, JG 26, JG 27, JG 53, JG 54, JG 77 and SG 4 – 12 Geschwader with 36 Gruppen in total, operating around 850 fighters and fighter-bombers between them. Among these were around 110 Focke-Wulf Fw 190D-9 'long noses' and 50 Fw 190F-8s, the latter being flown exclusively by SG 4. The remainder were a mixture of Fw 190A-8s and A-9s, and Messerschmitt Bf 109G-10s, G-14s and K-4s, plus at least one G-6.

In addition, 24 Me 262A-2 jet fighter-bombers of I./KG 51 and 10 Arado Ar 234B-2 jet bombers of E.Staffel III./KG 76 were due to take part.

Rather than allow the fighter formations to make their own way to their targets, it was decided that Junkers Ju 88s seconded from night fighter units should be allocated to help the fighters form up and then guide them there. A total of 72 Ju 88s were used for this purpose, with two each per Gruppe.

The formations were to attack 17 airfields. Five were in Holland: Eindhoven (Advanced Landing Ground B-78), Gilze-Rijen (B-77), Heesch (B-88), Woensdrecht (B-79) and Volkel (B-80), and one was in France, Metz-Frescaty (Y-34).

The remainder were in Belgium: Gent-St Denis Westrem (B-61), Grimbergen (mostly abandoned, although the Germans did not realise this at the time), Maldegem (B-65), Melsbroek (B-58), Ophoven (Y-32), Ursel (B-67), Asch (Y-29), Deurne (B-70), Evere (B-56), Le Culot (A-89/Y-10) and St Trond (A-92).

> *"The first casualty was Feldwebel Heinz-Jürgen Kilian of 3./JG 1."*

Based at these airfields were 58 RAF squadrons from 2, 83 and 84 Groups of the 2nd Tactical Air Force, variously operating Hawker Typhoons and Tempests, Spitfire IXs, XIVs and XVIs, Mustang IAs and IIs, Mitchell IIs, Wellington XIIIs and Mosquito XVJs. In addition, there were 31 squadrons from the USAAF's Ninth Air Force – 24 of them operating P-47 Thunderbolts, six P-51 Mustangs and a single photo recon squadron flying F-5 Lightnings.

The 2nd Tactical Air Force had been moved on to the Continent during the autumn of 1944 to provide ground forces with constant aerial support as they advanced through territories formerly occupied by the Germans. The USAAF units were under the operational control of the RAF.

First thing in the morning on January 1, 1945, most of these aircraft were likely to be on the ground and it was hoped that they would present easy targets for the attacking forces.

At 8.12am, 23 Fw 190s of I./JG 1 took off from Twenthe in Holland on a course that would take it over Ursel and Maldegem. Their Ju 88 guides were already airborne, waiting

for them. Three minutes later, the dozen or so Bf 109s of III./JG 1 also took off, and followed its Ju 88s along roughly the same course.

At first, as the two Gruppen flew along just 330ft above the snow-covered Dutch countryside, nothing stirred. Then the German flak batteries along the route, which had not been pre-warned about the attack due to the strict secrecy with which it had been organised, opened fire on them.

The first casualty was Feldwebel Heinz-Jürgen Kilian of 3./JG 1. He succeeded in bailing out as his flak-damaged aircraft plunged towards the ground, but at 330ft there was no way his parachute could have opened in time to save him.

Unteroffizier Egon Comtesse's died after his aircraft was hit and crashed into the sea and Oberstleutnant Herbert

ABOVE: Oberfähnrich Wilhelm Ade of 2./JG 1 battle with Spitfires close to B-65 Maldegem airfield.

RIGHT: The Fw 190A-8 flown by Wilhelm Ade on January 1, 1945, WNr. 960553 'Black 3'.

Ihlefeld managed to belly land his Fw 190 after it took serious but not immediately fatal flak damage. Unteroffizier Heinz Böhmer was killed when his 'Yellow 15' was also shot down by flak.

Following on behind, III./JG 1 was also hit by the flak gunners but this time it was the leading Ju 88 that went down first. The pilot, Leutnant Josef Hettlich, was killed when the aircraft crash-landed on an area of flooded land. The other two crew members were seriously injured but survived. III./JG 1's second Ju 88 was then also destroyed by flak, this time with all three crew members killed.

There was another problem when the Ju 88s they had been following peeled off and disappeared. Fw 190 pilot Oberfähnrich Wilhelm Ade later recalled: "We flew from the Zuiderzee to the coast where the coastal batteries had not been informed and they opened fire. We lost more aircraft at that stage than we did later. The Ju 88 was still leading us so we did not watch where we were as we usually did.

"Suddenly this Ju 88 turned away and we had to find the target for ourselves."

At the last turning point of I./JG 1's route, the four Fw 190s of 4. Staffel broke off and headed for Ursel while the remainder – down to around 12 fighters – flew directly towards Maldegem. The airfield was rather closer than expected, however, and the aircraft initially overshot it.

Ade remembered: "I was already over the airfield with my Staffel before I could react. We banked and went in. I remember seeing about three four-engine bombers at Maldegem. Together with my Staffel, I followed the others. Now we flew no longer next to each other, but behind each other.

"Stupidly enough, we still had to maintain radio silence and therefore could not give any instructions. We simply had to assume that the others did the same as we did. I

> *"The pilot, Leutnant Josef Hettlich, was killed when the aircraft crash-landed on an area of flooded land. The other two crew members were seriously injured but survived. "*

do not understand why we had to maintain radio silence over the target.

"They knew we were there so what was the point? No one dared to break radio silence fearing repercussions. Later I discovered that my radio hadn't worked at all. At this stage we were still with about 10 aircraft. Everything was covered in smoke now and it was difficult to orientate.

"Strafing the airfield, I fired at the parked aircraft, achieved hits at some of them and pulled up again. There was a considerable mix-up over the airfield and aircraft of 1. Staffel and even of II. Gruppe mixed with my Schwarm. It seems that we also flew over St Denis-Westrem. Suddenly somebody broke the radio silence and shouted: 'Spitfires!' and I thought 'This one is for me'.

"I got hits on the Spitfire but could not follow him as my fuel indicator already showed that I had to return. Later a 4. Staffel pilot confirmed my victory. I banked to the right and suddenly I was alone. I looked around for other pilots of my Staffel but looking at my fuel indicator I had to fly back to base if I did not want to end up a POW."

Although I./JG 1 seemingly had little success at Maldegem, the Bf 109s of III./JG 1 fared much better. They spotted rows of Spitfires belonging to 349 and 485 Squadrons and methodically destroyed them on the ground, one by one. They got 14 in total before running out of ammunition and having to depart. The Gruppe's only loss had been when the Bf 109 flown by Lt Anton Guha suffered engine failure and he was forced to make a belly landing before being captured by the British.

There had been no anti-aircraft batteries at Maldegem and although the RAF pilots, many still wearing their pyjamas,

BELOW: Burned out remains of a Spitfire IX – one of 12 destroyed during the JG 1 attack on Maldegem. Most of them belonged to 485 Squadron, which lost nearly all of its aircraft.

ABOVE: Boeing B-17G-40-BO Flying Fortress 42-97059 'Marsha Sue' of the 533rd Bomb Squadron, 381st Bomb Group, was another four-engine aircraft destroyed at St Denis-Westrem. It had made a forced landing at the airfield on December 12 and was still there when the January 1 attack commenced.

BELOW: This Short Stiring V, serial LJ986, 8Z-Y, was another St Denis casualty.

or sweaters and underpants, opened fire with revolvers and rifles, none of the attackers were hit.

When 4. Staffel got to Ursel, having lost one of their number to anti-aircraft fire, they shot up a B-17, two Lancasters and a Mosquito – seriously damaging all four.

After the confusion of the attack, the survivors of I. and III./JG 1 tried to make their way home. Most had become separated and were flying alone. Four were shot down by anti-aircraft fire and a fifth crash-landed after running out of fuel. In total, the two Gruppen lost 16 aircraft and 12 pilots. They had managed to destroy around 20 Allied aircraft and no pilots – a poor exchange rate.

UNWELCOME GUESTS

While their JG 1 comrades were being picked off by 'friendly' flak, something worse still awaited the pilots of II./JG 1 at their target airfield, St Denis Westrem. The unit's 36 Fw 190s took off from Drope airfield at 8.10am and headed for their first turning point near Spakenburg behind their Ju 88 guides.

The journey passed without incident and they turned towards Rotterdam. They followed the coast down to Zeebrugge before heading inland directly towards St Denis Westrem. Arriving at 9.30am, they found the airfield undefended and set about shooting up the many Spitfires and other aircraft parked around it. Soon a pall of dense smoke hung in the air but still the Fw 190s circled the base, strafing every target that presented itself.

This was the scene that greeted the 12 Spitfire IXs of 308 Squadron when they return to the airfield, their home base,

after having set off at 8.15am to bomb a ferry. First to come back was Flight Lieutenant Waclaw Chojnacki in MJ281 ZF-P. He had encountered problems with the aircraft's bomb release mechanism and resolved to come back early and get it sorted out.

As he was coming in to land he saw Fw 190s coming the other way and immediately shot one of them down. Flight Sergeant Bogdan Strobel saw what happened from the ground: "Approximately seven minutes after the attack had begun, I noticed a single Spitfire arriving over base at 2000ft height in a port turn. Three Fw 190s were just coming in to strafe.

"Flt Lt Chojnacki noticed these enemy aircraft and while still in the turn fired at the rearmost from about 800 yards range. The enemy aircraft was hit in the tail and a large part of the tail flew off. The enemy pilot lost control over the aircraft and being low, below 200ft, and diving for the attack hit a tree with its starboard wing, then hit the top of a small building on the airfield perimeter, finally coming to rest inside a B-17 Flying Fortress standing on the ground.

"I lost the Spitfire behind the smoke from the burning Fortress but saw him a moment later chasing another Fw 190 with three other Fw 190s on his tail. The Spitfire broke off his attack with a starboard turn and I last saw him, in that turn, with three Fw 190s on his tail."

The Fw 190 shot down was that of Feldwebel Karl Hahn and he is presumed to have been killed on impact and his body thrown clear, because although his personal possessions were found in the wreck, his body was not. He was never seen alive again.

Despite his courageous lone attack, Flt Lt Chojnacki could not hope to win against such overwhelming odds. The trio of Fw 190s shot him down and he was killed.

Then another solitary Spitfire showed up – this time it was Flight Sergeant Jozef Stanowski who had run short of fuel. He saw the Fw 190s still at it and flew in to attack. He got two before his tank ran completely dry and he was forced to make a belly landing near Ghent. By now the other 10 Spitfires had returned and laid in to the attacking Focke-Wulfs.

Flight Lieutenant Ignacy Olszewski, who had earlier spotted a formation of Fw 190s from JG 26 and JG 54 en

TOP: B-24s burn on the airfield at St Denis-Westrem. Most of the casualties at the airfield were Spitfire IXs, however.

ABOVE: Luftwaffe pilots taking part in Operation Baseplate were ordered to destroy enemy aircraft on the ground but also any stores of ammunition or fuel they could identify. This fuel dump at St Denis made an ideal target.

LEFT: More ruined Spitfires litter the aircraft at Maldegem after the Baseplate attack.

ABOVE: Most of the aircraft destroyed at Eindhoven were Hawker Typhoons – including this 137 Squadron example.

ABOVE MIDDLE PICTURES: The P-47 flown by 1st Lieutenant John W Ginder, 'Hershey Hellion No. 2', when he shot down a Ju 88 that had been acting as a guide for JG 2.

ABOVE: B-78 Eindhoven received the most severe punishment of any Allied airfield during Operation Baseplate. This 400 Squadron photo recon Spitfire PR.XI survived but was damaged.

BELOW: A huge explosion rocks St Trond as P-47s attempt to take-off. Ten Thunderbolts were destroyed on the ground during the attack, with another 31 suffering varying degrees of damage.

Fw 190 each. The last victory was by Pilot Officer Andrzej Dromlewicz. He reported: "I turned towards base and saw one Fw 190 attacking one of our Spitfires.

"I closed in and opened fire with cannon and machine guns from dead astern, range 600-700 yards and at 2000ft height. The enemy aircraft broke off his attack and made a starboard turn. I followed, closing in to approximately 300 yards. I continued to fire in short bursts with all armament and saw hits on the fuselage and wings of the enemy aircraft.

"Then my cannon gave out. The enemy aircraft straightened out and started to climb. I fired another long burst from machine guns only and saw pieces flying off the enemy's starboard wing. The Fw 190 then turned on to its back and the pilot baled out."

This last pilot was Feldwebel Fritz Hofmann of I./JG 1, who had suffered engine problems earlier in the morning, delaying his takeoff my 10 minutes. Before long, without the rest of his unit and the Ju 88 guide, he was lost and when he spotted II./JG 1's aircraft he had decided to tag along.

He successfully parachuted from his doomed Fw 190, which exploded when it hit the ground, only to be captured by angry Belgian civilians who, along with police officers, gave him a severe beating. He was then locked up in a Belgian jail cell for two hours before finally being handed over to the British.

This was not the end of II./JG 2's problems however. Shortly after 308 Squadron returned in force from their early morning mission, another squadron came back – No. 317.

Sergeant Kazimierz Hubert of 317 Squadron reported: "On my way back from the operation I heard over the R/T that B-65 was being attacked by enemy aircraft. The squadron patrolled the area for approximately 10 minutes before another message came through that it was B-61 which was attacked.

"We flew immediately over, arriving over base at 2000ft. I attacked a red-nosed Fw 190 which was flying at 300ft from astern and opened fire with all armament at a range of about 400 yards. I fired one long burst and the Fw 190 caught fire, turned over on its back and crashed in a street in Ghent."

After a series of rapid dogfights, the two squadrons' pilots claimed a total of 14 Fw 190s destroyed. Two Spitfires had been shot down, both of their pilots being killed. Another seven Spitfires either crash-landed or made emergency landings across the area due to damage sustained or through running out of fuel.

Another 18 Spitfires had been destroyed on the ground at St Denis Westrem and five damaged. The B-17 was burned out, alongside a Short Stirling, a quartet of Avro Ansons, a Mosquito and an Auster which had belonged to 85 Group Communications Squadron.

On the flight back to Drope, II./JG 1 suffered still more casualties from Allied flak and battle damage. Seventeen of the 36 Fw 190s that had set out failed to make it back – nearly half.

In total, JG 1 lost 33 aircraft and 24 pilots, only seven of whom had been taken prisoner, the remainder being killed. This compares to around 60 Allied aircraft destroyed and two pilots killed.

A SIMPLE MISTAKE
During the last two weeks of December, I./JG 2 had taken delivery of 54 Focke-Wulf Fw 190D-9s to its base at Merzhausen on the south-western tip of Germany. With one

being destroyed during a bombing raid and others out of action due to mechanical unserviceability, I./JG 2 had 29 available on December 31, plus six Fw 190A-8/R6s.

II./JG 2 had 20 Messerschmitt Bf 109s: 13 G-14s and seven K-4s. III./JG 2 had been even more fortunate with its supply of D-9s and had 34 available, in addition to a single A-9 and five A-8s. It only had enough pilots to fly 28 of the D-9s however. Stab JG 2 had one A-8/R6 and three D-9s.

On January 1, the target of all three Gruppen was St Trond – thought to be home to about 130 Republic P-47 Thunderbolts. Also to be involved in the attack was a specialist ground attack Geschwader, Schlachtgeschwader 4 (SG 4).

This had around 152 Fw 190F-8s on its books but only around 60 were serviceable due to the constant attrition of operations throughout December. The entire assault would be led by Hauptmann Franz Hrdlicka.

On the morning of January 1, I./JG 2's 35 aircraft took off just after 8am and headed for their initial assembly point at Koblenz in western central Germany. III./JG 2 set off at 8.19am, one of its D-9s crashing on takeoff, and II./JG 2 set off a little later, forming up over their airfield at 8.30am. Each formation of fighters was led by a Ju 88 or 188.

Arriving over Koblenz, II./JG 2 aircraft were fired on by German AA gunners but no casualties were taken. En route to Koblenz, another of III./JG 2's D-9s went down. The engine of Unteroffizier Fritz Altpeter's 'Yellow 4' caught fire and he peeled away from the formation but was too low to bail out and died when his aircraft hit the ground.

II./JG 2 was swiftly joined over Koblenz by the other two Gruppen before all three set off, flying separately from one another, for their next waypoint – the Eifel mountain range on the Belgian border.

When they got there at about 9am, their Ju 88s turned for home. One of them, however, was shot down 15 minutes later by 1st Lt John W Ginder of the 10th Fighter Squadron, flying his P-47 'Hershey Hellion No. 2' – which had a Hershey chocolate bar painted on the side of it.

At 9.05am, all JG 2 aircraft were nearing the front line near Malmedy in Belgium. The plan was for them to cross over into enemy territory at right angles to the line, heading straight for St Trond, so that as little time as possible would be spent lingering over the warzone.

Seconds after the 84 aircraft crossed the line flying at about 1000ft they were abruptly subjected to the most intense anti-aircraft fire any of the pilots had ever seen. Attack leader Hauptmann Hrdlicka was apparently unaware that the area around Malmedy and Aachen had been filled with AAA guns by the US Ninth Army in an attempt to protect

the city of Liège, to the west, from the V-1 flying bombs that German artillery units had been regularly launching at it.

As soon as the gunners spotted the huge formation of fighters flying their way they opened fire with devastating consequences. Dozens of fighters were hit and their altitude was so low that few of the pilots could even bail out.

Some of the survivors, now flying individually or in small groups, still attempted to reach St Trond and carry out their mission. However, it is believed that not a single one actually reached the correct target. It is thought that they mistakenly attacked Asch and Ophoven instead. Further casualties were then inflicted by Mustang fighters already in the air and the AAA guns of those airfields.

Making their way home after this unmitigated disaster, still more JG 2 aircraft were shot down or succumbed to damage sustained during the outward flight and crashed. In total, I./JG 2 lost 18 Fw 190s with another six heavily damaged. II./JG 2 lost five Bf 109s and had three damaged, and III./JG 2 lost a staggering 19 Fw 190s with three more damaged – which meant only six came back unscathed out of 28.

JG 2 had paid a heavy price for a simple error of planning.

SG 4 did no better. Its mechanics had trouble with the engines of its battle-weary Fw 190F-8s first thing in the morning, attempting to start them in temperatures as low as minus 10 degrees. Some would not start at all. Twelve of III./SG 4's Fw 190F-8s took off at 8.53am but almost immediately two had to turn back due to mechanical failure.

Then without warning the formation crossed the flight path of another large group of Fw 190s heading west and was forced to dive into cloud to avoid a collision. During this

> ## "Seconds after the 84 aircraft crossed the line flying at about 1000ft they were abruptly subjected to the most intense anti-aircraft fire any of the pilots had ever seen."

TOP: Another shot from St Trond shows the airfield strewn with damaged P-47s after the Luftwaffe's attack.

ABOVE: Smouldering remains of Typhoons litter the airfield at Eindhoven as a ground crewman poses for a photo.

BELOW: Fw 190D-9 pilot Feldwebel Werner Hohenberg of I./JG 2 was shot down on his way home after attacking St Trond.

ABOVE: After making a single pass over St Trond, the engine of 19-year-old Gefreiter Walter Wagner's Fw 190A-8/R2 'White 11' cut out and he was forced to belly-land it just beyond the perimeter of the airfield. The damage caused to the aircraft was minimal, however, and it was quickly repaired by mechanics of the 404th Fighter Group. It is pictured here under 'new ownership'.

ABOVE: A rear-side view of Walter Wagner's 'White 11', WNr. 681497.

BELOW: Having managed to find a replacement BMW 801D-2 engine, the Americans got 'White 11' running again – though they never flew it. After press photographers and a film crew arrived, it became one of the most photographed Fw 190s then in existence.

ATTACK ON EINDHOVEN

The objective of JG 3, led by the famous ace Major Heinz Bär, was Eindhoven – home to the Second Tactical Air Force's 124 and 143 Wings, comprising 137, 181, 182 and 247, and 168, 438, 439 and 440 Squadrons respectively. All eight were equipped with Hawker Typhoon fighter-bombers. Being a substantial ex-Luftwaffe airfield, it also accommodated 39 (Recce) Wing's 400, 414 and 430 Squadrons, flying Spitfires and Mustangs.

First thing in the morning on January 1, 1945, around 300 aircraft were parked out on the airfield, covered with frost. Most of them were in lines and around them were ammo dumps, fuel tanks, vehicles and assorted equipment.

At 8.20am, four Typhoons of 439 Squadron set off for a reconnaissance mission over German-held St Vith.

The first Luftwaffe pilots off the ground to begin attacking their large and inviting base, at 8.22am, were the 19 heavily armed Fw 190A-8/R2s of IV./JG 3 led by Leutnant Siegfried Müller. Once all were airborne, they flew south to meet up with rest of the Geschwader. Shortly thereafter, the 15 Bf 109s of III./JG 3 and the 22 Bf 109s of I./JG 3 took off and headed for the rally point over Lippstadt in western central Germany.

Meeting up on schedule at 8.45am, the three Gruppen formed a single large formation of nearly 60 aircraft, including the Fw 190A-9s of the JG 3 Stabsschwarm. Major Bär himself had taken off separately in a Fw 190D-9 – the only one his Geschwader possessed – and began making his own way to Eindhoven.

At 8.50am, six more Typhoons took off from Eindhoven, this time from 137 Squadron en route for an armed reconnaissance of the Minden area. Five minutes later, six Spitfire IXs of 414 Squadron took off. Another two embarked on tactical reconnaissance at 8.59am.

A minute later, as the JG 3 formation was passing Dorsten and heading for Helmond, six 168 Squadron Typhoons took off bound for targets in Prüm. Another six minutes passed before a single Typhoon, MN486 QC-D, piloted by Flight Lieutenant Howard Plaistowe 'Gibby' Gibbons took off for a flight test. It was now 9.06am and other aircraft were taxiing up in readiness for takeoff.

At 9.15am, JG 3 had just passed Helmond when Leutnant Hans-Ulrich Jung's Bf 109 suddenly burst into flames and then fell apart before its remains fell to the ground. As he passed low over a power line, it had caught on his drop tank, tearing it away and engulfing the rest of the aircraft in fire.

The formation was now approaching Eindhoven and suddenly Major Bär appeared, overtaking the formation on its right hand side in his D-9. The Stabsschwarm pilots opened the throttles of their A-9s and caught Bär just as he arrived over the Allied airfield.

Making a sharp left hand turn, Bär targeted a pair of Typhoons in the process of taking off and shot them up. One of

manoeuvre, five III./SG 4 pilots got lost and some actually joined the passing formation, which was JG 11 heading for Asch. All this happened in strict radio silence, so no one could check what was happening.

Now just five of III./SG 4's Fw 190F-8s reached the SG 4 rendezvous point at Zülpich at 9.05am. Waiting for them were about 25 other F-8s, circling above the town, but no one turned towards the target. Ten minutes later they were still circling. After another five minutes, a small number of Fw 190s were seen to peel off and head west but none of the others followed. They assumed that the mission was cancelled and returned to base.

Of the five pilots who got lost, two were shot down and killed, one was shot down and taken prisoner, and two managed to return home.

the pilots, Flight Lieutenant Pete Wilson, powered down his stricken aircraft and rolled it off the runway before dragging himself from the cockpit with a severe bullet wound through his torso which claimed his life just minutes later.

The other Typhoon pilot, Flying Officer Ross Keller, throttled up and took off but either he or the aircraft had taken a fatal hit and his body was later found in its burned out shell where it had crashed shortly afterwards.

Wilson and Keller's six 438 Squadron colleagues, who had been behind them in the queue to take off, leapt from their Typhoons and took shelter as the full force of IV./JG 3 arrived and opened fire with their MK 108 cannon, shooting up four of the aircraft.

Panic immediately set in. Several Typhoon pilots attempted to take off, while others tried to escape their stationary aircraft. As the Bf 109s and Fw 190s passed over, Pilot Officer R A Watson opened fire with his Typhoon's cannon and damaged one of them before his own aircraft was hit and set on fire.

Two 430 Squadron Spitfire XIVs were hit and damaged on the perimeter, both of their pilots being injured. The Spitfires of 83 Group Communications Squadron, also on the airfield, were strafed. Pilot Officer Lance Burrows of 137 Squadron was killed as bullets entered the cockpit of his Typhoon, JR260 SF-Z on the perimeter track.

At this moment, Flight Lieutenant Gibbons returned in MN486 QC-D. Seeing the airfield under attack, he picked out the closest Fw 190, probably 'Black 16' piloted by Feldwebel Gerhard Leipholz, and fired into it from above and behind. He was at 100ft, his target at 50ft and they were so close that Gibbons' four 20mm cannon blew the German fighter's tail off before the two halves span into the ground.

Within seconds, a trio of Bf 109s were on Gibbons' own tail and there could be no escape – his Typhoon going in close to Leipholz's aircraft.

The four anti-aircraft units around the field opened up, along with ground personnel who grabbed Bren guns and joined in, and over the next 23-25 minutes, the duration of the attack, shot down three Bf 109s and two Fw 190s.

In the midst of this chaos of strafing aircraft and hammering AAA guns, a lone Spitfire IX appeared overhead. It was flown by Flight Lieutenant Robert C Smith of 442 Squadron, who had taken off from Heesch airfield at 8.57am but had been forced to turn back due to a problem with a drop tank. He had heard that one of his colleagues had gone down near Eindhoven and went looking for him.

Within seconds he was caught up in the maelstrom of combat. He later reported: "I identified Fw 190s and Me 109s flying in a circle at about 200ft. I went down to 400ft and circled over the top of them. When I could pick one out that wasn't followed too closely by another, I would nip in and fire a quick burst, then break and climb up again.

"In this way I attacked three Me 109s, however I could not observe strikes all the time being on the lookout for other

enemy aircraft. I had not yet seen any other Allied aircraft. After firing at the third Me 109, I noticed a Fw 190 closing in on me from the port side. He had already opened fire as I broke port.

"He stayed with me so I climbed steeply and he fell off to port. I came down on his tail and gave him a short burst from about 200 yards, no strikes observed. I then broke port again into a Me 109 which I chased down to the deck. My windscreen had oiled up so I broke off the attack and climbed to about 800ft.

"I then noticed a Fw 190 coming up from the deck at the port side. I dove and made a head-on attack. We both opened fire at about 300 yards, no strikes observed. He broke to port at the last second and passed over the top of me going away. I sighted another Fw 190 on the deck going away. I chased him and we had a bit of a do.

"He was a very good pilot and I couldn't get in a shot. He finally straightened out. I closed in, but my ammo had run out. I broke off the attack and headed for base, as my fuel was low. My engine cut at 7000ft and I glided to base making a successful wheels-down landing."

Smith later claimed one Bf 109 destroyed and another damaged, after witnesses on the ground said they saw rounds from his Spitfire fatally damage a Messerschmitt, its pilot bailing out, but neither claim was acknowledged.

With Smith gone, another single Spitfire IX arrived over the airfield – one of the 414 Squadron machines that had taken off at 8.55am, flown by Squadron Leader Gordon Wonnacott. He had become separated from his wingman and was coming home when he was confronted by an incredible scene of carnage.

His report stated: "I immediately went into attack with cannon only from about 5000ft. I opened fire at about 450 yards using 20-30° deflection on the first enemy aircraft I saw – either a Fw 190 or a Me 109. I saw no strikes and broke off the attack as my aircraft seemed to be skidding and I was unable to hold my line of fire correctly (one cannon had stopped firing).

"I pulled up and saw a Me 109 which I attacked using machine guns only. I opened fire at 100 yards seeing strikes

> *"I immediately went into attack with cannon only from about 5000ft. I opened fire at about 450 yards using 20-30° deflection on the first enemy aircraft I saw – either a Fw 190 or a Me 109."*

BELOW: 'White 11' was repainted in garish red after the 404th's commanding officer Colonel Leo Moon was heard to remark that he had always wanted a red aircraft. The 'L' on the fuselage was for 'Leo'.

TOP: A pair of Fw 190D-9s belonging to 3./JG 26 during the winter of 1944-45. The unit attacked Grimbergen on January 1 – an airfield that had largely been abandoned. It achieved very little but lost 21 D-9s and 11 of its pilots were killed.

ABOVE: A pair of Hawker Tempests from 3 Squadron undergo servicing at B-80 Volkel in Holland. Though JG 6 was sent to destroy the aircraft at Volkel, they simply never got there. A few lost aircraft from other units destroyed a single Typhoon on the ground but the airfield was otherwise unscathed.

TOP RIGHT: The remains of Leutnant Theo Nibel's Fw 190D-9 'Black 12' with its engine bay hatches thrown open for inspection by Allied technicians. The 10./JG 54 aircraft was brought down near Grimbergen by a partridge hitting its radiator – rather than by enemy fire.

and the enemy aircraft took evasive action. I again closed, firing from below and using 10° deflection. Strikes were again seen and after more evasive action the pilot jettisoned his coupe top and then bailed out.

"I then attacked another Me 109, opening fire at 300 yards and using some deflection. I saw strikes, the enemy aircraft took violent evasive action, doing a loop and pulling out very close to the ground. I dove after this enemy aircraft, closing from 250 to 100 yards, taking short bursts and seeing many strikes, black smoke and flames issuing from the enemy aircraft.

"I did not see this aircraft hit the ground as I had to take evasive action to avoid three Fw 190s which were attacking me from astern. I turned into these aircraft, attacking No. 1 from 200 yards, saw strikes, broke hard left to avoid the two behind me which had opened fire and attacked the last of the section.

"My machine gun ammunition gave out after 10 rounds were fired and I tried to get my cannon to fire, but it ceased after about three or four rounds. No strikes were seen. I saw a large column of smoke about 1½ miles distance and on the track of the last Me 109 which I had attacked. I claim two Me 109s destroyed and one Fw 190 damaged."

Wonnacott's victims are likely to have been Feldwebel Walter Rutowski of 4./JG 3, who bailed out and was taken prisoner, and Oberfeldwebel Freidrich Hameister, acting Staffelkapitän of the same unit who crash-landed 15 miles from Eindhoven and was eventually captured and taken prisoner.

There were further furious skirmishes away from Eindhoven as JG 3's remaining aircraft attempted to return home and more losses were incurred on both sides. The overall damage caused at the airfield had been significant – with 44 aircraft destroyed and at least another 60 damaged. Fifteen men were killed and another 40 wounded. The airfield itself was barely touched, however, and once the debris had been bulldozed off the runway it was ready for use again that afternoon.

JG 3 lost 15 fighters, with three more damaged. Nine pilots were killed and six taken prisoner.

ALL CLEAR AT LE CULOT

The two airfields of Le Culot, 30 miles northeast of Charleroi, were being used by the Ninth Air Force. The 36th and 373rd Fighter Groups, comprising the 22nd, 23rd and 53rd, and the 410th, 411th and 412th Fighter Squadrons respectively, were on the first airfield, A-89. All six operated P-47 Thunderbolts.

The second, smaller auxiliary airfield, Y-10, was occupied by the 363rd Tactical Reconnaissance Group's 33rd and 155th Photo Recon Squadrons, operating the F-5 version of the Lockheed P-38 Lightning.

Assigned to attack these targets was JG 4. Rather than meet up and attack as a single formation, it was decided that the Geschwader's four Gruppen would attack individually.

Beginning at 8.08am, 17 Fw 190A-8/R2s of II.(Sturm)/JG 4 took off from Babenhausen airfield and began to follow their assigned Ju 88s. Shortly after takeoff, one Fw 190 returned with radio problems. After these were fixed the pilot, Unteroffizier Walter Hübner, crashed on takeoff, suffering injuries from which he died nearly two weeks later. Two more aircraft took off 10 minutes after the others and were then unable to find them.

Near Malmedy, the 16 remaining Fw 190s entered the same heavy AAA barrage that devastated JG 2. Their leading Ju 88 was the first aircraft hit, then one after another, a dozen others went down – leaving just four Fw 190s still flying, all of them damaged. They found an Allied airfield, probably Asch, and made a brief strafing run, shot up two trains and then dispersed to try and find somewhere to land. None of them made it back to Babenhausen.

IV./JG 4, led by Major Gerhard Michalski, had six serviceable Bf 109G-10s, 11 G-14s and two K-4s. In the event, at 8.20am on January 1, only 16 Bf 109s were ready. These, and another from Stab/JG 4, set off from Rheim-Main and followed a Ju 88 in the direction of Bingen. A few minutes later, Michalski suffered mechanical problems and had to turn back.

His command was taken up by Oberleutnant Lothar Wolff, Staffelkapitän of 15./JG 4. Another 15 miles further on and the Messerschmitts were joined by the two Fw 190A-8/R2s from II.(Sturm)/JG 4 that had been delayed taking off and were now lost.

Close to the front line, the 18 aircraft began to draw heavy AAA fire and the large cumbersome Ju 88 was forced to leave. Two of the Bf 109s were shot down and as the remainder flew into clouds to escape, some got lost. Unteroffizier Werner Anetzhuber of 13./JG 4 completely lost touch with his unit and ended up near Eindhoven, where he was shot down and killed by a pair of Tempests from 56 Squadron.

The survivors travelled on and on. Just when Wolff had all but given up hope of finding Le Culot, an airfield suddenly appeared below. It wasn't Le Culot, however, it was St Trond – which JG 2 had failed to find.

Believing they were in the right place, Wolff led the attack. Rows of P-47s belonging to the 48th and 492nd Fighter Groups were strafed, including several aircraft that had been taxiing into position for takeoff.

Numerous American aircraft took hits but the airfield's AAA gunners' concentrated fire exacted a heavy toll on IV./JG 4. Both of the Fw 190s accompanying the unit were shot down. Obergefreiter Hans Peschel made three strafing runs before taking a critical hit, climbing as high as he dared and bailing out. He landed safely and was quickly apprehended by the Americans.

Gefreiter Walter Wagner, 19, belly landed his Fw 190A-8/R2 'White 11' in a beet field after his engine cut out. Gefreiter Karl Noppeney's Bf 109K-4 was hit in the cockpit by AAA, probably killing him outright before his aircraft crashed near Wilderen. Oberfähnrich Arnolf Russow's 'Yellow 13' Bf 109G-14/AS suffered severe damage from an AAA hit and although he was able to leave St Trond, his aircraft went down a few miles further on. He survived and was taken prisoner.

Only Wolff and another pilot, Leutnant Josef Kunz, actually managed to return to German-held territory after the attack, the latter despite being intercepted by P-51 Mustangs on the way home and suffering damage to his oil tank which caused him to make a forced landing near Idar-Oberstein.

Wolff alone landed back at Rhein-Main. An American report on the attack stated: "It is believed from the tactics employed that the squadron was led by an experienced pilot and that the remainder were young and inexperienced.

"The leader got away and his flying was reported as being far superior to the others. After completing a strafing run, he would make a tight low-level turn while the others did not turn as tightly or at as low an altitude. All AA claims were made on hits inflicted on the turns. Some of the enemy aircraft were carrying belly tanks but no bombs were dropped or observed. At no time during the attack did the altitude exceed 500ft."

The aircraft of I./JG 4 and III./JG 4, both based at Darmstaft-Griesheim, also began taking off at 8.20am. III.'s nine Bf 109K-4s went first, followed by the 26 Bf 109s of I. Gruppe, a mixed group of G-10s, G-14s and K-4s.

Following their Ju 88s, the formation of 35 aircraft headed for Bingen, just as the other JG 4 Gruppen had. Within moments, they had run into intense AAA fire – from their own side. This caused the leader, Hauptmann Friedrich Eberle, kommodore III./JG 4, to give the order to cancel the mission.

His own III./JG 4 aircraft turned for home and the bewildered pilots of I./JG 4 were unsure of what to do.

> ## "Gefreiter Walter Wagner, 19, belly landed his Fw 190A-8/R2 'White 11' in a beet field after his engine cut out."

Two were shot down. Some tried to continue the mission but it is unlikely that any of them reached Le Culot. In fact, no German aircraft attacked Le Culot on January 1, 1945. Eberle was hauled before a military court and stripped of his rank before being sent to an infantry unit.

THE UNNOTICED AIRFIELD

Volkel, aka B-80, was another former Luftwaffe station now crammed with Allied aircraft – 121 and 122 Wings of the RAF. The former was composed of three Typhoon squadrons while the latter boasted five squadrons all flying Tempests.

Ordered to destroy as many of them as possible was JG 6. The Geschwader's III. Gruppe began taking off at 8.19am on January 1 and by 8.31am its three Bf 109G-10s and 18 Bf 109G-14/ASs were all airborne and following their assigned Ju 88s. Four minutes later they were over Quackenbrück, where they collected the 25 Fw 190A-8s of II./JG 6.

At around the same time, the last of I./JG 6's 20 Fw 190A-8s was taking off. One of the unit's aircraft suffered engine failure on takeoff and crashed, killing its pilot, but the rest flew on to join up with the other JG 6 aircraft. Once all three Gruppen were together, the huge formation of some 70 aircraft set off in the direction of Volkel.

What they did not know was that between them and their target, the Allies had actually built another airfield, B-88, also known as Heesch. Construction had taken place from October to November 1944 and it seems likely that German intelligence had simply failed to notice it.

The pilots flew right over it at low level at 9.15am, only the back markers realising they were over an Allied airfield and firing on to it as they passed.

Heesch, however, had already been busy that morning. Eleven 411 Squadron Spitfires had taken off for a fighter sweep at 8.50am, followed at 8.57am by 13 442 Squadron Spitfires on an armed recce mission.

When JG 6 appeared suddenly overhead, 10 Spitfires from 401 Squadron were already on the runway about to take off. It was the ideal opportunity for the RAF pilots. They took off as quickly as they could and gave chase.

One of them, Flying Officer Doug Cameron in MJ448, a Spitfire IX, later reported: "I took off and turned slightly starboard and sighted two Me 109s on my port side on the deck at 100ft.

"I attacked the starboard one from astern, about 10° starboard and 300 yards with a very short burst. I saw an explosion on the fuselage near the cockpit and the aircraft

ABOVE: Leutnant Theo Nibel, who attempted to destroy his Fw 190D-9 after crash-landing but failed. His aircraft was subsequently captured and thoroughly examined by the Allies.

BELOW: Emerging from their dispersed positions are Fw 190D-9s of 7./JG 26. The unit attacked Brussels-Evere on January 1, 1945.

dove straight down towards the deck at less than 50ft. I immediately turned on the other about 15° starboard, about 200 yards and fired a short burst. I saw a large explosion on the fuselage behind the cockpit followed by flames.

"This aircraft also dove down to port, with flames, at less than 50ft. I then sighted another Me 109 to starboard. I at once chased him and opened fire at about 400-500 yards, from about 30-40° port. I saw a small flash on the rear fuselage. I continued to fire short bursts with no results seen.

"I then chased to about 200 yards astern and after a fairly long burst (2-3 seconds) saw glycol streaming out. I was out of ammunition and flew very close on his starboard until he crash-landed in a large field approximately two miles north of the aerodrome. This aircraft smoked but was not burning. After two orbits of the crash I took a short cine camera shot of this aircraft. I claim three Me 109s destroyed."

Ground control had by now recalled 442 Squadron's 13 Spitfires from their mission and on arrival they were in time to shoot down at least one Fw 190 of JG 6.

Confusion now reigned in the JG 6 formation. So much so that all three Gruppen missed Volkel. I./JG 6 ended up joining the Eindhoven attack, II./JG 6 stumbled across an unfinished and unoccupied, but AAA defended, airfield B-86 at Helmond, and attacked it instead, and III./JG 6 flew into heavy AAA fire elsewhere. All three also suffered further losses from Spitfires and Tempests that were already airborne when they had arrived in the area.

Overall, Stab JG 6 lost one of its three Fw 190A-9s, I./JG 6 lost seven Fw 190s, II./JG lost eight Fw 190s and III./JG 6 lost 12 of its 21 Bf 109s. Not long after its utter failure against Volkel, JG 6 was withdrawn from front line operations in readiness for a transfer to the Eastern Front.

THE DISASTER UNFOLDS

It was a similar story for JG 11 attacking Asch (Y-29). Through a combination of AAA fire and P-51 Mustangs already being ready to fight, it lost 24 Fw 190s and Bf 109s out of 60, 20 of their pilots killed and only four taken prisoner. Among the dead were Major Günther Specht – who had led JG 11 since May 1944 – and his wingman Unteroffizier

> ## "This aircraft also dove down to port, with flames, at less than 50ft. I then sighted another Me 109 to starboard. I at once chased him and opened fire at about 400-500 yards, from about 30-40° port."

Sophus Schmidt. Their aircraft, and indeed their bodies, have never been found.

There was more success for the highly experienced JG 26 and III./JG 54, who attacked Brussels-Evere and Grimbergen. II. and III./JG 26 hit Evere as planned and managed to destroy 31 single-engine aircraft, 21 twin-engine types and nine four-engine aircraft, for a loss of 13 Fw 190D-9s and six Bf 109s.

I./JG 26 and III./JG 54 did rather less well in their attack on Grimbergen – which had been home to the Spitfires of 132 Wing but which was now largely abandoned. They destroyed a single Mustang, one twin-engine aircraft and four B-17s. To achieve this, they lost 21 Fw 190D-9s plus another 10 damaged. Eleven pilots were dead.

There was more success for JG 27 and IV./JG 54 at Melsbroek. Seventeen of the former's Bf 109s were destroyed along with three Fw 190s of the latter. In exchange, they managed to destroy more than 50 Allied aircraft, including 12 Mitchells, 13 Wellingtons, five Spitfires, four Mosquitos, four B-17s, two B-24s and an assortment of other types.

Attacking Metz-Frescaty and Etain, JG 53 suffered heavy casualties. Out of 80 Bf 109s taking part in the mission, 30 were shot down and another eight were damaged. The aircraft heading for Etain never reached it, having been intercepted and badly disrupted by American P-47s beforehand.

Those that made it to Metz-Frescaty managed to destroy 22 P-47s and damaged another 11 – losses that were made good within a week. JG 53 itself also received a full complement of replacement aircraft but the pilots it received were raw recruits unfit for front line duties, diminishing its effectiveness despite its apparent renewed strength on paper.

Antwerp-Deurne was the target of JG 77 and its attack also proved to be a failure. It managed to destroy 14 aircraft, most of them Typhoons, and lost 11 Bf 109s along with their pilots – six of whom were killed and the remainder taken prisoner.

Finally, the jet aircraft of KG 51 and KG 76 also participated in Operation Baseplate. Four of KG 76's Arado Ar 234B-2s flew a weather reconnaissance mission in darkness at 4am on January 1, 1945 – the first night time operation by jet aircraft in history – followed by a bombing mission.

This was to have involved 10 Ar 234s but four suffered mechanical failures so only six participated in the attack, on Gilze-Rijen, in the end. They reached their target and each opened its AB 500 container, dropping 24 SD 15 bombs per aircraft. These did little damage, however, destroying just one Typhoon, but at least all six jets made it back to base.

KG 51's Me 262A-2s were to carry out bombing and reconnaissance missions to Eindhoven, Gilze-Rijen and Volkel, so each of the 22 available machines was fitted with two 250kg bombs on its nose racks and a robot camera. Certainly, individual Me 262 were spotted by observers at all three airfields but damage caused by their bombs – those that dropped them – was again minimal. All 22 of KG 51's jets also returned safely home.

BOTTOM RIGHT: Burning Spitfire PR.XI slowly disintegrates after the attack on Melsbroek.

BELOW: A Vickers Wellington XIII of 69 Squadron burns at Brussels-Melsbroek. After Eindhoven, Melsbroek was next hardest hit.

BOTTOM: A 16 Squadron Spitfire PR.XI at Melsbroek beside another that has become completely engulfed in flames.

COUNTING THE COST

When the dust had settled and every German fighter that was going to fly home had done so, the mammoth task of assessing what damage had been inflicted on the Allies was begun. Overall, based on reports of pilots and aerial reconnaissance, the Luftwaffe believed that it had destroyed 479 aircraft and damaged another 114. Its own casualties amounted to 271 fighters and nine Ju 88s destroyed and 69 more aircraft damaged, with 213 fighter pilots killed or missing, including those captured, plus 21 wounded.

In reality, Allied losses were closer to 305 aircraft destroyed and 190 damaged. Just 15 Allied fighters were shot down, with only a handful of pilots being killed, including those who died on the ground.

While both the Germans and the Allies were able to replace their material losses – the Germans with considerably more difficulty – the loss of 213 pilots, including more than 60 highly experienced fighter pilots, was a grievous blow indeed.

The greatest single cause of Operation Baseplate's failure was Allied anti-aircraft fire. Some 47% of the German aircraft lost were shot down by it. The second largest contributing factor was attacks by Allied fighter aircraft, accounting for 23% of the Luftwaffe machines lost.

Why were the Allies so effective in these two areas? Poor route planning meant several formations flew directly over some of the heaviest flak coverage to be found anywhere on the Western Front. A lack of night and instrument flying training meant that the attack had to be carried out in daylight – when numerous Allied units were already in the air or ready for takeoff.

Having the fighters follow Ju 88s that were unable to proceed all the way to the targets was also a recipe for disaster. The pilots failed to check their own maps and trusted to their guide, who then departed some miles away from their ultimate destination.

An insistence on radio silence might have helped to maintain secrecy but it also resulted in total confusion in several instances where proper coordination by experienced leaders might have saved the day.

Instead, the operation was a failure that the Jagdwaffe would spend the next four months living to regret. ●

ABOVE: The jet-powered Arado Ar 234B-2 bombers of III./KG 76 pictured in December 1944. Like the Me 262s of KG 51, they had little effect during the January 1 mission.

LEFT: Me 262A-2a fighter-bombers from KG 51 were involved in the fighting on January 1 but their effect was minimal and none were destroyed during the attacks.

TOP LEFT: The body of 24-year-old Unteroffizier Herbert Maxis, a pilot of 13./JG 53, lies beside the wing of his Bf 109G-14. He was forced to make a belly landing near an American AAA position and was shot as he climbed from the cockpit. No identification was found on his body and he was buried in an unmarked grave, the location of which is unknown today.

MIDDLE LEFT: The wreckage of a P-47 lies on the temporary airstrip mesh at Metz following the attack by JG 53.

BELOW: Harsh winter conditions and delicate near-prototype jet engines do not mix well. Here technicians of KG 51 prepare to get to work on their charges.

DICING WITH PIGGYBACKS

FEBRUARY 3, 1945: THE DOUBLE NICKEL'S MISTEL ENCOUNTER

After escorting B-17 bombers to Berlin, four P-51 Mustang pilots of the 55th Fighter Group, Eighth Air Force, went hunting for targets of their own. Diving down to strafe a pair of locomotives, none of them expected what happened next…

ABOVE: Two of the three Mistel combinations encountered by four P-51 Mustangs from the Eighth Air Force's 55th Fighter Group on February 3, 1945. They are still flying in formation with both aircraft attached to one another, suggesting that this gun camera image was taken at the beginning of the Americans' attack.

The USAAF went all out to destroy the Tempelhof rail marshalling yards in the centre of Berlin on February 3, 1945 – it was believed that the German Sixth Panzer Army was passing through them on its way to the Eastern Front.

A total of 937 B-17s were send to destroy it with an escort of 575 North American P-51 Mustangs. Arriving in waves throughout the late morning and into the early afternoon the bombers did their work well, shattering a large area and starting a fire that would last for days.

Among the P-51s that had escorted the B-17s were squadrons of the 55th Fighter Group, the 'Double Nickel', led by the unit's flamboyant executive officer Lieutenant Colonel Elwyn C Righetti.

With fuel still in their tanks and the bombers well protected by others, Righetti decided that his men could conduct a ground sweep on the way home to Station 159 – the 55th's base at Wormingford in Essex. Strafing was his speciality and he organised two flights before setting out to look for targets.

His men were all members of the 343rd Fighter Squadron: 1st Lieutenant Bernard H Howes, 22, from Brockton, Massachusetts, was flying P-51K CY-C 44-63745 'My Li'l Honey', 2nd Lt Patrick L Moore from Griffin, Indiana flew P-51D CY-Y 44-14235 'Lil Jan' and 2nd Lt Richard G Gibbs, from Nantucket, also in Massachusetts, flew P-51D CY-Q 44-14175 'Cherry'.

'Eager El' Righetti himself, from San Luis Obispo, California, flew P-51D CL-M 44-72227 'Katydid'.

At about 12.30pm, near Boizenburg, Germany, the Americans spotted two locomotives and dropped down through a low layer of cloud to attack. What happened next was a remarkable free-for-all as the Mustangs vied with one another over a fresh set of targets that suddenly presented themselves.

A formation of Mistel combinations, each a fighter fixed atop a Junkers Ju 88, appeared flying at low level beneath the clouds.

Howes reported: "I was flying White 3 on the mission of February 3. At about 1230 we dropped to the deck to strafe. On pulling up from the first pass on a locomotive I sighted a formation of three pick-a-backs, Fw 190s on Ju 88s, in string formation at about 400ft.

"I turned into the second combo with my wingman Lt Moore behind me. I fired a short burst from 90° at about 350 yards, observing a few strikes on the 190. As I fired on this, the 190 on the third unit was released.

"The prop was windmilling, and on release the 190 seemed to nose up for a minute and then, apparently out of control, the nose went down and it headed for the ground. I claim this Fw 190 as destroyed. As soon as the 190 was released, the 88 turned sharply left. I followed, firing a short burst but observed no strikes. I fell outside the turn and lost sight of the 88 momentarily.

"My wingman behind me was in position and shot the 88 down. When I looked back I saw it crash into the ground. On pulling up I saw the first unit I had fired at about 300 yards in front of me. There were flames coming out of the 190, so I went after it again. I started firing and the combo turned into me, dropping to the deck.

"As I fired, another large burst of flame came from the 190. On making a second pass, the right engine of the 88 burst into flame, and I saw them both crash into the ground. From this entire encounter I claim two Fw 190s and one Ju 88 destroyed. Ammunition expended: 1440 rounds."

The aircraft attacked by Howes are clearly visible on his gun camera footage.

Righetti reported: "Near Boizenburg on the Elbe River I located a small hole in the unbroken overcast. Through the

hole I could see two locomotives and called them in and started down.

"Visibility was about two miles and scattered fuzz on the overcast ran down in some places to 500 to 600ft. I rolled out of my turn and started my final approach to the locos about four miles off. I had already assigned the locos and parts of the train to the flight. We were echeloned to the right with my position on the extreme left.

"At a distance of two miles from the train I spotted three piggy-back aircraft at 10.30 to me, at our same altitude of about 600ft, heading almost directly at us, and half a mile off. I mistakenly identified them as buzz bomb equipped He 111s and broke off rapidly, left and up, in a 200° chandelle,

ABOVE: Lieutenant Colonel Elwyn G Righetti sits on his P-51 Mustang 'Katydid'. He flew as Tudor White Leader on February 3, 1945. Note the unusual victory markings on the nose of his aircraft – a smaller version of his 'Katydid' logo with wings spread over a stylised swastika.

RIGHT: Tudor White 4, 2nd Lt Patrick L Moore, gives the photographer a cocky grin.

FAR RIGHT: The Ju 88 section of a 6./KG 200 Mistel backs to the left to avoid the P-51 Mustang firing on it from behind. The Bf 109 that had been attached to its back has already detached. None of the three Bf 109s involved in this encounter survived.

positioning myself on the tail of the middle one.

"I started firing two short bursts at 600 yards and missed. I swung into trail and closed to point blank range, firing a long burst, I saw many excellent strikes on the fuselage and empennage of the large aircraft and scattered strikes and a small fire on the fighter.

"Both aircraft, still fastened together, went into a steep dive straight ahead. I was about to overrun them and did not see them crash, but a few seconds later I saw a large explosion and spotted considerable burning wreckage.

"I still did not know what we were attacking; I turned slightly to port for another look. As I closed, and before I could open fire, I discovered that the buzz bomb was actually a Focke-Wulf 190 fastened atop the heavy twin-engined aircraft. As I was closing to fire, the heavy aircraft seemed to be jettisoned, went into a shallow diving turn to the left, and crashed and burned in a small hamlet.

"Apparently it carried no bombs, for the gasoline thrown from its tanks burned for some time, and I did not observe any unusually large explosion. The Fw 190, relieved of its load, snapped to the right and then began a wild evasive action, I drove up to 200 yards directly in trail, firing intermittently, and secured excellent strikes along the fuselage, wing roots, canopy, and induced good fire.

"Jerry went out of control and crashed straight ahead. At this time I noticed a few tracers too close and coming behind. I broke sharply left and up into a low cloud. I don't know who or what was firing at me, but it might have been the third Fw 190 having jettisoned its bomber."

Gibbs was also attacking the Mistel combinations. He reported: "I was flying Tudor White 2 on the mission of

February 3, 1945. We were on the deck and about to strafe a loco in the vicinity of Boizenburg, when Tudor Leader Lt Col Righetti called in a gaggle of three Fw 190-bomber combos, flying a sloppy 'V' formation at about 600ft. We attacked from a level turn port stern.

"Lt Col Righetti took the middle combo of the three, and I took the third and last one of this gaggle. I started firing on the Ju 88 at about 45° from about 800 yards, closing to about 300 yards with a two second burst. I observed many strikes on the left wing root of the Ju 88, where it began to burn.

"After a short dive the Fw 190 was released. The 190 appeared rather unstable in the air, but managed to conduct violent evasive action during the ensuing combat. I fired a short burst from astern, beginning at about 200 yards and closing to zero yards. I saw strikes all over the aircraft and observed parts of the cowling and canopy fly off.

"There was also a fire in or around the cockpit. I then overran the enemy aircraft and skidded out to the right. As I looked back I saw where the 190 had crashed into the ground."

As stated by Howes, Moore also claimed a Ju 88.

There had been three Ju 88s and three fighters but the four US pilots had claimed one Ju 88 each and a total of five Fw 190s – two for Howes, two for Righetti and one for Gibbs. In the confusion of combat, it was difficult to decide who had destroyed what.

In fact, German records show that at least two of the combinations were Mistel 1s, with Messerschmitt Bf 109s mounted atop Ju 88s rather than Fw 190s. The Ju 88 pilots were Feldwebel Willi Kollhoff, Oberfähnrich Franz Pietschmann and Feldwebel Fritz Lorbach of 6./KG 200, based at Kolberg but on their way to Tirstrup in Denmark.

Lorbach managed to put his Ju 88 down safely in the woods, albeit with the left engine on fire. Pietschmann was killed when his Ju 88 dived into the ground and Kollhoff was injured after he made a forced landing and was strafed by a P-51. His gunner, who also survived the landing, was killed. All three of the fighter pilots were shot down and killed.

WHERE THE MISTEL CAME FROM

The three combinations shot down on February 3 had been on their way to participate in Unternehmen Drachenhöhle or Operation Dragon's Lair, a plan devised by Hermann Göring with the goal of attacking the Royal Navy's home fleet at Scapa Flow and inflicting a high profile Pearl Harbor-style blow against the British.

The genesis of the Mistel, however, had come about three years earlier in 1942, when work was carried out in Germany to enable a glider to carry a full military load by launching it into the air using a smaller powered aircraft mounted on its back.

This combination was eventually to become known as the Mistel (mistletoe) since the powered aircraft could be given an extended range using fuel drawn from the glider below – like mistletoe drawing sap from its host tree.

The upper portion was to be a Bf 109E fighter, the lower a DFS 230 glider. Both were piloted.

In June 1943, it was decided that this technology could be used for launching a 'grossbombe' or large bomb at a ground target. The Bf 109 would still be the upper portion, now a 109F, but the lower would be a 'war weary' unmanned Junkers Ju 88A-4 filled with 3.5 tons of high explosives.

The Bf 109 pilot would control the whole Mistel up to its arrival over the target, whereupon the Ju 88 would be aimed and an autopilot unit within it activated. The Bf 109 would separate from the Ju 88 by firing explosive bolts and then peel away as the flying bomb flew serenely down to its target.

> *"The Bf 109 would separate from the Ju 88 by firing explosive bolts and then peel away as the flying bomb flew serenely down to its target."*

The Ju 88's high explosive warhead was a huge hollow charge with a plunger detonator at its tip which was fitted in place of the aircraft's cockpit. They were to be used against high value targets such as capital ships, power stations or bridges.

When a Ju 88 was converted for Mistel use, its crew compartment was removed at the aft bulkhead. Four quick-release bolts were then fitted which allowed the compartment to be re-attached for training or for ferrying the combination around. The warheads were moved separately by road or rail for safety.

ABOVE: 'Eager El' Righetti's P-51D CL-M 44-72227 'Katydid'.
ART BY MARK STYLING

ABOVE: A closer study of the nose art on Lt Moore's P-51.

TOP: Lt Gibbs's P-51D, 44-14175 CY-Q 'Cherry'.

RIGHT: The 'female' grasshopper logo on the nose of Righetti's first P-51D 'Katydid'. The pilot, who became the 55th Fighter Group's commanding officer in 1945, is pictured standing beside his machine.

FAR RIGHT: P-51D 44-14243 CY-Y 'Lil' Jan' was flown by Lt Patrick L Moore.

Once the aircraft and the warhead were both at the operational airfield, the crew compartment could be easily removed using the quick-release bolts and the warhead attached.

The Mistels being flown on February 3, 1945, therefore had their crew compartments in place complete with working controls, rather than warheads.

OPERATION DRAGON'S LAIR

Fifteen Mistels from 6./KG 200 were intended to form the strike force for Göring's ambitious 'British Pearl Harbor', supported by 12 flare-dropping Ju 88s and 188s from 5./KG 200 to illuminate the target. They were to set off from Tirstrup on a date after January 20, 1945.

Everything initially went to plan and Mistels from II./KG 200 arrived at the Danish base without any problems in mid-January 1945 along with the Ju 88s and 188s.

One of the pilots due to take part, Feldwebel Rudi Riedl of 6./KG 200, recalled: "As far as the Scapa Flow attack plan was concerned we only received one proper briefing which took place in a large room of the country house near the airfield, in which was a large map of the Scapa Flow area.

"Each pilot was assigned an individual target since we received regular reconnaissance updates on British shipping movements – I knew exactly where my target ship was anchored. To help us further, at our base at Tirstrup, we had a large, specially built model of the harbour on which were laid scale models of all the ships known to be there.

"The real prize was to be assigned an aircraft carrier. It was felt among the pilots of 6./KG 200 that if the Mistel had been introduced earlier and in greater numbers, its effect against certain pinpoint targets – such as ships – could have been far more decisive. Any ship – no matter what size – if hit by a Mistel would have gone under.

"There were to be 12 aircraft – no reserves – and the idea was to fly to the target in cloud so as to minimise the risk of being spotted by British patrols or flak. Fuel for the outward flight would be drawn from the Ju 88 lower

"Once the attack had been made, the plan was for our Fw 190s to climb as fast as possible to 7000m and make for Stavanger."

components and the amounts required had been calculated down to the last drop.

"Marker buoys had been laid out to guide us in. We were to adopt a line astern formation. We all wanted the mission to work, because we knew we would be decorated when we got back – there was even talk of the Ritterkreutz.

"Once the attack had been made, the plan was for our Fw 190s to climb as fast as possible to 7000m and make for Stavanger which was closest point for a safe landing. Both our forces in Norway and the navy had been warned to expect us and the navy had been briefed to watch out for any pilot unable to make it as far as Stavanger who might have to bail out due to lack of fuel."

Bad weather prevented the attack from going ahead however and it was decided that more Mistels would be needed.

Four fresh combinations were sent from 6./KG 200's Kolberg station, one flying separately from the other three. The Mustang attack by Righetti and his men was only the first disaster to befall the mission.

Eleven days later, a pair of de Havilland Mosquito Mk.VIs from the RAF's Fighter Experimental Flight attacked the airfield at Tirstrup. Two of the Mistel combinations were destroyed and on the same day Operation Dragon's Lair was cancelled.

HOWES' RESCUE MISSION

The pilots of the 55th who had shot down the three Mistel combos on February 3 continued to fly front line missions.

Exactly a month after the attack, on March 3, 1st Lt Howes was flying one of seven P-51s taking part in another hunt for targets of opportunity on the ground, this time in the vicinity of Prague, Czechoslovakia. One of the other aircraft was flown by his friend Lt Brooks J Liles. They had trained together, gone overseas together and then ended up in the same unit.

It was about 1pm and the Mustang pilots, organised into Red and Yellow flights, were cruising at 2000ft when they spotted rows of enemy aircraft parked out in the open at Prague-Letnany airport.

Another 343rd pilot, 1st Lt Marvin Satenstein, later reported: "My flight, Red flight, and the remainder of Yellow flight decided to attack it. We did so, making our passes individually.

"On Lt Liles' pass from north to south he was hit on the right side of his engine by light flak from the guns at the southwest end of the field. I observed flame coming from the engine. Lt Liles said that he had been hit.

"I was directly above and behind him and could see that he had the aircraft under control but could not get much power. He flew the aircraft for about three or four miles south of the airdrome where he bellied it in successfully on an open field. I saw Lt Liles get out of the aircraft, just after that it caught fire.

"The remaining six aircraft circled the spot, and Lt

Howes, Tudor Yellow 3, called over the R/T that he was going to land to try to pick up Lt Liles. After one try, Lt Howes made a successful landing in the same field.

"After discarding their parachutes both Howes and Liles were able to get into the aircraft. It appeared as if it was hard to get the plane started rolling from its parked position. As they started to roll, Howes called, 'Gang, keep your fingers crossed and we'll make it.' The aircraft rose into the air once, but apparently didn't have enough flying speed because it settled to the ground again.

"Then it bounced into the air, dropped off on its left wing in a stalled attitude, and cartwheeled to the left eventually flattening out. The aircraft caught fire but when I buzzed the wreck I saw both Howes and Liles walking away in an easterly direction towards a large highway. Both pilots looked all right and they waved to me as I passed over them."

Interviewed after the war, Howes said that what his colleagues had not seen was bursts of small arms fire being directed at his aircraft from the direction of the airport as he tried to take off.

The aircraft hesitated just before take-off and its undercarriage hit a ditch, causing it to crash. Liles had a broken nose and Howes took a blow to the head that rendered him blind for two days. Examining the wreck, Liles saw that it had taken a bullet in the throttle quadrant, probably causing a reduction in power during take-off.

A few hours later, both men had been taken prisoner by the Luftwaffe and were transported to Prague for

ABOVE: The first operational Mistel combinations utilised a Bf 109F, in this case WNr. 10130, paired with a Ju 88A-4, WNr. 10096.

BELOW: Eleven Mistel 1s of 6./KG 200 on the runway at Burg in readiness for an operation in late 1944 or early 1945.

medical treatment and interrogation. From there, they were moved to Oberursel in Frankfurt, Germany, for further interrogation, then to the nearby Dulag Luft transit PoW camp at Wetzlar and then to Stalag Luft III at Sagan, 100 miles south-east of Berlin.

Finally, they saw out the remainder of the war at Stalag VIIA at Moosburg. With the German war situation worsening dramatically by now, there was no fuel to drive the prisoners to Moosburg so they were forced to walk – a 19 day march. During their two months of imprisonment, the pair subsisted on bread and barley soup. Howes had weighed nearly 11 and a half stone when he was captured but was only nine stone when he was freed.

MOORE, RIGHETTI AND GIBBS

Patrick L Moore was promoted to 1st Lieutenant after the Mistel attack and awarded the 1st Oak Leaf Cluster to his Air Medal.

At 2.30pm on April 16, 1945, he was flying P-51D CY-Y 44-14235 'Lil Jan' with Tudor Yellow flight on a bomber escort mission to Salzburg, Austria, with fellow 343rd pilots 1st Lt Lloyd D Boring and 2nd Lt Raymond G Allen. The weather was clear and visibility was unrestricted.

The pilots had completed their main duties and were once again flying at low level looking for targets of opportunity in the area south-east of Munich.

Moore then crashed and was killed. A Missing Air Crew Report was filed on his crash and in a section of the report

marked "aircraft was lost, or is believed to have been lost, as a result of: (check only one) enemy aircraft, enemy anti-aircraft, other circumstances as follows" the first two boxes are unchecked and the 'circumstances' are given as "unknown".

Boring reported: "I was flying Tudor Yellow Three, April 16, on a bomber escort and strafing mission. We were driving along over an autobahn south east of Munich at approximately 3500ft when suddenly I noticed a plane in a steep dive ahead of me.

"It went out of view under my wing; about this time someone called over the R/T and reported a plane from White Flight had spun. Coming to the scene of the incident, I dipped my left wing and investigated. It appeared that he had set a large portion of the woods on fire where he went in. I saw no chute."

Another pilot, 1st Lt Walter Strauch, also saw Moore go down. He reported: "I was flying Tudor Red Three on April 16, 1945, on an escort and strafing mission. We were flying along over an autobahn south and east of Munich at 3000ft when suddenly Tudor White Four flipped up a wing to see below, and the plane snapped upside down and started a split-S. Lt Moore tried to roll out and pull up at the same time, and succeeded in doing both, but as he levelled out he hit the ground and exploded. I called Tudor Leader about the accident. I saw no chute."

It is believed that Moore crashed while strafing at extremely low level and was killed. Not long afterwards, two of his colleagues were still in the area, now over Chiemsee, a large lake.

Tudor Yellow Leader had been forced to return to base but Boring and Allen, the remainder of the four-man Tudor Yellow fight, attacked what they later reported as a pair of Blohm & Voss Ha 140 seaplanes, of which only three were ever built, nearly eight years earlier in 1937-8. They reported destroying an Ha 140 apiece before returning home.

During the same mission, Tudor Red had also lost a pilot. Captain Chester E Coggeshall Jr, 25, had also been flying with Strauch, who was Tudor Red 3, strafing an airfield at Ainring west of Salzburg, when his aircraft suffered flak damage and he was forced to make a belly landing. His fate is recorded later in this publication under 'April 16'.

The following day it was Lt Col Elwyn Righetti's 30th birthday. He had been promoted to commanding officer of the 55th Fighter Group on February 22, 19 days after the Mistel attack, but still flew missions with the callsign 'Windsor'. This time he was flying P-51D CL-M 44-72227 'Katydid' looking for an aerodrome to attack near Dresden with his wingman 1st Lt Carroll D Henry.

> ## "The following day it was Lt Col Elwyn Righetti's 30th birthday. He had been promoted to commanding officer of the 55th Fighter Group on February 22".

Henry later reported: "I was flying Acorn White 2 position off Lt Col Righetti's wing. We broke and started looking for aerodromes. One was called out at 10 o'clock. We let down under about 5/10 clouds with base at 5000ft and made one 360° port turn at 3000ft. Windsor called in and told the rest of White flight to orbit while he went down and checked for flak. I then called and asked if I could come down with him and he said 'yes'.

"We were going across north edge of the aerodrome at about 500ft from east to west. One Fw 190 was landing at the time from north-east to south-west, and he told me to go in after it since I was between him and the aerodrome.

"I made the pass and drove past the field on the deck for about three miles avoiding flak. I then came back around and made a pass on a large field, which was a large dispersal area about one half mile north-west of the aerodrome. I pulled up and was orbiting aerodrome again when I saw a P-51 streaming coolant as he was making a pass on the field from west to east.

"I called him and told him. He called in saying, 'This is Windsor and I am hit bad, oil pressure dropping. I can't make it back I have enough ammo for one more pass.'

"He then made one more pass from west to east destroying a Fw 190. I called him telling him that I was tacking on. He acknowledged saying that he was heading out on 270°. I was about 3000ft and overran him due to excess speed gained while letting down. He was at six o'clock to me and I rolled out on 270°. I chopped my throttle and when I looked back I couldn't locate him.

"About 30 seconds later he called in saying 'I broke my nose but I am okay, I got nine today, tell my family I am okay, and it has been swell working with you.' I made one orbit and couldn't locate him on the ground. Being by myself I then headed out."

Righetti is believed to have been hit by flak before being forced to make a belly landing. He survived the crash and radioed Lt Henry to say he was all right. After that, he was never heard from again and his body has never been found. It is speculated, based on anecdotal evidence, that as he climbed from his wrecked aircraft he was surrounded by a crowd of angry civilians who lynched him.

The only one of the four men who engaged 6./KG 200's Mistels on February 3, 1945, to survive the war without being captured was Lt Richard G Gibbs. He was promoted to 1st lieutenant in March/April 1945 and destroyed a pair of Fw 190s on the day that Righetti was killed.

Three weeks after the war's end however, on May 29, 1945, he had a close shave in his P-51 when according to an East Suffolk Police report he was "stunting in mid air and collided with another plane". He bailed out and came down safely near Chediston Hall. The report notes that he did suffer a sprained ankle, however. His aircraft was completely destroyed. ●

BELOW FROM FAR LEFT: A mugshot of Lt Bernard H Howes taken by the Germans who captured him after his failed attempt to rescue his downed friend Lt Brooks J Liles.
NATIONAL ARCHIVES VIA KURT SPENCE

Lt Howes was blinded for two days by the head injury he sustained during the crash of his P-51D.
NATIONAL ARCHIVES VIA KURT SPENCE

Lt Brooks J Liles, who was captured by the Germans alongside his friend Lt Howes on March 3, 1945.
NATIONAL ARCHIVES VIA KURT SPENCE

ABOVE: Lt Richard G Gibbs, left, was the only one of the four Mustang pilots of February 3's Tudor White flight who saw out the war alive and free.

LEFT: Lt Patrick L Moore, right, was killed during a strafing mission in April 16, 1945.

FAR LEFT: Lt Col Righetti was shot down the day after Moore, April 17, 1945, and survived the crash, radioing his wingman to tell him he was all right. He was never heard from again and it is speculated that he was lynched by German civilians.

FIGHTING JETS WITH SPITFIRES

FEBRUARY 14, 1945: FLIGHT LIEUTENANT TONY GAZE DESTROYS A MESSERSCHMITT ME 262

The first Spitfire victory over a Messerschmitt Me 262 was on October 5, 1944, and it had taken five of the piston engine aircraft to bring it down. Yet despite the jet's superior speed, it was possible for a lone Spitfire to best it if the circumstances were right, as Aussie fighter ace Tony Gaze discovered…

WORDS: SQUADRON LEADER CLIVE ROWLEY • PHOTOGRAPHY: VIA RAY BERGHOUSE

LEFT: Australian fighter ace Tony Gaze joined the elite group of Allied pilots who had shot down a German jet when he destroyed a Me 262. VIA CLIVE ROWLEY.

On St Valentine's Day, February 14, 1945, there was still not much love lost between the Allied fighter pilots and their Luftwaffe opponents. During that afternoon, Flight Lieutenant 'Tony' Gaze, the flight commander of 'B' Flight of 610 (County of Chester) AuxAF Squadron RAF, led a two-aircraft section of Mk.XIV Spitfires, call-sign 'Wavey Black', on a standing patrol over Nijmegen, from their base at airfield B78 Eindhoven, in the Netherlands.

Over a year before, in January 1944, 610 Squadron had re-equipped with Rolls-Royce Griffon-engined Mk.XIV Spitfires. The Griffon engine rotated in the opposite direction to the earlier Merlin, the torque causing the aircraft to swing the other way to the Merlin-engined Spitfires, so it took pilots familiar with the earlier variants time to get used to it.

The Mk.XIV was noticeably heavier (1100lb heavier) than the Mk.IX Spitfire, but the 2000hp Griffon endowed this version with a top speed in the region of 450mph, an extra 35-40mph over the Mk.IX, making it a match for any other piston engine fighter flying at the time, although not the equal of the new Luftwaffe jets.

The enormous power and torque from the 37 litre V12 Griffon made the Mk.XIV more of a handful for its pilots than previous Spitfire variants and flying it required more attention than its predecessors. The Griffon engine growled rather than purred like a Merlin; it also reduced the Spitfire's directional stability and changes of power or speed caused the aircraft to swing markedly, requiring large and frequent rudder inputs by the pilot to keep the aircraft flying in balance and pointing exactly where it was going.

At about 4.30pm on February 14, Gaze sighted an Arado Ar 234B-2 twin-jet bomber of III./KG 76 flying below him as it pulled up from a dive-bombing attack in the Cleves area, in northwestern Germany, close to the Dutch border.

These attacks by III./KG 76, the first Luftwaffe unit to be equipped with the bomber version of the Ar 234, had been a considerable nuisance of late and were among the reasons for the standing Spitfire patrols, although intercepting these jet bombers was another thing entirely.

Powered by two Junkers Jumo 004 axial-flow-compressor turbojet engines, the same as those fitted to the Messerschmitt Me 262 fighter, the Ar 234 had a top speed of just over 460mph, so they were difficult to catch even with the speed of the Mk.XIV Spitfires.

Gaze jettisoned his drop tank and chased after the bomber, but even though he tried to 'cut the corner', the Ar 234 pulled away easily at 7000ft. He subsequently reported: "After that, we continually chased Arados over this area. I fired at two without result."

After half an hour of this, it became apparent that the Arados were diving through the cloud layer, which was a solid sheet from 9000-11,000ft, when they were threatened. Gaze decided to leave his No. 2 below the cloud while he climbed above, hoping to warn 'Black 2' when the next jet was on the way down.

On the way up through the winter cloud Gaze picked up some ice on his windscreen, so once in the clear sky above he flew an orbit at 13,000ft while the ice cleared in the sunshine.

As he did so, he suddenly spotted three Me 262s of I./JG 51 'stooging along' below him at cloud top level. He immediately set his Spitfire into a dive behind them and then closed in with the excess speed gained in the descent, crossing behind the formation to attack the 262 on the left, which was lagging slightly behind the others.

This was likely to be a fleeting opportunity as, if or when the German pilots saw him they would open up their engines and accelerate away easily using the Me 262's amazing top speed of 540mph, far in excess of any other aircraft of the time.

Heading west into the low winter sun, it was now 5.10pm, Gaze could not see the illuminated graticules of his reflector gun sight properly. Using his years of experience, honed since he first became a fighter pilot almost four years earlier, he aimed by instinct and fired his two 20mm cannons and four 0.303 machine guns together, from dead astern, at a range of about 350 yards.

His second burst hit the 262 in the starboard engine. Reacting to the danger, the other two German jet fighters immediately dived into cloud. The stricken victim of Gaze's guns pulled up slowly and turned to starboard. Gaze fired at it again and obtained more strikes on the fuselage and on the starboard engine, which caught fire.

The 262 rolled on to its back and dived almost vertically through the cloud. Gaze turned through 180° and dived after it, calling on the radio to warn his No. 2. As he broke cloud, Gaze saw an aircraft hit the ground and explode about a mile ahead of him, near Emmerich am Rhein, inside Germany. His No. 2 also witnessed the explosion. The pilot of the Me 262A-2a shot down by Gaze, WNr. 500064, 9K+CL, was 26-year-old Feldwebel Rudolf Hoffmann of 3./JG 51, who was killed in the action.

After returning to base, Gaze claimed a rare Spitfire versus Me 262 air-to-air kill; the first jet kill for 125 Wing of which 610 Squadron was a part. For Gaze, this was another kill to add to his score which up to then had been nine and a half confirmed destroyed, the half being shared with another pilot, four probably destroyed and five damaged. His jet kill resulted in him being awarded the Distinguished Flying Cross for the third time, an exceptional honour.

This was not the first time that a RAF Spitfire had destroyed a German Me 262 in an air-to-air engagement,

however. That distinction had gone to five Spitfires of 401 Squadron RCAF over Nijmegen on October 5, 1944, whose pilots (Sqn Ldr Rod Smith, Flt Lt Robert M Davenport, Flt Lt Hedley Everard, Fg Off John Mackay and Fg Off Andrew L Sinclair) shared in the destruction of the Me 262A-2a WNr. 170093, 9K+BL of 3./KG(J) 51's Hauptmann Hans-Christoph Büttmann, 24, who was killed in the engagement.

Most Allied fighter claims against the Me 262s were made from strafing attacks against the jets while they were on the ground at their airfields, or diving attacks made during their take-offs or landings, when they were most vulnerable, slower and least manoeuvrable.

Gaze had now joined a small and elite band of Allied fighter pilots who managed to down one of the German jets in an aerial combat engagement.

"After returning to base, Gaze claimed a rare Spitfire versus Me 262 air-to-air kill; the first jet kill for 125 Wing of which 610 Squadron was a part."

TWENTY-FIVE YEARS EARLIER

Frederick Anthony Owen 'Tony' Gaze was an Australian of British roots, born into a well-off family on February 3, 1920, in Melbourne, Australia, to parents Irvine and Freda Gaze.

Tony's father Irvine had been an Antarctic explorer who supported Ernest Shackleton's Trans-Antarctic Expedition

ABOVE: Spitfire Mk.XIVs of 610 Squadron in January 1944. Flt Lt Gaze rejoined the squadron in July 1944.
VIA CLIVE ROWLEY

RIGHT: Another gun camera still, this time from Flt Lt Gaze's 129 Squadron Spitfire Mk.IX, shows the death throes of the Focke-Wulf Fw 190 he shot down on August 17, 1943, while he was officially being 'rested'.
VIA TONY BERGHOUSE

BELOW: The same four 610 Squadron Spitfires from the side. During this time Flt Lt Gaze was still recuperating after being shot down and escaping back to Britain through occupied Europe.
VIA CLIVE ROWLEY

and had survived being stranded in Antarctica for two years before being rescued. Irvine Gaze then became a fighter pilot with 48 Squadron RFC, flying Bristol Fighters on the Western Front during the First World War. Returning to Tangmere, near Chichester, after the war had ended, Irvine met his future wife, Freda, a WAAF driver. Flying, it seemed, ran in the blood of the Gaze family.

Tony was educated at Geelong Grammar School, in Australia, and was already in the UK as an undergraduate at Queen's College Cambridge when the Second World War broke out in September 1939. He was a man of means, courtesy of the family's shoe making businesses, which enabled him to list his occupation on his passport as 'Gentleman'.

Tony's younger brother, Irvine Junior, known as 'Scott', who was two years younger, was also studying at Cambridge when war was declared. Both brothers immediately enlisted in the RAF.

TRAINING, TRAGEDY AND A DFC
The Gaze brothers both graduated from 5 Flying Training School at RAF Sealand in January 1941, and then from 57 Spitfire Operational Training Unit (OTU) at Hawarden, Cheshire, in March 1941, following in their father's footsteps to become RAF fighter pilots.

They were both posted as pilot officers to 610 Squadron AuxAF to fly Mk.IIa Spitfires operationally at

RAF Westhampnett, upon part of which the Goodwood race circuit would later be built. The squadron was about to become part of Wing Commander Douglas Bader's celebrated Tangmere Wing, 'Bader's Bus Company'.

Tragically, only two weeks after joining 610 Squadron, on March 23 and just after his 19th birthday, Tony's younger brother was killed when his Spitfire flew into the South Downs while chasing two Junkers Ju 88s in bad weather.

It was a terrible blow for Tony, but there was little time to mourn as he was in constant action that summer, shooting down his first enemy aircraft, a Messerschmitt Bf 109E on June 26 over Gravelines, northern France.

The squadron re-equipped with Mk.Vb Spitfires in July 1941 and continued to take the fight to the enemy with fighter sweeps over France.

Gaze was awarded the first of his three DFCs on August 5, 1941, having destroyed three and a half Bf 109s, plus two probably destroyed and one damaged. The citation said: "This officer has shown a persistent desire to engage the enemy on all occasions.

> *"Gaze was awarded the first of his three DFCs on August 5, 1941, having destroyed three and a half Bf109s, plus two probably destroyed and one damaged."*.

"In a recent combat he undoubtedly saved his squadron commander from being shot down over enemy territory by destroying his two attackers. He has now destroyed at least three enemy aircraft."

The incident referred to in the citation, when Gaze saved Squadron Leader Ken Holden from being shot down in a dogfight over France, occurred on July 10, 1942. He was flying Spitfire Mk.IIB 'DW-G' and claimed both Bf 109s destroyed. He had more than proven himself as a good wingman. Gaze remained with 610 Squadron until November 1941, when he was posted for a break from operations to be an instructor at No 57 Spitfire OTU.

FLIGHT COMMANDER

In June 1942, Gaze was posted back to operational flying as the flight commander of 'B' Flight on 616 (South Yorkshire) Squadron AuxAF, with the rank of acting flight lieutenant. During his time with 616 Squadron, the unit was variously based at Kings Cliffe, West Malling, Kenley and Great Sampford and was equipped with the high-altitude Mk.VI Spitfire.

This version of the Spitfire had been developed to counter German high altitude bombers and reconnaissance aircraft and was fitted with extended, pointed wing tips, a pressurized cockpit and a Rolls-Royce Merlin 47 engine driving a four-bladed Rotol propeller intended to provide increased power at high altitudes. More often than not though, this limited-edition variant of the Spitfire (only 100 were built) was used as a conventional fighter at lower levels.

Gaze flew with 616 Squadron, leading 'B' Flight, until the end of August 1942. During this time he was credited with destroying a Focke-Wulf Fw 190, probably destroying another and damaging two more. He also shot down a Dornier Do 217 bomber during the ill-fated Dieppe Raid, Operation Jubilee, on August 19, 1942.

Neither Gaze nor his colleagues could confirm the destruction of his first victim with 616 Squadron, a Fw 190 which he attacked west of Abbeville on July 13, so he claimed it only as probably destroyed. In 1994 the wreck of this particular Fw 190 was discovered during excavations, so it is now known to have been a definite kill and not the 'probable' with which Gaze was originally credited.

GAZE DEMOTED

In September 1942, Gaze was promoted to acting squadron leader and given command of 64 Squadron, flying Mk.IX Spitfires out of Hornchurch. On September 26, he led a wing of Spitfires, including 133 (Eagle) Squadron, in support of a USAAF Boeing B-17 daylight bombing raid on Morlaix, France.

BELOW: The members of 610 Squadron pictured September 1944 – Tony Gaze is in the front row, second from left. VIA TONY BERGHOUSE

ABOVE: In April 1945, Gaze joined 41 Squadron flying Spitfire Mk.XIVs, some of which had the new 'low back' design, which afforded significantly improved visibility.
VIA CLIVE ROWLEY

The sortie briefing led the Spitfire pilots to expect little cloud and a strong headwind outbound. In the event, when they were over the Channel, they encountered heavy cloud cover obscuring the ground features and, unknown to them at the time, a 100mph tailwind, which blew the formation much further south than intended and out of radio contact with England.

Returning into the headwind, with fuel running low, the American pilots of 133 Squadron decided to descend below the cloud to look for land, despite being told by Gaze not to do so. The Eagle Squadron pilots flew directly over Brest and were subjected to all that the German defences could throw at them.

The unit lost 11 of their 12 brand new Mk.IX Spitfires; the 12th crash landed on the south coast of England having turned back early with an engine problem. Four of the American pilots were killed and six became POWs. Three RCAF Spitfires also failed to return, but the remainder of the wing, including all of the 64 Squadron Spitfires, reached England safely.

This unfortunate and tragic incident weighed heavily on Gaze's mind for some time and, as the leader, he took the blame for it even though he had ordered the 133 Squadron Spitfires not to descend. He continued in post and damaged another Fw 190 during a combat on October 11.

The official inquiry that ensued, eventually concluded that the debacle was the result of many contributing factors, especially the incorrectly forecast weather and the inexperience of some pilots. Nonetheless, Gaze was made something a scapegoat for the event and in November he was transferred back to 616 Squadron as a flight commander, back down to the rank of flight lieutenant.

Officialdom eventually forgave him, it seems, and when he was rested from operations again in January 1943 Gaze, who was now officially an ace, was awarded a second DFC for his "high skill and fine fighting spirit".

SHOT DOWN

While officially being rested from operational flying, between May and August 1943, Gaze flew as a supernumerary pilot with 453, 222 and 129 Squadrons, which made up the

Hornchurch Wing. During combats in August, he destroyed a Fw 190, damaged another and claimed a 'probable' against a Bf 109G.

Towards the end of August he was formally posted back to the front line as the flight commander of 'A' Flight on 66 Squadron, which was flying Mk.Vb Spitfires at Kenley

On the morning of September 4, 1943, flying Spitfire Mk.Vb 'LZ-A' on fighter escort duty for RAF Boston bombers raiding Amiens, Gaze became embroiled in a dogfight with several Fw 190s. He shot down one of the enemy fighters, but was then attacked himself by six more.

He radioed for help from the rest of the squadron and endeavoured to escape, but was forced to turn and face his adversaries each time one of them attacked. Eventually, after some 10 minutes of fierce and increasingly desperate combat, the engine of Gaze's Spitfire was hit

BELOW: Flt Lt Gaze was flying Spitfire Mk.XIV RM797 EB-E when he scored two and a half victories with 41 Squadron – over a Junkers Ju 52, an Arado Ar 234 and a shared Focke-Wulf Fw 190. The aircraft is pictured at Eindhoven. VIA CLIVE ROWLEY and critically damaged by a burst of cannon fire from one of the Fw 190s.

He was forced to crash land at high speed, with the undercarriage retracted, near the town of Le Tréport, 20 miles west of Dieppe, in enemy occupied France. His conqueror was Luftwaffe fighter ace Leutnant Gerhard Vogt of 6./JG 26.

Despite head and facial wounds suffered in the high-speed crash landing, Gaze managed to evade capture and with the help of the French Resistance he embarked on the difficult and dangerous journey through occupied France and over the Pyrenees into Spain.

From there he was transferred to Gibraltar and thence flown back to England in a RAF C-47 Dakota. He arrived back in the UK two days short of eight weeks after he had taken off on the ill-fated mission, and was admitted to hospital for surgery to repair his facial damage.

FIGHTING THE LONG-NOSE

Having recovered from his injuries, Gaze completed a rest tour on fighter affiliation duties, training bomber crews to defend themselves against fighter attack. He then rejoined his first operational squadron – 610 – in July 1944, as a flight commander. The squadron was now flying the Griffon engined Mk.XIV Spitfire and, on August 5, Gaze shot down a V-1 flying bomb over Kent.

Towards the end of 1944 the squadron was transferred to Belgium as part of the RAF Second Tactical Air Force and, during Bodenplatte on January 1, 1945, Gaze added to his rising score with a Fw 190D-9 destroyed. The Fw 190 'Dora' was the latest variant of the successful and robust German fighter, with a longer nose to accommodate the inline, liquid-cooled Jumo 213 engine that produced 2100hp in some variants.

> *"The squadron was now flying the Griffon engined Mk.XIV Spitfire and, on August 5, Gaze shot down a V-1 flying bomb over Kent.".*

Its performance made it a worthy adversary for any of the latest Allied fighters, including the Spitfire Mk.XIV and the P-51D Mustang.

On January 1, Gaze had taken off on patrol at 8.50am but had been separated from the rest of his section having taken evasive action against intense and accurate flak from Allied ground forces near Liege, Belgium.

He said later: "I found myself alone when I got to our base. I was amazed to find several aircraft on fire as was the fuel dump. As I turned round the aircraft a group of 30 plus Fw 190s and Me 109s came by a low level but as we were flying in opposite directions, they had gone a long way by the time I had rolled round and started to chase them.

"After a short time I saw eight Fw 190Ds in a better position, so turned after them. I caught them just after crossing the River Meuse but, as they were so low, I had trouble shooting because of the slipstreams. After a while they crossed a wood and as they lifted, I was able to get a good burst at one, hit it and the flaps and one undercarriage leg came down.

"It then crash-landed at high speed. I started after the others for a few seconds then decided I was well into Germany and outnumbered so I climbed away. I was followed to the river by flak and picked up by American AA when I crossed, so formed up on a Mustang: then they stopped."

The pilot of the Fw 190D-9, WNr. 600380, Leutnant Christfried Clemens of 10./JG 2, was killed.

INTO GERMANY

After achieving the feat of destroying the Me 262 jet fighter on February 14, Gaze was transferred to 41 Squadron in April 1945, for his fourth operational tour as a flight commander.

41 Squadron also operated the Mk.XIV Spitfire and, in April 1945, it moved forward with the advancing Allied front to its first base in Germany, just southwest of the town of Celle (140 miles west of Berlin), only a short distance from the Nazis' former concentration camp at Bergen-Belsen.

During April and early May, German resistance crumbled and in the 23 day period up to May 3, 1945, the squadron claimed 33 enemy aircraft destroyed in the air; its pilots also shot up 21 Luftwaffe aircraft on the ground at their airfields.

Gaze claimed a Junkers Ju 52/3m transport aircraft destroyed near Bremen on April 10, making him a double ace. Two days later he shared in the destruction of another of the Luftwaffe's jets with a kill against an Arado Ar 234 jet bomber, shared with Flight Lieutenant Derek Rake.

His combat report from April 12, 1945, tells of the dramatic combat: "I was leading Red section of four aircraft on a patrol Delmonhorst-Verden. At about 1700 hours Red 2 sighted an aircraft which I identified as an Arado 234 and chased, managing to drop my tank.

"The enemy aircraft, which was flying south, turned north and I cut the corner closing to 800 yards. I opened fire and got strikes on fuselage and starboard wing. I continued firing closing slowly and more strikes were followed by the starboard jet catching fire.

"I closed to 100 yards and broke away as the enemy aircraft flicked inverted after some wild jinking. It spun violently down flicking one way and then another and I last saw it disappear in the haze inverted at about 1000ft. Red 3 saw it recover at 300ft and finished it off. I claim one Arado 234 destroyed shared with Flt Lt D V Rake."

After being credited with another shared, half-kill, against a Fw 190D-9 on April 28, the final combat victory of the war for Gaze was against a Fw 190 that he described as 'short nosed' near the Elbe Bridgehead, Germany, on April 30, 1945.

BRITISH JETS

For the last few days of hostilities Gaze moved to 616 Squadron, the only unit flying the new Gloster Meteor Mk.III operationally on the Continent and by now based at Fassberg in Germany.

> *"Tony Gaze finished the war with a total score of 11 destroyed and three shared destroyed, including two of the Luftwaffe's jets – a Messerschmitt Me 262 and an Arado Ar 234."*

BELOW: Tony Gaze, wearing his hat, with members of 616 Squadron and a now camouflage painted Gloster Meteor. VIA TONY BERGHOUSE

The Meteors were painted white all over to aid identification and avoid confusion with the Me 262. During the last days of the war and just prior to the unconditional German surrender, Gaze landed his Meteor on a stretch of autobahn where Luftwaffe Me 262s were stationed, to meet with the German pilots.

After the airmen, former enemies, had looked over each other's aircraft and Gaze had been photographed standing by a Luftwaffe Me 262 similar to the one that he had shot down, he took off and flew back to his base, having declined an invitation from the German pilots to attend a party being held that night.

He remained with 616 Squadron and flew in various victory parades after the war had ended, including performing what was reported as "a superb solo show" in his Meteor during the celebrations in Copenhagen before a crowd of more than 100,000 people.

FINAL RECKONING

Tony Gaze finished the war with a total score of 11 destroyed and three shared destroyed, including two of the Luftwaffe's jets – a Messerschmitt Me 262 and an Arado Ar 234 – he also claimed four enemy aircraft probably destroyed, one of which is now known to have been destroyed so his score was actually 12.

In addition, he shot down a V-1 flying bomb. He had flown Spitfires operationally from March 1941 to April 1945, spanning four years of war fighting and 488 combat missions in Mk.II, Mk.V, Mk.VI, Mk.IX and Mk.XIV Spitfires.

He is one of fewer than 50 people to be awarded three DFCs (DFC and two bars) during the Second World War. He was still only 25 years old when the war ended.

WHEN THE WAR ENDED

After the war, Gaze stayed in the RAF for two more years, flying the Meteor jet as a squadron commander and as a test pilot, before returning to Australia.

During his time in England he had got to know Kay Wakefield, the 30-year-old widow of Johnny Wakefield, a successful prewar English racing driver, who had been killed flying with the Fleet Air Arm in 1942. Kay had been involved in racing circles since before the war and Tony Gaze was drawn into the motor racing world.

Kay visited him in Australia and on her second trip in 1949 they were married and then returned to England together. They set up home at Caradoc Court, a Jacobean manor house with extensive estates and stables, overlooking the River Wye in Herefordshire, which Kay had inherited from her father. It is now a hotel.

Gaze raced an Alta Formula 2 car at various events all over Europe and in 1952 became the first Australian to compete in a Grand Prix at the Circuit de Spa-Francorchamps in Belgium. In 1953 he drove a Holden FX in the Monte Carlo rally.

He acquired an ex-Ascari Ferrari 500 F2 car and other Grand Prix races followed. He had Jack Brabham in his own racing team, and came second to Stirling Moss in the 1956 New Zealand Grand prix. Gaze won the Australian Grand Prix four times in 1954, 1957, 1958 and 1961. He also raced an Aston Martin DB4GT Zagato at Le Mans in 1961.

After his first wife Kay died in 1976, Gaze sold up in the UK and moved back to Australia. A year later he re-married Diana Davison, widow of Lex Davison, a fellow Australian racing driver who was killed during practice for a race in 1965.

Gaze's contribution to Australian motorsport was recognised in 2006 when he was awarded the medal of the Order of Australia (OAM). His second wife Diana died in 2012 aged 86.

Tony Gaze DFC and two bars, OAM, fighter pilot, jet killer and racing driver, whose life reads like a Boy's Own adventure, passed away peacefully on July 29, 2013, at the age of 93. ●

ABOVE: Gaze soon familiarised himself with the Gloster Meteor and flew it during end of war celebrations in Copenhagen before a crowd of more than 100,000 people. VIA TONY BERGHOUSE

LEFT: Celebrating a racing success in 1956. From the late 1940s to the early 1960s Gaze raced all over the world – winning the Australian Grand Prix four times. VIA CLIVE ROWLEY

BELOW: Tony Gaze at the wheel of his Ferrari 500 F2, with which he won seven Grand Prix races in a row. VIA CLIVE ROWLEY

THE FATAL MISTAKE OF LOTHAR SIEBER

MARCH 1, 1945: BACHEM-WERK M23 TEST FLIGHT

The career of talented Luftwaffe pilot Lothar Sieber was on the rise when charges of drinking on duty saw him arrested and stripped of rank. To redeem himself, he undertook one hazardous mission after the next until on March 1, 1945, he took on the most dangerous of them all…

ABOVE: Test pilot Lothar Sieber speaks with a man identified in most sources as Erich Bachem shortly before his first and only flight in BP-20 M23. The fully prepared rocket-powered vertical take-off aircraft awaits him in the distance.

H aving been interested in flying from a young age, 14-year-old Lothar Sieber attended a rally at his home city of Dresden in 1936 and found himself shaking hands with First World War flying ace and recently appointed Reich Aviation Minister Hermann Göring.

It was an inspirational moment, and afterwards Sieber was determined to become a pilot in the newly formed Luftwaffe. Four years later, as soon as he was old enough, he signed up and before long he had not only qualified as a pilot but had also specialised in large bombers, mastering a wide variety of aircraft including captured Allied examples such as Boeing B-17s and Soviet Tupolev TB-3s.

He was promoted to leutnant and given his first command in 1942 – a meteoric rise. His world fell apart in February 1943, however, when he was caught drinking on duty. He was demoted to ordinary pilot and sentenced to

four months in prison. His father wrote to Göring himself, explaining the circumstances and pleading for clemency, and the sentence was reduced to six weeks' close arrest – but the demotion stuck.

Back on duty, Sieber threw himself into his work as never before. In April 1944, he was involved in trials of the Arado Ar 232A, which was designed for short-distance take-off on rough terrain using its centreline row of 10 smaller wheels mounted beneath the fuselage. He also carried out rocket-assisted take-off trials using the aircraft and was so confident of his skills that at one point he looped the loop in a Junkers Ju 52. In August 1944 he was posted to I./KG 200.

While Sieber's quest to regain his original rank continued, work was going on elsewhere which would ultimately ensure that he never succeeded.

RISE OF THE SNAKE

It was during Sieber's period of close arrest that the Allied bombers began causing disastrous damage to German cities and industry. The Luftwaffe seemed unable to stop them by conventional means, so a number of unconventional ideas were examined by the Reichsluftfahrtministerium (RLM) – the German Air Ministry.

An aircraft was needed which could climb at high speed to intercept the bombers as they appeared, inflict maximum damage, and then return quickly and safely to earth.

The idea of a vertical take-off rocket-powered interceptor had originated with a 27-year-old Dr Wernher von Braun in 1939. Already working on a number of rocket projects for the Luftwaffe, he had submitted a proposal to the RLM outlining a fighter that could be launched vertically from the back of a lorry, up to an altitude of 26,250ft in 53 seconds before switching to horizontal flight.

The aircraft's main engine would then cut out and a smaller secondary unit would take over. When the mission was over, the aircraft would land on a skid. The RLM turned von Braun's report over to Heinkel, the company already responsible for building the world's first liquid rocket powered aircraft, the He 176, for assessment.

The firm's development team was sceptical about the idea, suggesting that the engine envisioned by von Braun would not be powerful enough, its fuel would run out too quickly, and there was no tactical benefit to having a very short range high-altitude fighter.

The proposal was not rejected however, and was next handed to Gerhard Fieseler's engineers, led by the firm's technical director Erich Bachem, modified the idea to form the basis for a pair of 'rider and horse' designs, where a rocket would be used to boost a jet-powered aircraft to high altitude.

This was purely a paper exercise, however, as Fieseler was busy with other projects such as expanding production of the highly successful Fi 156 Storch. Von Braun resubmitted his idea in 1941, only to have it finally rejected outright by the RLM a few months later.

By now, the RLM was already backing a different team, led by Alexander Lippisch, building a different rocket interceptor – the Messerschmitt Me 163 Komet.

Work on the Me 163 was slow, however, and disagreements between Lippisch and Willy Messerschmitt led to the former leaving the company in 1943. When the bombs started to fall on Germany in earnest, the Komet was woefully behind schedule and beset with teething problems.

It was also complex and at best offered only four minutes, 11 seconds of powered flight at full throttle.

A requirement was therefore issued in 1944 for an even smaller fighter that could be built from basic materials such as wood and powered by a Walter 109-509 liquid rocket unit – the same power plant as that fitted to the Me 163. It would also have to be capable of being flown by a pilot who had received only minimal training, since all qualified fighter pilots were urgently needed by the front line units.

Meanwhile, Bachem had left Fieseler in 1941 with the intention of setting up his own business, Bachem-Werk GmbH being formally established on February 10, 1942, at Waldsee, Upper Swabia, by Bachem and his business partner, former Fieseler test pilot Willy Fiedler. The new company specialised in wooden aircraft parts and was initially kept busy with contract jobs – eventually designing and making parts for the Dornier Do 335 Pfeil and Heinkel He 162. It may also have manufactured parts for Fieseler's Fi 103 V-1 flying bomb.

The only uniquely Bachem aircraft at this time was an ultralight known as the Lerche. When the RLM requirement was issued for a small wooden rocket fighter, Bachem found himself in an excellent position to draw up a proposal that could successfully fulfil it. He said later that he vaguely remembered seeing von Braun's proposal during his days at Fieseler and resolved to design something similar, which he named 'Natter' or 'Snake'.

He began with a rough sketch of something resembling a manned missile on July 16, 1944. The parachute-wearing pilot lay prone within a cigar-shaped fuselage, a rocket projectile weapon ahead of him in the 'aircraft's' nose.

Further design drawings fleshed out this concept and it was given the factory designation BP-20-01. Bachem wrote up a terse outline of his design's purpose in a document headed 'Projekt Natter': "Annihilation of enemy aircraft especially bombers by bringing up a gunner within the immediate vicinity of the enemy and discharging rocket projectiles at him with the smallest possible amount of manoeuvring and propellant.

"No self-destruction of the pilot, on the contrary, armoured protection of him. Smallest possible production cost, maximum use of wooden parts, reduction of iron. No burden on standard aircraft industry. Exploitation of the large, partly free, timber resource. Repeated use of the most critical airframe and propulsion unit parts by parachute recovery.

"Little requirement of the pilot, due to the omission of a normal landing. Little ground input. Little transport cost. Easy

transferability. Good camouflage potential."

With Bachem providing the outline, the project's chief designer was Dutchman Henri Frans Bethbeder. At an early stage, it was envisioned that the Natter's nose would house 19 55mm R4M rocket projectiles but no firm decision was made on armament. As for the rest of the aircraft, several design variations were worked on simultaneously.

The overall cost of the Natter was expected to be about 1/50th of that for a normal fighter aircraft and it was further anticipated that full production could begin within six months. By September

> **"Little requirement of the pilot, due to the omission of a normal landing. Little ground input. Little transport cost. Easy transferability. Good camouflage potential."**

LEFT: The first manned test of the Bachem BP-20 was carried out using the M1 glider towed by a Heinkel He 111. It took off from a trolley with Flugzeugführer Erich Klöckner at the controls but was destroyed on landing, Klöckner having already bailed out.

ABOVE: Lothar Sieber was an outstanding pilot but had his career ruined by a charge of drinking on duty. He was looking for any opportunity to redeem himself and regain his original rank.

BELOW: Erich Bachem and famous test pilot Hanna Reitsch on July 17, 1938, at an air show in Kassel-Waldau. Bachem, then the technical director of Fieseler, oversaw the day's events. Just six years later he would be responsible for building one of the most dangerous aircraft ever flown.

the favoured design had shifted to that of a manned rocket aircraft, BP-20-09, rather than a manned missile – the pilot now seated rather than prone. The single rocket engine in the rear of the fuselage was augmented by a pair of disposable Schmidding SG 34 solid fuel boosters attached on to each side of the aircraft.

The launch sequence was to involve the pilot bracing himself against padded head and back rests and gripping handles on either side of the rear nose frame. On the left handle was the button to fire the boosters.

Once this was pressed, the Natter would rise under the control of a basic autopilot and after 10 seconds it would be at an altitude of 4000ft and a speed of 550mph. The exhausted boosters would then automatically detach and the Walter engine would take over.

Within another 50 seconds, the Natter would reach the same altitude as the bomber formations. The pilot would then turn off the autopilot, grab the control column and bring the aircraft around in a shallow curve to line up a target.

> ## "Within another 50 seconds, the Natter would reach the same altitude as the bomber formations."

At a distance of 300m he would fire the Natter's weapons at the bomber. The Walter engine would then run out of fuel and the pilot would put it into a dive. Pulling out at low level, the pilot would activate a mechanism to detach the aircraft's nose, which would fall away, and he would then be catapulted out by the sudden deceleration – activating his parachute.

The Natter's fuselage, minus the nose, would then descend to earth on its own parachute, ready to be refurbished and reused.

Tendering for the RLM requirement had, however, ended in August and Bachem's early design was the one submitted for consideration. It was up against advanced designs from three much larger firms – Messerschmitt, Junkers and Heinkel.

FRIENDS IN HIGH PLACES

In early September, the RLM awarded Heinkel a contract for 20 prototypes of its P.1068 vertical take-off rocket aircraft design – later to become the P.1077 'Julia'. Messerschmitt

and Junkers, which had both tendered horizontal take-off designs, and the Natter were seemingly out of the race.

Bachem refused to accept this rejection however. He took his idea to SS-Obergruppenführer Hans Jüttner and Sturmbannführer Otto Skorzeny who, excited by it, took it directly to the leader of the Waffen-SS, Heinrich Himmler. Himmler granted Bachem an audience and offered him the full support of the SS for his "war deciding device".

Now under pressure from the SS, in mid-September the RLM was forced to give Bachem a contract for 15 BP-20 aircraft. Himmler sent some of his own people to oversee the project too – SS-Obersturmführer Heinz Flessner, who led a team of 120 Waffen-SS construction workers

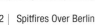

seconded to Bachem-Werk, and SS-Obersturmführer Gerhard Schaller.

The first Natter V1 prototype was finished on October 4, 1944, and on October 28 it was given the official RLM designation 8-349, later Ba 349, though this name was seldom if ever used at the time. The aircraft was known as the BP-20. Construction was now well under way on the 15 aircraft 'ordered' by the RLM. The Natter's basic dimensions now featured a stubby wingspan of 11ft 9in, a short fuselage of 19ft 2in and a fuselage width of 2ft 11in.

Various different armaments were discussed including a pair of MK 108 30mm cannon, a battery of 28 R4M rockets and a cluster of 32 single-shot 30mm cannon barrels, but again no satisfactory conclusion was reached.

On November 3, a manned gliding trial took place with an engineless Natter airframe designated M1. It was towed along the runway behind a Heinkel He 111 on a take-off trolley with Flugzeugführer Erich Klöckner at the controls.

A Junkers Ju 87 was used as an observation platform. All three aircraft became airborne at around 4pm but Klöckner struggled to control the M1 until he moved a trim weight inside it, altering the centre of gravity. Even so, he was forced to bail out when he realised that the aircraft could not be brought into a normal towed position and therefore its parachutes could not be deployed.

The M1 landed behind the He 111, twisted, detached and then span away, coming apart in the process.

A second gilder, the M3, was fitted with an undercarriage so that it could be properly landed and reused. It was competed on November 20 and test-flown by Klöckner on December 14. Again, he was forced to bail out but this time the Natter glider landed safely without its pilot.

The first attempted vertical take-off test of the Natter was on December 18 at Heuberg – a military training area about 40 miles west and slightly north of Waldsee – using prototype M21. While the boosters went off as planned, the release clamps failed and the aircraft was engulfed in flames and burned out on the ground.

On December 22, 1944, the first successful launch took place with prototype M16. It flew up to about 230ft before tipping over onto its side. It crashed 5250ft away. That same day, a new test pilot arrived at Bachem-Werk – Lothar Sieber.

LAST WILL AND TESTAMENT

Sieber had been recommended for the job by Sturmbannführer Skorzeny. He had met the 22-year-old after he had gone behind enemy lines in an Ar 232 to rescue 23 of his KG 200 comrades who had become encircled by the Soviets in Ukraine. It was a close-run thing. Despite being under heavy fire, Sieber managed to get the transport aircraft off the ground and then flew it at low level all the way back to base.

This feat earned him a personal letter of commendation from KG 200 commander Oberst Werner Baumbach and the Iron Cross 1st Class. After further heroics on the front line, Skorzeny recommended him for another bravery decoration, the German Cross in gold. He also offered him the opportunity of promotion to oberleutnant if he would undertake a mission for the SS – fly Bachem's new SS-sponsored rocket-powered interceptor.

After arriving at Waldsee, Sieber watched several vertical take-off trials of Natter prototypes, including the successful test of version M22 on February 25, 1945, where a dummy pilot was fired into the sky and then floated safely down on a parachute after the nose separation was activated automatically. The fuselage parachute also activated but traces of fuel left in the Walter engine's tanks ignited and M22 was burned out.

The first manned test, Sieber's first flight in the Natter, was scheduled for March 1. Asked how he felt about the prospect, he apparently replied: "In the course of this war I have already done riskier things, let me worry about this. I look upon the testing of the device as a self-imposed

LEFT: The Natter was design with a disposable nose but it was intended that the rest of the fuselage would float safely back down on a parachute once its mission had been completed.

BOTTOM: Camouflage netting clings to the tail of the M23 vehicle on the morning of March 1, 1945, as the aircraft is prepared for Lothar Sieber's test flight.

BOTTOM: Netting still in place, ground crew work to fill M23's tank with C-Stoff – the chemical which, when combined with a second chemical, T-Stoff, produced the violent reaction which provided the rocket engine's thrust.

ABOVE: Fully fuelled and ready to fly. M23 hangs from its launch ramp awaiting only its pilot. Sieber's padded head rest, attached to the cockpit hatch lid, can clearly be seen.

RIGHT: Lothar Sieber, having scrambled up a precarious wooden gangplank, grips a handle on the nose of M23 as he struggles to manoeuvre himself into the cockpit.

task that I would like to accomplish and I firmly believe in a successful outcome."

Despite this bullish attitude, he still prepared a last will and testament on February 28 which left all his worldly goods to his fiancée Gertrud Nauditt, who was four years his senior.

The day of the launch saw grey skies over the Heuberg launch site and mist on the ground which began to clear as the morning wore on. M23 was the Natter prepared for the launch and its design had been significantly altered from M22.

It had a safety chute to decelerate the fuselage as the pilot bailed out – in place of a parachute to 'rescue' the fuselage, which was to be sacrificed on this occasion – rudders were installed in the tail and the elevons were increased in size by 20%.

There was a pitot tube on the right wing for monitoring air speed and other sensors were fitted to monitor the aircraft's performance. There was no autopilot – the control column had been fitted with a slight depression of 2° but otherwise Sieber would be required to simply hold it in the neutral position during take-off.

> *"In the course of this war I have already done riskier things, let me worry about this. I look upon the testing of the device as a self-imposed task that I would like to accomplish and I firmly believe in a successful outcome."*

Take-off was scheduled for 11am and while final checks were being carried out on M23, Sieber stood on a low hill overlooking the launch site. He wore his full bulky flight suit and helmet. At some point he received final words of advice or encouragement from both Erich Bachem and Willy Fiedler.

Close to 11am, he walked over to the launch tower and climbed vertically up to a steeply angled wooden gangplank which took him up to the leading edge of M23's left wing. A trio of ground crew helped him awkwardly scramble around the outside of the machine and into the cockpit. Going in legs first, he lay on his back in the seat and buckled on his parachute before fastening his seat belts. He put on his oxygen mask and the canopy hatch was closed by the crew.

They then climbed down from the tower and retreated to a safe distance before signal rockets were launched to tell Sieber that it was time to start the Walter engine. This was allowed to build up to full thrust – a cloud of smoke enveloping the Natter in the process – before Sieber ignited the four boosters with a bright flash visible through the haze.

The Natter's locking mechanism released flawlessly and Sieber's machine shot upwards. After climbing to about 330ft, the aircraft began to curve onto its back at an angle of about 30° – then the canopy hatch flew off. Something had gone badly wrong but the aircraft continued its ascent to about 5000ft whereupon it disappeared into a bank of low-lying cloud.

Just 15 seconds into its climb, the Natter's engine stopped and it rolled right over on to its back before entering a nose dive. Several kilometres from the launch site, Lothar Sieber's first and last flight in the Natter ended when it crashed vertically into the ground. It had been in the air for less than a minute.

THE FINAL MOMENTS

After waiting an hour in the hope that Sieber had parachuted to safety and would come walking back, the Bachem team went in search of the crash site. Writing several years later, Bachem himself described the scene: "We found the machine completely destroyed. The pilot had made no attempt to escape. Of our comrade we found only

LEFT: With nothing between him and a plunge to the ground, Sieber clambers into the Natter's cockpit legs first, assisted by ground crew.

BELOW: The Natter launch procedure called for its Walter rocket engine to be ignited first. The thrust produced was insufficient, on its own, to lift the aircraft so it produced a dense cloud of smoke instead, completely enveloping the machine.

BOTTOM: Solid-fuel boosters ignited, M23 roars skywards with Lothar Sieber attempting to hold the control column in the neutral position, despite a 3G load on his arms. The production Natter was intended to have an autopilot for this stage of the flight but this was not yet ready on March 1.

ABOVE: With Lothar Sieber dead, the Natter test programme reverted to unmanned testing. Here, vehicle M52 is winched into position on a newly designed single-rail tower.

RIGHT: Another view of M52 attached to its pole launcher – essentially a straight tree trunk shorn of branches.

the left hand with a piece of forearm and a left leg that was ripped off below the knee."

The crater left by the impact was 5m deep and when it was excavated a small shard of Sieber's skull was found. When little remained of him was buried with full military honours in the cemetery at Nusplingen.

The investigation carried out by Bachem-Werk afterwards had little hard evidence to go on but attention was concentrated on the canopy hatch that had broken away from the aircraft during its ascent. It was recovered intact not far from the launch site and the latch meant to fasten it in place appeared to be bent.

Over the next few days a sequence of events was pieced together. It was suggested that for the first few seconds after take-off, Sieber's body would have been subjected to forces of about 3G – pinning him back in his seat and applying backwards force to his arms.

Since he was holding the control column, this would account for the aircraft curving steadily on to its back. As the aircraft became increasingly upside down, Sieber's body would have been pushed up against the hatch – his seatbelt having enough 'give' to allow this to happen. The latch might well have then given way, causing the hatch to be caught by the slipstream and spin away.

The pilot's headrest was a part of the hatch so when the hatch suddenly parted company with the aircraft, Sieber's head would have been violently flung back 25cm, against the wooden rear wall of the cockpit. This was likely to have concussed him, rendered him unconscious or even broken his neck.

It was considered possible that a dazed Sieber might have shut down the rocket engine himself after 15 seconds but it was equally possible that the odd angle of ascent might have caused air bubbles in the Walter engine's fuel, causing it to cut out.

Either way, the Bachem team felt they had been

pressured into conducting a manned launch too early.
It seemed as though Sieber's accident might have been avoided if an autopilot had been available to prevent the control column from moving.

This was small consolation to his family and his fiancée.

THE INFAMOUS NATTER
The first Natter to be flown with automatic guidance, M14, flew on March 16. After a successful take-off, it went into a spiral and was destroyed after its safety chute failed to prevent a hard landing.

A total of seven further vertical launches were carried out from the tower after Sieber's death and plans were advanced to bring the Natter into service under the code name Krokus. This was chosen because the crocus

> ## "We found the machine completely destroyed. The pilot had made no attempt to escape. Of our comrade we found only the left hand with a piece of forearm and a left leg that was ripped off below the knee."

blooms in March, when the attacks on bombers had very optimistically been expected to begin.

A mobile pole launcher was designed for use with the Ba 349A-1 and a test machine, M52, was successfully fired from it some time after April 5. Ten production Natters, still regularly referred to as BP-20s, were under construction during late March and into early April. The final armament of a nose-mounted honeycomb type launcher for 24 Henschel Hs 297 Föhn rockets was fitted.

A handful had been completed by mid-April when French ground forces entered the vicinity of the Bachem-Werk factory. Attempts were made to put the Natters into operation but in reality the personnel involved were only just able to keep the aircraft away from the advancing Allies by driving them around on the back of trucks.

Four lightly damaged Natters and the personnel accompanying them were captured at St Leonhard in Austria on or around May 6, 1945.

After the war, Bachem's factory was closed by the French and the firm was dissolved, its holdings being sold to the Wolf Hirth company. Bachem tried various subsequent business ventures but died in 1960 after a long illness. Willy Fiedler got a job working for the American military and after some initial involvement with Northrop, ended up working for Lockheed. He helped to design submarine-launched missiles such as Polaris and died in California in 1998. ●

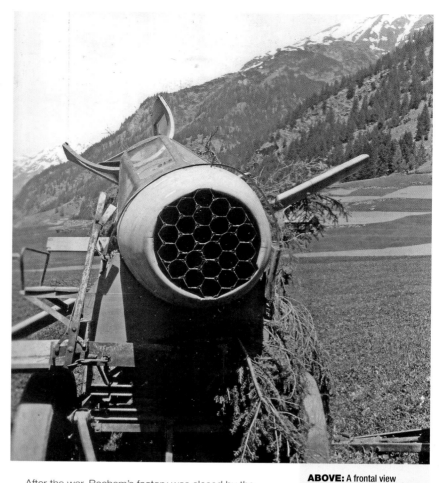

ABOVE: A frontal view of a Natter captured by the Americans, showing the honeycomb Föhn rocket launcher finally chosen as the aircraft's armament.

LEFT: Americans examine one of four damaged production Ba 349A-1 Natter aircraft captured in Austria.

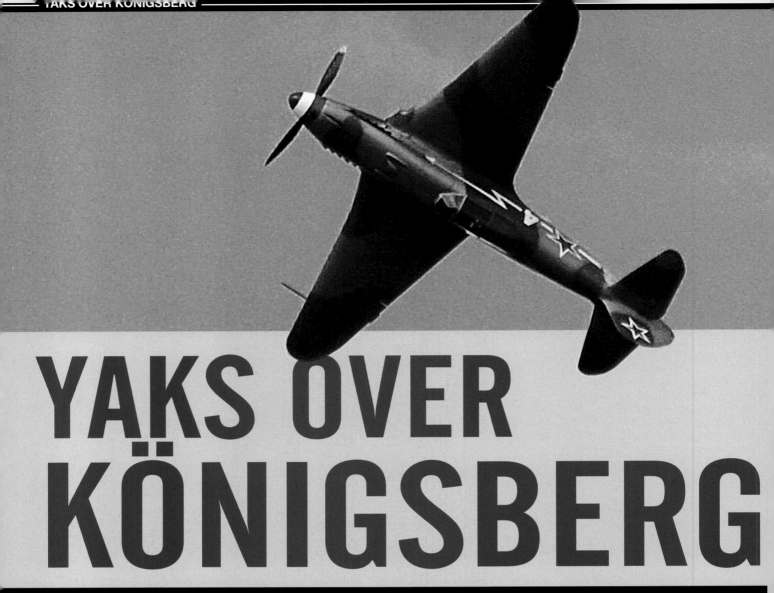

YAKS OVER KÖNIGSBERG

MARCH 31, 1945: NORMANDIE-NIEMEN JOINS THE LAST BATTLE FOR EAST PRUSSIA'S CAPITAL

Général Charles de Gaulle sent a Free French Air Force group to serve alongside the Soviet Air Force on the Eastern Front in November 1942. This was Groupe Normandie. By 1945 the Frenchmen were battle-hardened Yak-flying veterans about to face their sternest test – the advance on Königsberg.

ABOVE: A Yakovlev Yak-3M painted in the colours of the Normandie-Niemen regiment. Deliveries of the original Yak-3 began in late 1944 but Normandie pilots were still flying the Yak-9 until the beginning of 1945.
SEBASTIAN TENGUY

Königsberg was a fortified city that marked the furthest eastern extent of the old German Empire. It was the capital of East Prussia and an important port on the Baltic Sea. Since 1941 it had been on the front line of the war against the Soviet Union – being repeatedly bombed by the Soviet Air Force.

Being close to the departure point for Germany's invasion of first Poland, then the Soviet Union, the city had become a centre for slavery and a collection point for looted treasures from the east.

Within and around the city were around 85,000 Polish and Soviet slaves as well as Allied prisoners of war, working in labour camps.

The summer of 1944 had also seen two devastating night raids on the city by the RAF, which destroyed the historic old city, gutted the cathedral and severely damaged the castle and other large civic buildings.

Nevertheless, Königsberg maintained huge fortified positions on its landward side that remained untouched by aerial attack. These included three defensive rings – the outermost consisting of 12 fortresses linked by subterranean tunnels and concrete structures, a secondary ring around the outskirts of the city itself and the main city fortress in the centre.

All three were protected by an impressive array of anti-tank positions and structures, barricades and minefields.

In addition, there were a number of other heavily fortified positions both within and immediately outside the city.

Manning all these positions were five full divisions of German infantry – 130,000 men all together.

There was also strong support for Königsberg in the air. As of January 11, 1945, Luftflotte 6, based in East Prussia and western Poland was the strongest Luftwaffe formation to be found anywhere on the Eastern Front.

Luftflotte 6 boasted JG 51 with 108 Bf 109s (78 serviceable), and 86 (70) Bf 109s of JG 52. It also had two night fighter units, NJG 5 and NJG 100 with 94 (76) aircraft between them, a mixture of Bf 109s and Ju 88s.

KG 55 was still equipped with 14 (10) He 111 bombers, and perhaps most importantly Luftflotte 6 had three large ground-attack units – SG 1, SG 3 and SG 77. Between them they had 294 (262) Fw 190 fighter-bombers which could also serve as pure fighters if need be. In addition, 10./SG 77 still had 19 (16) Ju 87s.

There was also the night ground-attack unit NSGr. 4 with 60 (47) Ju 87s and Si 104s, the maritime reconnaissance unit SAGr. 126 with 21 (11) Ar 196 floatplanes and nine (six) Bv 138 flying boats, strategic reconnaissance units FAGr. 1, FAGr. 3, AGr. 22, AGr. Nacht and AGr. 122 with 124 (88) Ju 188s, Me 410s, Ju 88s and Do 217s, and tactical reconnaissance units NAGr. 2, 3, 4, 8 and 15 with 159 (126) Bf 109s and Fw 189s.

Finally, Luftflotte 6 could also call on a single depleted transport unit – I./TG 3 with 36 (27) Ju 52s. Overall this amounted to 1024 (817) aircraft, 582 (486) of them fighters.

GROUPE DE CHASSE 3

At the beginning of 1945, the front line was less than 50 miles to the east of Königsberg. Ranged against the German forces in East Prussia were more than 1.6 million Soviet troops commanded by Ivan Chernyakhovsky – at 38 the youngest commander of an entire front during the Second World War.

His forces included large tank armies and four air armies – the 1st, 3rd, 4th and 15th. Each of these comprised more than a thousand aircraft.

Within the 1st Air Army was a highly unusual unit. The Free French Air Force's Groupe de Chasse 3 (GC3) had been sent to Russia in November 1942 at the behest of Général Charles de Gaulle. The Free French leader had set up the National Committee in 1941 as a sort of war cabinet and was determined that the Soviet Union should give official recognition to Free France.

Part of this was offering military assistance. Soviet leader Joseph Stalin had been cautious at first but with the formation of the National Committee opted to encourage mutual military assistance between the two nations.

De Gaulle signed the order forming Groupe de Chasse 3 on September 1, 1942, and shortly afterwards it was agreed that the unit should also use the title 'Normandie' so that its members would always remember that region of France and the fact that it was under German occupation.

By early December the unit's pilots and equipment had been incorporated into the Soviet Air Force and on January 19, 1943, its first fighters, six Yak-1Ms, were delivered.

The unit's first operational mission, involving 13 of the new Yak-1Ms, took place on March 22, 1943, and its first aerial victory was on April 5: Lieutenants Albert Préziosi and Albert Durand shot down a Fw 190 each in the Smolenski area. Both would themselves be killed in action later that year.

Having started out as a single escadrille or squadron, Normandie expanded to two in August 1943 – named Rouen and Le Havre.

After eight months of incredibly fierce fighting on the front line, nine of the groupe's original 15 pilots had been killed in combat, including its commandant Jean Tulasne. And of the 23 replacement pilots received between May 10, 1943, and the end of November 1943, 12 had been killed.

The 38 pilots had accumulated 72 victories between them, however. Up to March 1944, this total was further raised to 84.

Now the groupe was expanded to a regiment, with third and fourth squadrons being added – Caen and Cherbourg. The Yak-1Ms were replaced by Yak-9Ds and more front line combat quickly followed during what became known as the regiment's second campaign.

It was during this campaign that Stalin ordered the regiment, which was operated under Soviet control and frequently made appearances in Soviet propaganda publications such as Pravda, to call itself Normandie-Niemen. This was to commemorate its role in the fighting to liberate the Niemen river – traditionally regarded by Germany as the marker of its true eastern border.

Deliveries of a remarkable new lightweight fighter, the Yak-3, began on August 17, 1944, gradually replacing the Yak-9Ds, which continued to be used in combat until the end of the year.

By the beginning of 1945, the regiment had amassed 201 'kills' but had been reduced back to just three squadrons as a result of personnel shortages. It had been stationed at Gross-Kalweitchen on the southern fringes of Lithuania and close to East Prussia since the end of November 1944.

Little flying was done during the first 12 days of 1945 but Normandie was moved to Dopenen, closer to the front. January 13 saw the beginning of Chernyakhovsky's East Prussian Offensive. His vast armies, including Normandie-Niemen, were unleashed against Germany's battered forces along the northern sector of the Eastern Front – and drove towards Königsberg.

FIRST FIVE DAYS

Weather on the first day of the offensive was too poor and those Normandie-Niemen patrols that were sent up had to turn back within minutes of takeoff as dense fog shrouded the region.

ABOVE: Sous-Lieutenant Roger Sauvage was a fighter pilot during the Battle of France. In April 1940 his twin-engined Potez 631 was shot down by a British pilot flying a Hawker Hurricane who mistook it for a Bf 110. He bailed out but landed badly and suffered total amnesia for four days. The following month, however, he scored his victory – shooting down a Dornier Do 17. A Heinkel He 111 followed in June.

ABOVE: The commandant of Normandie-Niemen from December 12, 1944, to the end of the war was Lieutenant-Colonel Louis Delfino. He was a highly experienced pilot who had joined the Armée de l'Air in 1931 and by the beginning of 1945 had racked up 12 aerial victories, though 10 of them were shared with other pilots.

ABOVE: Sous-Lieutenant Jacques André was one of Normandie's most successful pilots. During the third day of the Soviet push along the 3rd Belorussian Front he shot down four Focke-Wulf Fw 190s single handed and claimed another 'probable' in the Gumbinnen/Kussen area.

ABOVE: An ace with only two victories. Sous-Lieutenant Francois 'The Baron' de Geoffre also contributed to five more, giving him a tally of seven under the French scoring system. De Geoffre gained a reputation for getting into scrapes during the war and survived several near-death experiences – particularly when he was shot down and landed in the Friesches Haff.

ABOVE: Captain Gabriel Mertzisen was among the first Normandie pilots to score a victory during the opening stages of the Soviet East Prussian Offensive, shooting down a Messerschmitt Bf 109 on January 14 east of Insterburg.

BELOW: The Yak-3 of French ace Sous-Lieutenant Roger Sauvage, photographed shortly after the war's end. His aircraft shows his 16 'kills' in three rows of five with one more to the right just behind the cockpit canopy.

This had cleared by the following day, however, and at 1pm on January 14, a patrol from the 1st Escadrille encountered a pair of Bf 109s near Gumbinnen, about 80 miles directly east of Königsberg.

The Germans attempted to turn away but the Frenchmen followed in hot pursuit. Sous-Lieutenant René Martin hit one with his 20mm cannon and it began to burn before abruptly breaking up in mid-air. The second dived to extreme low altitude as Martin turned to fire on it too – attempting to lose him by hedge hopping. Instead, the pilot brought himself into range for both Sous-Lieutenant Pierre Dechanet and Aspirant Lionel Menut, who each scored several hits on his machine and then watched as he ploughed into the ground.

Three more Bf 109s were then engaged over a nearby railway line but although Martin and Sous-Lieutenant Roger Versini both claimed hits, the result was inconclusive.

A squad from the 3rd Escadrille found four Bf 109s near Insterburg but then lost them. Captaine Gabriel Mertzisen found them again but became separated from the rest of the squad. In spite of this, he doggedly followed them unnoticed until he got close enough to take the rearmost Messerschmitt by surprise and fired into it from point blank range, rapidly destroying it.

While this was going on, the rest of his squad encountered 15 Fw 190s north of Gumbinnen and shot two of them down before disengaging. Late in the afternoon, as darkness was falling, yet another Bf 109 was downed, this time by Aspirant Charles Miquel. Returning to base, Miquel then forgot to put his undercarriage down and landed his aircraft on its belly instead.

Snow started falling on January 15, which reduced patrols to a minimum, but on the 16th Sous-Lieutenants Jacques André, Francois de Geoffre and Pierre Lorillon, and Aspirant Roger Penverne, happened upon 12 Fw 190 fighter-bombers and attacked immediately. They got one each in the ensuing battle.

Another dozen Fw 190s were encountered by the pilots of the 1st Escadrille. Aspirant Léon Ougloff fired into one which seemed to release a shower of small metal fragments and Sous-Lieutenant Roger Sauvage hit and fatally damaged another at close range which then dived into the ground. Then he did the same to a second. Ougloff then claimed another blown up in mid-air.

On the way back to base, one of the 1st's pilots, Captaine Marc Charras, spotted some Pe-2s being attacked by Bf 109s. Also engaged in the battle were some P-39 Airacobras. Charras joined one of these to jointly claim a Bf 109.

The 2nd Escadrille fought still more Fw 190s, Sous-Lieutenant Georges Lemare opened fire on one only to see the pilot immediately eject his canopy and take to his parachute. The German's wingman was shot down by Aspirant Georges Henry. At this point, Miquel was seen going down, his engine struggling and billowing white smoke.

The leader of Normandie-Niemen himself, Commandant Louis Delfino, and four other pilots then caught a large formation of Fw 190s flying at low level by surprise. Delfino dived into them and used his cannon on one at very close range, causing pieces of the aircraft to fly off and hit his left wing. What was left of the Fw 190 then fell to earth.

André, attacking close by, had a similarly frightening experience when the Fw 190 he was firing into suddenly erupted into a ball of fire right in front of him. Quick reflexes narrowly prevented the resulting large chunks of debris from crashing through his aircraft's canopy.

On a second patrol towards the end of the day, André and three comrades engaged another group of around 20 Fw 190 fighter-bombers. Again, André poured fire into one at close range but this time it simply dropped its bombs, peeled off and crashed into the ground.

Aspirant Pierre Bléton, André's wingman, shot down two more. André's own total for the day was four Fw 190s destroyed and one 'probable'.

There was no let-up the next day as the battle raged on the ground below – the depleted German forces fighting a desperate delaying action against overwhelming odds. The Soviets found they were taking heavy casualties and making only painfully slow progress.

During a morning patrol, a squad of four from the 1st Escadrille found 12 Fw 190s strafing Soviet positions and ploughed into them. Captaine René Challe severely damaged one fighter and saw it go down before a second caught him in its crosshairs and blew a hole in his Yak, wounding him in the left arm. Sous-Lieutenants Robert Marchi and Robert Iribarne destroyed another Fw 190 each.

As part of a second patrol that caught up with some Fw 190s just as they were beginning their bombing run, Sauvage shot yet another down in flames – its pilot successfully bailing out.

This time though, it was Normandie's turn to be surprised. A formation of 20 Bf 109s appeared and attacked – sending Sauvage's comrade Aspirant Jean Piquenot crashing to his death. Captaine Charras was also lost, missing in action.

Flying had to be curtailed in the afternoon as a powerful snowstorm blew in and made further missions impossible.

January 18 was the opposite, with the morning written off due to heavy fog and flying commencing early in the afternoon. Close to Kussen, Captaine Pierre Matras and

de Geoffre caught up with a formation of four Fw 190s and managed to down two of them.

On a separate patrol, Sous-Lieutenant Gaël Taburet got a third. As part of another patrol from the 1st Escadrille, Sous-Lieutenant Marcel Perrin destroyed one Fw 190 and damaged a second before the remaining eight Fw 190s from the formation closed in on him and forced him to withdraw. His comrade Aspirant Pierre Genès was killed when the Luftwaffe pilots shot his Yak to pieces.

Delfino led a squad comprising Sous-Lieutenant Pierre Douarre, Mertzisen, Penverne and Bléton against 20 Fw 190 fighter-bombers, only to be bounced by another 20 that were flying escort. The French swiftly withdrew as the fighter-bombers dived away but Douarre managed to catch up with a straggler and shot him down about three miles northwest of Insterburg.

Later in the day, Charras made a surprise appearance at Normandie's base. He had evaded the Bf 109s of the previous day and then spotted a single one flying on its own.

He surprised the German pilot, who saw him at the last second and dived to the deck, attempting to flee at treetop height. Charras told his fellow pilots that he had been just about to open fire when the Bf 109's wingtip struck a branch and span the aircraft into the ground.

> **"André, attacking close by, had a similarly frightening experience when the Fw 190 he was firing into suddenly erupted into a ball of fire right in front of him."**

ABOVE: Russian by birth, Léon Ougloff's parents moved to settle in France when he was a one-year-old and he became a naturalised French citizen in 1933. He is pictured at the controls of another pilot's Yak-3 in this rare air-to-air photo taken by fellow Normandie pilot Roger Sauvage. The aircraft in question was the regular machine of Captaine René Challe. When the photo was taken, some time in March 1945, Ougloff and Sauvage were flying over Königsberg.

BELOW: Whenever Normandie was called upon to put on a display of its aerial prowess, its commanders called on Sous-Lieutenant, Lieutenant from March 1945, Roger Marchi, pictured here in the cockpit of his Yak-3. One of Normandie's highest scoring aces with 13 victories, seven of them shared, he had a reputation for being able to perform incredible aerobatics that wowed even his fellow pilots.

ABOVE: Captaine Marc Charras served with the French air force both before and after the Battle of France until his unit was dissolved by the Germans in 1943. He then escaped to Spain but was imprisoned by fascists. After being liberated by the British, he volunteered to serve with Normandie. He survived the war, only to be killed in combat during the First Indochina War in 1949 – the French Vietnam War.

BELOW: Ahead of the final battle for Königsberg, Normandie pilots watch one of their number making a pass over their airfield.

In the afternoon, Lieutenant Robert Castin, André, Bléton and Sous-Lieutenant Maurice Challe flew another patrol. Again, they happened upon a large group of bomb-laden Fw 190s heading for the front. Challe damaged one but then part of his fairing came away, forcing him to return to base – a common problem with the lightly built Yaks.

Bléton chased two, shooting one down and damaging the other, while André saw something very strange happen. He was pursuing a pair of Fw 190s and was about to open fire when his quarry suddenly opened fire on his comrade. The second Fw 190 burst into flames and crashed.

Hardly able to believe his eyes, André double checked that the aircraft he was following was, in fact, a Luftwaffe liveried Fw 190 and when he saw that it was he opened fire.

The apparently treacherous German fighter began to belch out smoke but André had to break off before he could finish the job. Castin, meanwhile, had spotted an Il-2 being set-upon by an Fw 190. He flew in, guns blazing, and forced the German to break off the attack – only for a second Fw 190 that he hadn't seen to shoot his Yak's engine dead.

He was forced to make a belly landing near Naumiestis in Lithuania.

On January 19, a squad from the 1st Escadrille found another 20 Fw 190 fighter-bombers being escorted by 20 more Fw 190s and while Charras claimed one, Sauvage claimed two.

A short while later, André, Challe and Bléton spotted a trio of Henschel Hs 129s tankbusters flying in formation at low level. Attacking together, they put two of them down but the other escaped.

Sauvage was in action again during his second patrol of the day – attacking nine Fw 190s with Iribarne, Marchi, Perrin and Taburet. He got one to begin with, then took another with the aid of Iribarne.

Marchi destroyed a third and a fourth was claimed by Perrin and Taburet together. Finally Perrin shot down one that appeared to have already suffered damage elsewhere.

That evening, the regiment heard that Stalin had mentioned them in his order of the day.

BREAKTHROUGH

Bad weather hampered operations again on January 20 and on January 21, the Normandie pilots heard that Soviet forces had finally broken through into Silesia and were closing on Breslau. At midnight, they heard that, far to the south, the Red Army had also entered Tannenberg, Saxony, inside the German border.

Snow continued to fall on January 22 and 23. Fog took its place on the 24th and 25th. The following day,

Normandie relocated to another small airstrip, this time at Gross-Skajsgiren. The move was completed by the end of January 27 and operations could at last resume on January 28.

During the first patrol of the day – in the Königsberg region – Matras and de Geoffre spotted a pair of Fw 190s and went after them. The Germans fled but the Frenchmen caught one and shot it down. Rather than exploding, spinning or otherwise coming apart, the Fw 190 reportedly skidded 650ft on its belly before coming to rest.

A second patrol tangled with three Fw 190s but without success and a third found just a single Fw 190. Three Normandie pilots claimed hits on it but later acknowledged that the aircraft was being flown so skilfully that it was difficult to get near it. With a last burst of gunfire from Henry, the fighter began to give off black smoke and then vanished into cloud under 1000ft off the ground.

Patrols resumed on January 29 but without encountering any enemies.

January 30 was a write-off due to appalling weather but the snow cleared enough on January 31 to allow a strafing mission against the German airfield at Gross Kubuiken – resulting in a Junkers Ju 52 being destroyed on the ground.

Activity in the air reduced because the Germans had suffered a catastrophic series of reversals on the ground.

The German 4th Army had been pushed back to the Baltic, where Soviet forces had then encircled it, trapping it against the shores of the Vistula Lagoon in East Prussia in what became known as the Heiligenbeil Pocket. With these battered divisions now contained, the Red Army continued its relentless drive westwards into northern Germany.

At the same time, what was left of the 3rd Panzer Army had been pushed into Königsberg and Samland – the peninsula to the northwest of the city.

Normandie's efforts now became focused on helping to crack this tough but isolated defensive bastion.

A thaw arrived on February 1, bringing with it mud and heavy rain. Despite these conditions, Normandie flew several reconnaissance missions over Königsberg. Two days later, strafing missions were undertaken on the airfield at Gross Kubuiken and on February 4 Penverne was shot down and killed during an encounter with 12 Fw 190s.

Normandie was moved to Powunden, about 12 miles directly north of Königsberg on February 5.

The rain then intensified until the clouds finally relented on February 10. The first patrol saw Matras, de Geoffre and Lorillon all firing into a Fw 190, one of a group of six, which soaked up their bullets and caught fire but did not go down.

> *"Sauvage was in action again during his second patrol of the day – attacking nine Fw 190s with Iribarne, Marchi, Perrin and Taburet."*

On the second patrol, Perrin, Henri and Lieutenant Maurice Guido ganged up on a Bf 109 which had been attempting to escape with a comrade and saw it crash into the ground.

Another four Bf 109s were spotted north of Bladiau, to the southwest of Königsberg. Sauvage and Taburet hit one, only to see it disappear into the clouds, while Charras hit another on its left wing. Sauvage and Marchi then chased this damage machine towards Pillau before Marchi finished it off and watched it crash.

On February 11, Iribane was shot down and killed by a Fw 190. Guido shot down a Bf 109 after interrupting a huge turning dogfight between a large force of Messerschmitts and Yaks of a different unit, Martin finished off another and Perrin got a third. Aspirant Maurice Monge failed to return and no one was sure what had become of him.

Two days of still more bad weather followed and on February 14 Normandie transferred to Wittenberg – a former fully-fledged Luftwaffe airfield almost directly south from Königsberg, rather than a muddy airstrip.

However, this meant that although it could boast concrete buildings, hangars and properly built runways, much of this infrastructure was in ruins, and booby-trapped.

Soviet sappers took more than 12 hours to destroy all the German devices, blowing several up where they had been laid because they were in such a dangerous state.

Operations recommenced on February 15 and although the first three patrols encountered no enemy activity, the fourth found a dozen Fw 190s preparing to attack some Il-2s. They were caught napping, and Lemare got one straight away then damaged a second.

Sauvage and Aspirant Joseph Schoendorff worked together to turn another into a ball of fire, its left wing shot to pieces before it crashed.

Despite the earlier thaw, a snowstorm then blew up and only a handful of further missions took place before February 20. That day there were a number of uneventful patrols but during one 12 Bf 109s appeared and immediately shot down Bleton, who managed to bail out.

By now, with just 24 pilots to call on, Delfino decided to reduce Normandie to just two escadrille – the 1st being dissolved and its pilots redistributed to the other two.

The next day, Monge reappeared and told everyone how he had run out of fuel before he could return to Normandie's airstrip and how, having crash landed, he was forced to rejoin the unit on foot – which had taken all of 10 days.

The big freeze continued from February 22 to February 25, when it was announced that Normandie would be relocated again, this time to an airstrip at Friedland. This occurred the same day without incident, despite the icy conditions.

Normandie was temporarily stood down the following day due to the ongoing manpower shortage and the terrible weather. This lasted until March 7.

At 11am, the Soviet General Staff announced abruptly that Normandie would resume operations that day and ground crew immediately set to work clearing snow from the runway. This took until 3.30pm, leaving just barely enough time for four patrols to provide a few minutes' coverage over the front line some 190 miles away to the west in the Elbing region of West Prussia.

The next day Normandie provided cover for Pe-2s that were bombing the Braunsberg area inside the Heiligenbeil Pocket. During the third patrol, a group of 12 Fw 190s intercepted the Pe-2s and began attacking them.

Pierrot raked one with fire and it dived slowly away trailing smoke, the pilot making no effort to control it – leading André, who saw it, to later report that he believed the pilot had been shot dead.

He also saw a Fw 190 on its own, being pursued by the Yaks of Challe, Ougloff an Lorillon.

Challe fired a burst but then realised he had an oil leak and peeled off. Lorillon took a shot and then saw that he too had an oil leak. Ougloff could not target the Fw 190 and it sped for home at extremely low altitude out onto the waters of the Frisches Haff.

March 9-24 passed without contact with the enemy – for much of that time the Friedland runway was in a poor state and all but unusable.

At last, on March 25, the day dawned to clear blue skies and the runway was clear of ice and mud. Several patrols were flown, with André and Challe taking on three Fw 190s close to Königsberg at Pillau. The former managed to down one of them, which crashed into the sea.

On March 26, the second patrol of the day was set upon by half a dozen Fw 190s. During the lengthy dogfight that

TOP: Ground crew prepare to refuel one of Normandie-Niemen's Yak-3s.

ABOVE: Normandie's Yaks lined up shortly after the end of the war. The one nearest the camera is the aircraft of Lieutenant-Colonel Louis Delfino, the regiment's commandant. When he was a child his father was killed in the First World War and he was brought up by his mother. On August 12, 1942, under the Vichy government, his unit was ordered to prevent British incursions into French West Africa and he ended up shooting down an RAF Vickers Wellington bomber with his Curtiss H-75A Hawk for his eighth shared victory.

ABOVE LEFT: Three of Normandie's highest scoring pilots together, from left, Sous-Lieutenants Georges Lemare (13 victories), Jacques André (15) and Roger Sauvage (16). The photo was taken during a parade for Soviet generals on March 20, 1945.

ABOVE: There were several Luftwaffe airfields around Königsberg at the start of 1945 but all were destroyed by heavy and relentless Soviet bombing.

The second patrol of the day comprised 10 Yaks and was again flown over Pillau. Contact was made at 13,000ft – high altitude for aerial combat on the Eastern Front – and Delfino opened fire as he climbed into a formation of eight Fw 190s, hitting one.

This aircraft then dived directly into the guns of Perrin, who destroyed it and saw the wreckage crash into the sea far below. Lemare and Schoendorff spotted a Bf 109 and Lemare shot it down.

As daylight waned, Guido took part in a five aircraft patrol but failed to return. Marchi fired into a Fw 190 which was then finished by Henri after a lengthy chase. Sauvage and Ougloff destroyed another by working together, Lorillon downing yet another which then crashed on to the shore.

When the pilots finally returned to base it was realised that Challe was no longer with them.

The following day, Guido showed up at Normandie's airstrip. There were celebrations because everyone thought he was dead. It turned out that he had simply suffered engine problems and had been forced to land elsewhere – the area was not short of Soviet-controlled airfields.

THE FINAL BATTLE

March 31 saw Normandie ordered to occupy the airfield at Bladiau to the southwest of Königsberg, but bad weather closed in and made a move impossible. It was not until April 7 that the weather improved sufficiently for the unit to make the transfer.

Bladiau was close to the southern shore of the Frisches Haff, the lagoon directly to the west of Königsberg. Across the water could be seen Pillau – a seaport on a narrow spit to the north – southwest of which was Pillau-Neutief airfield where the Bf 109G-6 and G-14 fighters of III./JG 51 were based.

To the north-east, a vast column of black smoke could be seen rising from Königsberg – a clear indication that the ground assault was already well under way.

Having arrived, the Normandie pilots began patrols immediately. A four-strong squad, André, Sauvage and Ougloff, with Capitaine Charles de La Salle bring up the rear, were flying over the sector towards the city at 11,500ft during the afternoon when André spotted four fighter-bomber Fw 190s flying east towards the battlefront at 5000ft.

Diving to attack, the three aspirants flew into a wall of heavy flak and were forced to break off. The Fw 190s got away in the confusion that followed.

Moments later, André managed to spot them again and this time dived down accompanied by de La Salle. The French pilots noticed that the German aircraft, flying in a straight line, were still carrying bombs under their fuselages – which meant they had not detected the threat.

This situation only last a few seconds though, as de La Salle flew in too fast and caught the Fw 190 pilots' attention. Seeing the threat, all four dumped their bombs and attempted to flee. André closed in, chasing one of them towards the north-west of Königsberg. He put four bursts of gunfire into it but once again extremely heavy flak forced him to disengage and he never saw what became of his intended victim.

Then the weather closed in again. Schoendorff, who had been flying with another patrol, got lost and was forced to land some 10 miles away from Bladiau at Normandie's old base of Wittenberg.

Meanwhile, Normandie's DC-3 had been busily moving the regiment's staff and supplies from Friedland to Bladiau. At 7pm, Normandie personnel went to their quarters in the only three nearby houses that had not been gutted by bombing, only to have their dinner interrupted by a massive bombardment taking place over the Frisches Haff at Pillau.

Wave after wave of Petlyakov Pe-2s and Il-2s bombed the seaport and nearby airfield and several Normandie pilots went outside to watch.

The following day, three patrols were sent up but found no targets – probably unsurprising given the heavy bombing of the night before. Towards the end of his patrol however, André

followed, Marchi damaged one of the enemy machines but then suffered a mechanical failure and was forced to crash-land his aircraft in a field near Normandie's airstrip. Monge was shot down and killed during the encounter.

During the fourth patrol, Perrin and Guido saw a pair of Bf 109s harassing an Il-2 before setting it on fire and speeding away before it crashed. They gave chase but their Yaks were initially outpaced by the Messerschmitts. They eventually caught up however and Guido destroyed one of them.

Late in the day, a commissar ordered Normandie to escort a group of Pe-2s that had turned up too late for its expected fighter escort. Four of the unit's pilots went up but on arriving at the rendezvous point were attacked by a lone Fw 190. It dived on them at high speed but then failed to fire and banked away.

Two more Fw 190s then appeared and one was shot down by Sauvage and de Geoffre.

It was decided on March 27 that sorties should only be made in force – with the first mission of the day comprised of 16 Yaks. This was meant to be an escort run but the Pe-2s never showed up so it became a patrol over the Pillau region.

A number of Bf 109s and Fw 190s were encountered and sporadic dogfights broke out. Dechanet crippled a Fw 190 which then fell into the Frisches Haff but in return de Geoffre was lost.

He had been flying parallel to the coast when his aircraft began to shudder violently and then his engine caught fire. When it finally stalled he had no option but to bail out.

As he tried to leave the cockpit of his stricken machine, he discovered that his right leg was caught up in his harness. Freeing himself with only seconds to spare he jumped, opened his parachute and then smacked into the freezing cold water.

His aircraft had hit the water an instant earlier and sank immediately. Despite pains from his leg, he swam to the shore and was picked up by Soviet soldiers who gave him a swig of vodka and basic medical care.

spotted another four Fw 190s flying towards a group of Il-2s on a bombing mission. His squad engaged the Focke-Wulfs and he again chased one that attempted to get away.

It headed south then west towards the now distant German front line. André fired on it five times before it sank to the ground and landed on its belly in a marshy area near Königsberg.

At around 1pm, two squads of six Yaks each were sent up by Normandie to protect bombers making an all-out assault on the city's already shattered defences. Nearly every available Soviet Air Force aircraft capable of carrying bombs was sent on this attack.

Aspirant Lorillon was among those sent to protect the bombers. While flying cover for Il-2s, Pe-2s and Douglas Boston IIIs, he looked over and noticed a DC-3 among them. As he looked on in amazement, the crew opened the side door and began tossing bombs out by hand.

Looking down, Lorillon found it impossible to see what effect the bombs were having – the whole city was invisible beneath a blanket of smoke and flames.

For the rest of the day, Normandie pilots strafed ground positions and hunted for targets of opportunity. One spotted an E-boat attempting to escape the city's port and make a run for the Baltic. He flew down and attacked, watching his 20mm cannon shells cutting into it. He then made a second pass before leaving the wreckage of the vessel sinking into the icy waters.

> ## "Looking down, Lorillon found it impossible to see what effect the bombs were having – the whole city was invisible beneath a blanket of smoke and flames."

THE END OF KÖNIGSBERG

During the final assault on Königsberg, including the devastating bombing raids, some 40,000 German troops were killed and another 92,000 taken prisoner afterwards. Just 30,000 civilians remained within the city's ruined walls and an uncounted number of slaves.

Three Soviet armies were involved in the attack – the 11th, 43rd and 50th Guards Armies comprising some 106,600 soldiers. Around 24,500 of these were specially trained and equipped assault troops. Casualties on the Soviet side were comparatively light at 3700 killed.

Assessing the battle in its aftermath, the Soviets counted 193 tanks or SPGs on the German side compared to 538 of the Red Army, 120 aircraft to 2174 and 3216 field guns to 2567 – plus another 2358 heavy artillery pieces.

Normandie-Niemen saw out the war in the east and in June 1945 was allowed to return to France with a gift of 40 Yak-3s from Stalin himself. These modern fighters help to form the basis for the fledgling postwar French air force. ●

ABOVE: In honour of Normandie's achievements, Stalin himself presented the new French government with 40 Yak-3s. They are pictured here at Le Bourget in Paris.

RAM THEM!

APRIL 7, 1945: KOMMANDO 'ELBE' IS UNLEASHED ON THE EIGHTH AIR FORCE

Adolf Galland's Great Blow never took off but his idea was not forgotten. Influential ex-bomber pilot Oberst Hans-Joachim 'Hajo' Herrmann gave it a novel twist – why not send up fighters en masse and have their pilots simply ram them into the bombers? The attack went ahead, though not exactly as planned…

RIGHT: Famous or perhaps infamous for an unconventional approach to warfare, Oberst Hajo Herrmann was the mastermind behind the ramming attacks carried out on American bombers by Luftwaffe pilots on April 7, 1945. BUNDESARCHIV

One of the Luftwaffe's rising stars and a keen ideas man, Oberst Hajo Herrmann, was appointed Luftwaffe Inspector of Aerial Defence in December 1943, aged 30, after pioneering the innovative but risky Wilde Sau or 'wild boar' night fighter technique.

This had involved day fighters, unequipped or only lightly equipped for night-time operations, being sent up into enemy bomber 'streams' to find their own targets independent of radar guidance – seeking to make visual contact by the glare of specially directed searchlights or the glow of burning buildings below.

Herrmann had himself taken part in more than 50 Wilde Sau missions – practising what he preached.

In late 1944, the seeds of another idea began to grow. What if he could recruit a large force of idealistic if inexperienced young pilots – volunteers – to participate in an attack en masse against the American bomber force?

Given the Luftwaffe's burgeoning supplies of newly built fighters, such a force could be equipped without difficulty, he reasoned, and launched together in a single one-off assault.

So far, so like Adolf Galland's Great Blow. But where Galland's force actually was trained to attack bomber formations with their fighters' weapons, Herrmann's force would not require even this basic instruction.

The attack would be carried out with Messerschmitt Bf 109s fresh off production lines – Bf 109G-10s, G-14s and K-4s – but with their engine cannon and one machine gun removed. The remaining MG 131 machine gun would have just 60 rounds of ammunition, compared to the usual 300. All armour protection would also be removed and a metal propeller was fitted rather than a wooden one. The standard Revi 16 gun sight was also removed.

Lightened to this degree, the Bf 109's qualities as a fast and manoeuvrable high performance machine would be considerably enhanced – giving it a greater top speed and allowing it to achieve a higher service ceiling.

With such an aircraft, even a novice ought to be able to catch up with waves of high-flying bombers and then… crash into one of them.

When he put the idea to Hermann Göring, the Reichsmarschall gave it a lukewarm reception. But early in 1945 he finally gave it his backing. With this in hand, Herrmann secured a promise of 1500 fighter aircraft from General der Flieger and Luftwaffe chief of staff Karl Koller.

Next, at 3.25pm on March 8, 1945, he sent out an appeal for volunteers to all units of Luftflotte Reich – the home defence force – 'signed' by Göring. It read: "The fateful battle for the Reich, our people and our homeland has reached a critical stage. Almost the whole world is against us.

"They have sworn to destroy us in battle and, in their blind hate, to wipe us out. With one final effort we must stem this threatening wave.

"As never before in the history of the Fatherland, we are facing a final destruction from which there can be no rebirth. This danger can only be averted by preparing to fight in the highest German tradition. I turn to you, therefore, in these deciding moments.

"I ask you to rescue, with one conscious effort, the life of your nation from a final downfall. I call you to an operation from which there is little possibility of returning. Those of you who are called will be sent immediately to flight training.

"Comrades – a place of honour in the glorious history of the Luftwaffe will be yours. You will give the German people in this hour of grave danger a hope of victory and you will be an example for all time."

These stirring words elicited 2000 volunteers – more than the absolute maximum number of aircraft that would be available.

It seemed that Herrmann's operation, now named Elbe, had all the right ingredients but the big problem was fuel. With operational Luftwaffe units already exerting maximum effort on all fronts, there was precious little to spare. In addition, Koller first reduced the total number of aircraft available for Elbe to 1000, then down to 350.

The list of volunteers was pared back and those selected began arriving at Stendal airfield – about 60 miles directly west of Berlin – for training on March 24. Prior to briefing his men, Herrmann had visited the Luftwaffe test centre at Rechlin to get an idea of how a Bf 109 might best approach a B-17 Flying Fortress or B-24 Liberator, and how it might cause maximum damage by ramming it.

Serious consideration was also given to how the Messerschmitt's pilot might possibly escape its crippled remains in the immediate aftermath of the crash.

It was decided that the best option all round would be for the pilot to dive on to his target and use his aircraft's propeller as a saw to cut through control surfaces on the tail or wings – or even to chop the rear end of the fuselage off completely. How best to get out of the fighter as it fell away with, at the very least, its propeller shattered, proved to be a more difficult question to answer.

Pilots were given the option of jettisoning their canopy before the attack or leaving it on and hoping to get it open afterwards.

This 'training' lasted for 10 days. Although some Luftwaffe pilots belonging to the earlier Sturm units, which specialised in attack bomber formations, had successfully rammed their targets, little or no real research had been carried out on the topic. Much of what the young pilots were presented with was guesswork.

Training ended on April 4, and on April 6 Herrmann told his men that they would go into action the following day. Unfortunately many of the specially stripped aircraft had not yet been delivered to Elbe's airfields – Stendal itself, Gardelegen, Sachau, Delitzsch and Morlitz, plus Klecan and Rucin on the outskirts of Prague in Czechoslovakia to the south.

On a more positive note, the experienced Me 262 pilots of JG 7 and KG(J) 54, and the Fw 190 pilots of JG 301, were instructed to provide support for the Elbe mission by attacking escort fighters that might otherwise prevent the 'rammers' from doing their job.

April 7 saw a total of 1314 bombers and 898 fighters – the full might of the Eighth Air Force – sent against targets in central and northern Germany.

More than half of the 974 B-17s involved, 529 of them, were to attack airfields at Kaltenkirchen and Parchim, the oil depot at Buchen and a munitions centre at Gustrow, with secondary targets of the rail marshalling yards at Neumunster and Schwerin.

Another 442 B-17s were to hit airfields at Wesendorf and Kohlenbissen plus an oil depot at Hitzacker. The secondary

"Pilots were given the option of jettisoning their canopy before the attack or leaving it on and hoping to get it open afterwards".

target was Lundeburg. Three more B-17s were involved in scouting missions.

The other heavy bombers, B-24s, were despatched to destroy explosives plants at Krummel and Duneburg.

At around 11am, the leading bombers were flying over Holland and it was possible for Luftwaffe staff to plot their likely course and targets. It was apparent that they were heading into northern Germany and could therefore soon become targets for Herrmann's Elbe force. Herrmann gave the order and his plan swung into action.

He wanted to have Elbe forces to the north and south of the bomber stream so that the chances of interception were increased. Their rallying points were to be above Domitz to the north and Magdeburg to the south.

Even now, however, the pilots at Stendal had no aircraft to fly. At the last moment, 16 aircraft that had been held in readiness elsewhere were ferried over to them. This still left 40 pilots effectively grounded. There were enough aircraft at Delitsch, 30 Bf 109s, but they were still being refuelled and there was a shortage of drop tanks.

A force of 24 aircraft was available at Morlitz and 20 at Gardelegen. Sachau was the only station to field 30 fully prepared machines. Altogether, around 120 Bf 109s set off from the five bases to intercept the Americans at around 11.15am. Shortly after takeoff, the pilots were surprised to find that the Nazi party's official anthem, Horst-Wessel-Lied,

ABOVE: Aircraft such as this Messerschmitt Bf 109G-10AS were used in the Elbe attacks of April 7. This machine is marked up as belonging to IV./JG 301 but was captured at the Elbe base, Stendal, on April 27, 1945.

BELOW: Bf 109G-14 WNr. 465805 abandoned at Prague-Rucin airfield in May 1945. Rucin was one of two airfields on the outskirts of Prague in Czechoslovakia that served as a reserve station for the Elbe attack.

BOTTOM: Damaged Messerschmitt Bf 109G-10s of JG 301 hidden among the trees close to Stendal airfield. Bf 109s used in the Elbe attacks are believed to have been unmarked and were modified to make them lighter and faster. Those machines that survived would probably have been pressed into service with other units.

TOP: Probably the first American aircraft destroyed by a ramming attack on April 7 – B-24L-5-FO 44-49254 'Palace of Dallas'. It was named after its skipper Lieutenant Bob Dallas and as the leading B-24 of the 389th Bomb Group, the 'Sky Scorpions', was hit head-on by the Bf 109 of Unteroffizier Heinrich Rosner at around 12.30pm.

RIGHT: On board Lieutenant Bob Dallas's B-24 was the commander of the 389th Bomb Group, Lieutenant Colonel John B Herboth Jr. He, Dallas, and everyone else on board was killed when the bomber was rammed and veered off course into a second B-24, B-24L-10-FO 44-49533 flown by 1st Lieutenant Walter R Kunkel.

BELOW: Pictured left is 2nd Lieutenant Robert F Bare of the 563rd Bomb Squadron with his crew. On only their second mission, their aircraft, B-17G-95-BO 43-38869 'Paula Sue', was hit by the Bf 109 of Oberfeldwebel Werner Linder, formerly of training unit Ergänzungs-Jagdgeschwader 1. Linder, Bare and all his crewmen were killed.

and Deutschlandlied, the German national anthem since 1922, were being played directly to them on their radio sets.

This was eventually replaced with the sound of a woman's voice speaking to them. It told them to "remember the women and children burned under the ruins of our towns" and to "save the Fatherland".

The 60 fighters at Klecan and Rucin near Prague were also ordered to take off, even though they were probably too far away to reach the bombers.

It has been estimated that out of the 180 fighters that should have taken off, for one reason or another, only 143 actually did.

The Elbe pilots were now expected to climb, up to an altitude of 10,000 metres – 32,800ft – where the air was thin and the temperature was down to about –40°C. This would put them above the bombers and in an ideal position to dive on them when the opportunity arose.

By midday, around 70 Elbe machines had assembled over Magdeburg, ready for action. Herrmann, realising that the fighters from Prague were not going to be of much use at this stage, recalled them.

Even now, several American fighter units had begun to make contact with Bf 109s flying alone or in pairs at extreme high altitude. North of Celle at 11.55am, one was shot down by 2nd Lieutenant Charles McBath, flying a P-47 of 'Household White' flight of the 63rd Fighter Squadron.

Another was destroyed by P-51 pilot 1st Lieutenant James W Ayers of the 334th Fighter Squadron's 'Cobweb Blue' flight at 12.15pm.

There were soon more sightings and more battles but before long a Bf 109 managed to get through and struck a B-24 of the 330th Bomb Squadron a glancing blow, taking two feet off the port wingtip and damaging the No.1 engine. Another B-24 of the 467th Bomb Squadron had the fin and rudder from its starboard vertical stabiliser sliced off by a Bf 109. Both bombers were able to limp home.

At just after 12.30pm, Elbe pilot Unteroffizier Heinrich Rosner managed the unit's first major success of the day – slamming his aircraft into the cockpit of the leading B-24 of the 389th Bomb Group, the 'Sky Scorpions'.

This was B-24L-5-FO 44-49254 'Palace of Dallas' flown by Lieutenant Bob Dallas but with command pilot Lieutenant Colonel John B Herboth Jr, the commander of the 389th, also on board. Dallas and Herboth were both either killed or incapacitated by the attack and the stricken 'Palace of Dallas' careered to one side and crashed into the second aircraft in the formation, B-24L-10-FO 44-49533.

This was a radar-equipped pathfinder flown by 1st Lieutenant Walter R Kunkel, with Major James F Tolleson on board as command pilot. Both were in the cockpit when the aircraft began to disintegrate around them – the rest of the crew unable to bail out. Abruptly, the cockpit itself came apart and both Kunkel and Tolleson were thrown clear. They parachuted to the ground and were taken prisoner.

The rest of the crew were killed, along with Dallas, Herboth and all but two of their crew members, who also survived as POWs.

Remarkably, Rosner himself managed to bail out after the crash and survived the attack by taking to his parachute as his ruined Messerschmitt fell away.

At around the same time, B-17s of the 388th Bomb Group came under attack from Elbe fighters. The first hit was B-17G-95-BO 43-38869 'Paula Sue' of the 563rd Bomb Squadron flown by 2nd Lieutenant Robert F Bare. Oberfeldwebel Werner Linder, formerly of training unit Ergänzungs-Jagdgeschwader 1, had crashed his Bf 109 into it, causing fatal damage and a fire which rapidly engulfed it.

Unlike Rosner there was no escape for Linder, whose body was recovered from the Hüttensee, a collection of small lakes just outside Meissendorf, a few days later. All of the 'Paula Sue' crew members were killed – it was only their second mission.

A moment later a second bomber from the 388th BG was rammed, an aircraft from the 561st BS – the unnamed B-17G-40-BO 42-97105 flown by 2nd Lieutenant Lew A Hickman Jr. This time though the damage was severe but not immediately catastrophic and five crew members managed to parachute to safety – Hickman himself, navigator 2nd Lieutenant Arnold Wolf, bombardier Staff Sergeant Cawthon B Perdue Jr, ball turret gunner Sergeant Albert W Vawter and right waist gunner Sergeant Herman R Meyer. All were taken prisoner on the ground.

The other four crewmen were killed – co-pilot Second Lieutenant John A Hughes, top turret gunner Sergeant

Elwood P Eisenhawer, radio operator Sergeant Jim F Martin and tail gunner Sergeant Bob W Wetzel.

Following on behind the 388th came another large formation of B-17s, those of the 452nd BG. They were also set upon by Elbe fighters, seemingly from every direction. The first casualty came quickly when B-17G-15-BO 42-31366 'Old Outhouse – Never a Dry Run' aka 'Snake Eyes' of the 731st BS flown by Dave Owens suffered a head-on collision. The entire fuselage forward of the top turret was completely destroyed. After wavering for a second, the remains of the aircraft crashed down, all nine crew members being killed.

Another bomber, B-17G-95-BO 43-38868 of the 728th Bomb Squadron, was sliced in half by a Bf 109, its front and tail sections falling separately to earth. Eight of its crew were killed but two were thrown clear and managed to get their parachutes open – bombardier Technical Sergeant Vance P Urban and radar counter measures operator Staff Sergeant Stephen A Kiss.

Two more B-17s suffered damage that would eventually result in the aircraft being brought down. B-17G-75-VE 44-8634 'Ida Wanna' of the 731st BS, flown by Dabney W Sharp, suffered substantial damage including having its number four engine knocked out by an Elbe attacker. It crashed near Heide, killing all but two of its crew – top turret gunner Technical Sergeant Arris D Stephenson and radio operator Technical Sergeant Ralph W De Celle.

Most of the crew of B-17G-70-VE 44-8531 'Miassis Dragon' of the 728th BS were more fortunate. When an Elbe machine wrecked the number two engine and set the port wing on fire, pilot 2nd Lieutenant Bill H Gill gave the order to bail out. Everyone managed to get out safely except for tail gunner Sergeant Bill E Costley, whose parachute snagged on the aircraft's tailwheel, causing him to be dragged down to his death.

At 1.04pm, the action resumed with an attack on B-17G-55-VE 44-8225 'Hard To Get'. The 579th Bomb Squadron, to which it belonged, was part of the 390th BG which had so far avoided any fighter attacks. This time though, it was a Me 262 of I./KG(J) 54 which dealt the killing blow – a ruined and burning number four engine. Flames spread up the wing and quickly threatened to set the whole aircraft ablaze.

Pilot 2nd Lieutenant Bill Kotta from San Francisco told his crew to abandon ship and all nine men managed to get down safely, while the vacated bomber, actually loaded with leaflets rather than ordnance, hit the ground near Celle.

Another bomber shot down at this time, by a Bf 109 or Fw 190, was 2nd Lieutenant Warren P Whitson Jr's unnamed B-17G-100-BO 43-39070. The damage inflicted made the aircraft unflyable but there was enough time for Whitson and his nine-strong crew to take to their chutes before it went down. All 10 survived as prisoners of war.

It was well after 1pm when the B-17s of the 100th BG, the 'Bloody 100th', first came under attack. The Elbe pilot who crashed into B-17G-40-BO 42-97071 'Candy's Dandy' of the 418th BS, flown by Lieutenant Arthur R Calder, was unlucky. His terrific strike succeeded in igniting the bomber's load of six 1000lb bombs and both B-17 and Bf 109 were instantly annihilated in a huge fireball that ripped through the sky.

At around the same time, the crews of bombers flying with the 385th BG saw fighters closing in on their formations. Four Bf 109s flew in close, attempted some head-on attacks and then pulled away without making contact. Four Fw 190s made similarly unenthusiastic attempts to fire into the bombers, swerving away before any real damage was done.

Then a Bf 109, flying on its own, plunged out of the clouds above the 385th and sped down through the bombers, apparently taking hits from several gunners before crashing into the unnamed B-17G-80-VE 44-8744 flown by 2nd Lieutenant George E Burich Jr. The heavily damaged bomber began to fall out of formation but it only got a few hundred feet before, like 'Candy's Dandy', it exploded, killing all nine crewmen on board.

Attacks on the 490th BG began at 1.13pm and an unusually well-equipped Elbe Bf 109, believed to have been flown by Leutnant Hans Nagel, formerly of IV./JG 102, accounted for B-17G-80-BO 43-38082 'Lady Helene' by shooting it down with its machine guns.

One crew member, navigator 2nd Lieutenant Jack F Knox, was killed in action but the other eight survived. Pilot Lieutenant Dick L Druhot, radio operator Staff Sergeant Bob M Campbell, ball turret gunner Edgar L Plaeger, right waist gunner Sergeant Ralph F Hogan and Jim Kyser were all taken prisoner.

Three men evaded capture however. These were co-pilot 2nd Lieutenant Chas W Bowers, bombardier Staff Sergeant Carmen B Francis and top turret gunner Staff Sergeant Jim A Bobo. 'Lady Helene' came down over Stolzenau, west of Hannover, which was very close to the Allied front line on April 7.

After putting 'Lady Helene' out of action, Nagel then targeted a second B-17, presumably having now run out of ammunition, and rammed it in the right waist gunner's position. This machine, B-17G-75-BO 43-38058 flown by 1st Lieutenant Carroll D Cagle, reportedly shuddered as Nagel's machine was briefly dragged down the fuselage, opening a 6ft rent along its side, caught on the ball turret and then span away, ripping the supercharger from one engine and smashing the propeller from another as it went.

Somehow, Cagle managed to coax the machine to a forward air base in France and land it successfully. The only crewman injured was the turret gunner, who suffered a broken arm.

A group of civilians, who had witnessed Nagel's battle with the B-17s, saw the remains of his fighter tumbling away and rushed to the crash site. His body was swiftly recovered and identified from its papers before he was buried with full honours in a village cemetery.

> *"Remarkably, Rosner himself managed to bail out after the crash and survived the attack by taking to his parachute as his ruined Messerschmitt fell away."*

BOTTOM: Unnamed B-17G-40-BO 42-97105 of the 388th Bomb Group. Flown by 2nd Lieutenant Lew A Hickman Jr on April 7, it was hit by an Elbe rammer but was not immediately destroyed. Five crewmen made it to parachute to relative safety in captivity, but the other four were killed when the bomber went down.

BELOW AND MIDDLE: The damaged tail of B-17G-90-BO 43-38514 'E-Z Goin' of the 100th Bomb Group. The vertical slash marks were made by the propeller of the Elbe Bf 109 that crashed into it.

ABOVE TWO PHOTOS:
Inspecting the damage done to B-17G-90-BO 43-38514 'E-Z Goin'. To make matters worse, the aircraft's No. 1 engine was accidentally shot up by a gunner aboard a nearby B-17. It therefore had to fly home on only three engines – the damaged tail causing them to struggle against tremendous extra drag.

TOP RIGHT: Even seen from the opposite side, the damage to 'E-Z Goin's tail still looks severe.

RIGHT: The crew of B-17 'E-Z Goin' stand where the horizontal part of its tail should be.

At 1.23pm, the 'Bloody 100th' was targeted again. B-17G-90-BO 43-38514 'E-Z Goin' was singled out by another Elbe volunteer. In an article for the 100th Bomb Group Foundation, the co-pilot of 'E-Z Goin', Hank Cervantes, remembered: "Caarraash! The nose yawed left, we skidded right and the plane waggled like a dog shaking water off itself.

"Instinctively Carl (pilot 1st Lieutenant Joe Carl Martin) and I kicked hard right rudder – both pedals disappeared under the instrument panel then returned to dangle uselessly; the control columns were violently jerking back and forth, the number one engine was streaming white smoke and all the radios including the intercom were dead.

"We had no way to ascertain the crew's condition or to get their damage assessments. However, like the stubborn old war horse unwilling to give up the fight, 'E-Z Goin' seemed to still want to fly, so we stabilised the rocking and rolling with the ailerons and hung on.

"At 1.28pm over the target, toggler (bombardier) Ralph Spada released the bombs and the nose lurched up sharply. Carl rolled the elevator trim wheel forward to add nose-down trim, but the wheel spun ineffectively. Now we were on a collision course with a B-17 in the squadron above.

"Quickly we exerted our combined strength to push the control columns forward. But it was insufficient and at the last possible moment Carl retarded the throttles. 'E-Z Goin' shuddered into a stall and the B-17 slid by close enough for us to see the startled look on the tail gunner's face.

"By trial and error, we found that 'E-Z Goin' was most stable at an airspeed of 105-110mph. This is just above the stall speed at that altitude, but although we could not understand the reason at the time, drag induced by the damaged tail was causing the engines to labour even at that airspeed.

"As the strung-out remnants of the 100th disappeared into the haze, we wallowed through the sky alone. Now the number one engine oil pressure was dropping rapidly; to prevent a friction-induced fire in the engine, we feathered the propeller and shut it down.

"This put an additional strain on the three functioning engines. The battle ended and flight engineer William 'Dude' Dudecz toured the ship to assess our condition. He reported back: 'Everyone's okay. Paul (tail gunner Paul Gerling) says that a Me 109 crashed into us; it just missed hitting him. The left elevator and the top half of the rudder are gone. There are two big gashes in the fuselage aft of the left

gunner's window and the flight control cables and electric wire bundles are cut there. What's left of the tail is flapping up and down so hard that it looks like it might break off. Oh dear, there are bullet holes in the left side of the nose. We think a gunner in another B-17 shot out the number one engine and the master radio control box, that's why the radios are dead.'

"On a B-17, the tips of the horizontal stabilisers are visible from the pilots' side windows, and I looked back to determine what was causing the control wheels to jerk back and forth so violently. 'Carl,' I said, 'Dude's right. The tail's really bobbing up and down on my side. What's yours doing?' Carl checked his and asked, 'Are you sure we're supposed to be able to see the tail from here?' 'Yeah, I'm sure.' 'I don't have one.'

"Dude tapped me and asked, 'Do you want to come back and take a closer look at the damage?' 'No Dude,' I replied, 'I'm needed here. How's Paul doing? Is he still in the tail?' 'No, I ordered him out of there. He says that when parts from the plane went flying back, they knocked off the left horizontal stabiliser on another B-17 behind us. They're back there somewhere.'"

What remained of the 'E-Z Goin' remained in one piece all the way back to the 100th BG's base at Thorpe Abbotts in Norfolk. The landing gear had to be manually cranked down.

Cervantes wrote: "Carl made a perfect two-point landing, and as everyone held their breath, we gently lowered the tail-wheel to the runway. 'E-Z Goin' screeched, grated and groaned in protest (picture a giant beer can being scrunched on the sidewalk), but she held together and a fleet of emergency vehicles trailed us to our hardstand.

"Five hours had elapsed since the collision, but no one cheered, embraced or shook hands – we were all barely into our twenties and at that age everyone thinks he is going to live forever."

Flying close to 'E-Z Goin' had been another B-17 of the 100th, B-17G-60-VE 44-8334, with Lieutenant Bill E Howard at the controls and Lieutenant Genaro Delgado as co-pilot.

Seconds after the attack on 'E-Z Goin', Delgado noticed that 44-8334's starboard wing was burning. Exactly what caused the damage is unclear – it may have been debris from another aircraft, bullets from a Bf 109 or even bullets from the gunner of another B-17. Whatever the cause, the aircraft's No. 3 engine was on fire.

Howard banked 44-8334 sharply out of formation and ditched the load of bombs it had been carrying. He tried various manoeuvres to put the flames out but failed. Then the main wheel beneath the engine caught fire and began to produce a stream of thick black smoke. As the wing itself began to buckle, Howard set his autopilot and ordered his crew to abandon ship.

All nine men managed to get out and dropped to the ground beneath their parachutes. They all hit the ground safely too, but on his way down Howard was fired on by shotgun-wielding civilians. They missed but it gave the pilot a taste of what was to come. Quickly captured by armed civilians, he was beaten before being dragged to the local village hall where he had stones and mud thrown at him by an angry mob.

Already at the village hall was navigator 2nd Lieutenant Doug Jones, who had suffered a broken jaw during his beating. They were eventually taken to a Luftwaffe detention centre with four of their fellow crewmen but the other three were nowhere to be seen.

Much later, after the war, the bodies of the missing men were found – sergeants Mike A Maty, Lou A Lehrman Jr and George F Thomas had been killed after landing. Their killers were never found.

There were more casualties when the bombers finally reached their targets. B-17G-70-VE 44-8528 'Flak Sack' was destroyed, not by flak, but by bombs dropped from another B-17. Eight of its 10-strong crew survived and were taken prisoner. One man, top turret gunner Staff Sergeant Roland R Fricault, evaded capture and the 10th, right waist gunner Staff Sergeant Tom G McMahon, was killed in action.

Another aircraft, B-17G-105-BO 43-39163 'Happy Warrior', had the double misfortune of being hit by bombs from above and by flak gunners on the ground. From a crew of 10, six men survived to be taken prisoner. Two others reached the ground alive but were subsequently killed.

In addition to the B-17s rammed or otherwise shot down, many more suffered varying levels of damage which forced them to land on the Continent rather than flying back to their bases in England – in the 303rd BG alone three aircraft had to get down as quickly as possible, the unnamed 43-38763, 42-97944 'Daddy's Delight' and 44-6309 'The Duchess' Granddaughter'.

The raid was judged a success, with 1257 bombers successfully dropping their ordnance on target out of the 1311 that set off (not including the three B-17s on recon duties) – a total of 3446 tons of bombs. Some 850 people were killed on the ground, four airfields were badly damaged, rail infrastructure targets were destroyed and oil production at two sites was disrupted.

A report on the day's action produced for the Eighth Air Force's director of intelligence, Brigadier Charles Y Banfill, stated: "After a lapse of several weeks during which conventional single-engined enemy aircraft have largely been non-active partners in the air war, and even when encountered have shown very little fighting spirit, today in excellent flying conditions the Luftwaffe put up a force of some 115-130 single-engined fighters supplemented by 50-plus jets.

"From all reports it appears that this was a desperate attempt on the part of the enemy, and although enemy aircraft fought aggressively and made determined efforts to get through to the bombers, our losses were comparatively light while more than half the enemy force was destroyed or damaged.

"Signs of desperation are evidenced by the fact that Fw 190 pilots deliberately rammed the bombers, bailing out before their planes went into the formations and making fanatical attacks through the murderous hail of fire.

"Tactics were thrown to the wind and attacks were made from all positions, mainly in ones and twos."

Banfill himself added: "The desperation of the enemy attacks and the closeness and abandon with which they were pressed seemed to be evidence of 'suicidal ramming'. They were not suicidal ramming attacks, but in each case were aircraft clearly out of control either through injury to pilot or structural failure of attacking aircraft.

"The closeness of attack has given rise to rumours of ramming but review of complete division experience fails to substantiate the ramming theory."

Eighth Air Force fighter pilots claimed to have shot down 67 enemy aircraft on April 7, 1945. When Me 262s, Fw 190Ds, probables, a case of 'friendly fire' and multiple claims are removed, this boils down to 47 claimed victories over Bf 109s. Bomber gunners claimed a further six Bf 109s shot down, making a total of 53. Given the likelihood of overclaiming, this probably amounts to about 30 Elbe aircraft being shot down before they reached their intended targets.

It has been estimated that around 40 Elbe fighters managed to attempt a ramming attack on the American bombers. Some 10 bomber losses, two B-24s and eight B-17s were directly attributed to ramming by enemy fighters with overall losses to all causes of 17.

Herrmann hoped to carry out further attacks the following day but it was not to be. No further Elbe attacks were ordered and he turned his attention to his final wartime scheme – Sonderkommando Bienenstock or 'Beehive'.

This involved using Fieseler Fi 156 Storch light aircraft to carry demolition teams behind enemy lines where they could carry out attacks on Allied static targets such as bridges, supply depots and parked-up tanks.

The order to establish Bienenstock was given on April 14 and 15 personnel were ready for action four days later. Five aircraft took off for operations on April 25 with only four returning and with no concrete results.

The following day, nine Storchs took off between 1.45am and 2.30am carrying two man demolition teams. Two bridges were blown up but five of the aircraft and their crews were lost. Finally, on April 28, three Fi 156s took off to attack supply depots in south east Germany but none returned. ●

> *"Five hours had elapsed since the collision, but no one cheered, embraced or shook hands – we were all barely into our twenties and at that age everyone thinks he is going to live forever."*

LEFT: The final moments of B-17G-105-BO 43-39163 'Happy Warrior'. Missed by the Elbe rammers, the aircraft nevertheless had the double misfortune to be hit by bombs from above and by flak gunners on the ground. Six of its 10-strong crew survived, two of them reaching the ground safely but then being killed by German soldiers or civilians.

BELOW: Despite the best efforts of Kommando Elbe, the vast majority of Eighth Air Force bombers deployed on April 7, 1945, returned home safely. Some, such as 42-97944 'Daddy's Delight', were not shot down but suffered damage severe enough to force an early landing at Allied airfields on the Continent.

King of FIGHTERS

THE BEST SINGLE-SEATERS OF 1945

Technology was advancing rapidly towards the end of the war with the most powerful piston-engined types the world had ever seen fighting alongside or against the first jet aircraft. But how did they compare?

There were around 20 high performance fighter types at least nominally in service in Europe when the war there came to an end.

Each had its strengths and weaknesses – a higher top speed, a better rate of climb or simply being quicker in a turn, but it is worth bearing in mind that even the best aircraft in the hands of a novice was usually a poor match for a lesser machine in the hands of an experienced ace.

The 'official' statistics available for each machine have been endlessly scrutinised in the decades since the war's end and some of the figures, for example for top speed, were achieved only under special conditions – with particular equipment fitted and at a particular altitude.

The fastest Messerschmitt Bf 109, the K-4, for example, has an 'official' top speed of 440mph, but this could only be managed with methanol-water injection (MW-50) to allow increased boost pressure in its DB 605DB or DC engine, and then only for a maximum of 10 minutes. It also required a broad-bladed 3m diameter VDM 9-12159A propeller and then only at 24,600ft.

Without MW-50, even the Bf 109K-4 could only manage 416mph, at 26,528ft. These figures also relate to well-built aircraft running high octane fuel in engines allowed to run at full power. De-rating engines had been a common practice in the Luftwaffe, to reduce maintenance time, since the beginning of 1944. Fuel shortages meant there was no opportunity to test engines and aircraft thoroughly before they were accepted into service either. And by the end of the war, many if not all of Germany's aircraft manufacturers were relying on slave labour to produce components and assemble the finished product.

Sabotage and shoddy workmanship were routine – a situation that worsened as the end of the war approached. Hans Knickrehm of I./JG 3 wrote about the new Bf 109G-14/AS aircraft received by his group from the manufacturer in October 1944: "The engines proved prone to trouble after much too short a time because the factories had had to sharply curtail test runs for lack of fuel.

"The surface finish of the outer skin also left much to be desired. The sprayed-on camouflage finish was rough and uneven. The result was a further reduction in speed. We often discovered clear cases of sabotage during our acceptance checks. Cables or wires were not secured, were improperly attached, scratched or had even been visibly cut."

These issues were typical of many new aircraft being delivered to front line units.

The available statistics for the aircraft examined here, regardless of their origin, do not include measurements for some of the most important aspects of performance either – such as manoeuvrability, rate of turn, rate of roll or dive speed. For these, anecdotal evidence must suffice.

In addition, several of these aircraft were only available in tiny numbers and so were unable to make any real impact on the outcome of the war – such as the Heinkel He 162 and Focke-Wulf Ta 152. Some types, such as the Me 163 Komet, were of greater value for the fear they instilled in Allied bomber crews, and Allied intelligence, than for the pitifully small number of aircraft they were actually responsible for shooting down.

Had they been urgently needed, jets such as the Gloster Meteor F.3 and Lockheed P-80 Shooting Star could have been rushed to the front line and brought into action far sooner – hence their inclusion here. Similarly, the Bell P-63 Kingcobra was delivered to the French too late to see combat and was supposedly only used on the Western Front in small numbers by the Soviets. It was available in 1945, however, and did see combat against Luftwaffe types.

The aim here is simply to provide a statistical comparison between the most powerful and advanced aircraft available in Europe. Five British types have been chosen for inclusion – the Supermarine Spitfire LF.IX, the Spitfire Mk.XIV, the Hawker Typhoon Mk.1b, the Hawker Tempest V and the Gloster Meteor F.3. The four American types are the North American P-51D Mustang, the Republic P-47D Thunderbolt, the Lockheed P-38L Lightning and the Lockheed P-80A Shooting Star.

The four Soviet types are the Lavochkin La-7, the Yakovlev Yak-3, the Yak-9U and the Bell P-63A Kingcobra – an American fighter but initially flown almost exclusively by the Russians. Finally, seven German machines are included: the Focke-Wulf Fw 190A-9, the Ta 152H-1, the Fw 190D-9, the Messerschmitt Bf 109K-4, the Me 262A-1a, the Me 163B-1 and the Heinkel He 162A-2.

Some contemporary types, such as the Bell Airacomet, are omitted because they were never considered for front line duties, and others, such as the Hawker Tempest II and De Havilland Vampire, have been left out because they were simply not yet ready for action.

SUPERMARINE SPITFIRE LF.IX

FAR LEFT: A line-up of Spitfire LF.IXs at an advanced landing ground on the Continent in late 1944.
LEFT: Flying Officer George Lents of 341 Squadron pictured in front of his Spitfire LF.IX in Sussex, June 1944. By 1945, the Spitfire IX had been completely outclassed in straight line speed by newer types, but it could still climb faster and manoeuvre better than many of its opponents.

The Merlin 66-engined Spitfire LF.IX was the workhorse of the RAF's fighter squadrons from its introduction in 1943 through to the end of the war. The original Mk.IX had been introduced as early as mid-1942.

Compared against a captured Bf 109G-6/U2 with GM-1 nitrous oxide injection by the Central Fighter Establishment in late 1944, the LF.IX was found to be superior in every respect except acceleration in a dive. Manoeuvrability was found to be "greatly superior" and it was noted that the LF.IX "easily out-turns the Bf 109 in either direction at all speeds".

By 1945, the LF.IX was beginning to show its age. Figures given for its top speed vary but it was undoubtedly among the slowest of the 20 aircraft being assessed here in a straight line. It could out-climb and fly higher than most of its opponents, however, even out-performing many of the most advanced German types.

There were few to rival it for manoeuvrability either, making it worthy of inclusion here, and explaining why it remained on the front line for so long even when more 'advanced' types were becoming available to replace it.

BELOW: Later production models of the Spitfire LF.IX were fitted with the pointed tail fin that was also a feature of the Spitfire XVI. Production of the Mk.IX continued until the end of the war and it was the most numerous type of Spitfire built.

SUPERMARINE SPITFIRE MK.XIV

Combining the Spitfire Mk.VIII airframe with a two-speed, two-stage supercharged 2220hp Rolls-Royce Griffon 65 engine resulted in the Mk.XIV. Introduced in 1943, in appearance it was similar to the Spitfire XII with normal wings but with a five-bladed propeller. The rudder was also enlarged and an extra internal fuel tank was fitted.

The huge increase in power meant the XIV was a match for most of its piston-engined contemporaries, the only exception being the Ta 152, and the two are believed never to have met in combat. Its range was short and its manoeuvrability was inferior to that of the Spitfire LF.IX, but nevertheless the XIV was one of the best fighters of the war's final months.

Flight Lieutenant Ian Ponsford, who shot down seven enemy aircraft while flying a Spitfire Mk.XIV with 130 Squadron, remembered: "The Spitfire XIV was the most marvellous aeroplane at that time and I consider it to have been the best operational fighter of them all as it could out-climb virtually anything.

"The earlier Merlin-Spitfire may have had a slight edge when it came to turning performance, but the Mark XIV was certainly better in this respect than the opposition we were faced with. The only thing it couldn't do was keep up with the Fw 190D in a dive.

"It could be a bit tricky on takeoff if one opened the throttle too quickly as you just couldn't hold it straight because the torque was so great from the enormous power developed from the Griffon engine.

"One big advantage that we had over the Germans was that we ran our aircraft on advanced fuels which gave us more power. The 150 octane fuel that we used was strange looking stuff as it was bright green and had an awful smell – it had to be heavily leaded to cope with the extra compression of the engine."

During the Arab-Israeli War in 1948, Israeli pilots flew both Mk. IX and Mk. XIV Spitfires bought from Czechoslovakia against Egyptian Spitfires and concluded that the IX was better due to its superior manoeuvrability.

LEFT: The Spitfire XIV sacrificed some manoeuvrability for raw speed but was still capable of out-turning and out-climbing almost any opponent.

HAWKER TYPHOON MK.1B

The history of the Typhoon is too long and troubled to detail in full here, suffice to say that it was a failure in the high-altitude interceptor role for which it was designed. Although it was the RAF's first fighter capable of more than 400mph, climbing speed was regarded as inadequate and a series of structural failures in the fuselage caused significant delays in its production.

Having entered service in 1941, it is one of the oldest of the 20 aircraft examined here and was beginning to struggle against more advanced competition by 1945. Pilots had to wear an oxygen mask from the moment the engine was switched on due to heavy carbon monoxide contamination in the cockpit, and the level of noise and vibration made life at its controls doubly uncomfortable.

Nevertheless, as history shows, it proved to be a deadly fighter-bomber when armed with rockets or bombs, and many Fw 190 pilots were unpleasantly surprised to discover that despite its size and weight – being one of the largest and heaviest single-engined aircraft here – it had a very short radius of turn and rolled well.

It could also carry a heavy load with relative ease, which meant it could be fitted with four powerful 20mm Hispano Mk II cannon – a weapon originally designed as an anti-aircraft gun – in addition to its bombs/rockets.

ABOVE: It was uncomfortable to fly but the Typhoon was agile at low level despite being a large aircraft and could carry a heavy weapons load, making it particularly useful as a fighter-bomber.

RIGHT: Typhoon MN686 was one of Hawker's development machines, photographed here in late 1944. The Typhoon was fast but poor in a climb.

HAWKER TEMPEST V

Big, heavy and fast, this thin-wing upgrade of the Typhoon design was undoubtedly one of the best fighters of the Second World War and at low altitudes could give either of the two Spitfires detailed here a run for its money.

It had the same Napier Sabre IIA engine as the Typhoon but range was extended by moving the engine forward by 21in to make room for a 76 gallon fuel tank. Tail surfaces were enlarged and a four-bladed propeller was fitted. While the first 100 built had the Typhoon's four Hispano Mk II cannon, the Series II Tempest V got the Hispano Mk V cannon – the weapon's ultimate wartime development.

The first Tempests reached squadrons in January 1944 and they were initially used to combat Fieseler Fi 103 V-1 flying bombs. When they were moved on to the Continent, it quickly became clear that below about 8000ft the Tempest dramatically outperformed the very best aircraft that the Luftwaffe could throw at it – such as the Fw 190D-9 and the Bf 109K-4. Tempest pilots were also responsible for shooting down a number of Me 262s.

According to Hubert Lange, a pilot who flew 15 missions in Me 262s with JG 51, the Hawker Tempest was the German jet's most dangerous opponent, "extremely fast at low altitudes, highly manoeuvrable and heavily armed".

ABOVE: Similar to the Typhoon, the Tempest's redesigned wing and enlarged tail were big improvements. These 486 Squadron Tempests are pictured at Lübeck shortly after the war's end.

LEFT: Hawker Tempest Vs from 501 Squadron pictured in 1944. The Tempest V had a quartet of 20mm cannon, giving it a deadly punch, and at low level it was capable of overmatching even the Luftwaffe's finest fighters.

GLOSTER METEOR F.3

LEFT: The first Gloster Meteors on the Continent during 1945 were painted white to avoid 'friendly' fire. The jet's handling was described as pleasant but it suffered from directional snaking, particularly in poor weather.

BELOW: A Meteor in flight. The type was Britain's first operational jet fighter and while its performance on paper was not dissimilar to that of the Me 262, the Meteor's handling was probably inferior.

Powered by a pair of Rolls-Royce Derwent I jets with a static thrust of 2000lb each, the Meteor F.3 began to enter service in early 1945. Deliveries of its predecessor, the F.1, had begun in June 1944.

While the first Meteors were actually slower than the fastest piston-engined fighters then available, such as the Spitfire XIV, the F.3 offered much higher performance.

It was field tested from bases in Belgium with 616 and 504 Squadrons during the last weeks of the war primarily in the fighter reconnaissance and ground-attack roles. It never met the Me 262 in aerial combat but some were shot down by flak due to their superficial resemblance to the German machine.

As a result, Meteors were given an all-white paint scheme to make them more easily recognisable to Allied units.

Like all in-service jets in 1945, the Meteor was at the cutting edge of performance, and in good weather handling was described as "pleasant", but the F.3 suffered from 'snaking' – directional instability – which made it more difficult to target an aerial opponent effectively.

A report from the Central Fighter Establishment noted: "The failure of the Meteor to come within an acceptable standard is due to the directional snaking which occurs in operational conditions of flight so far experienced and the heaviness and consequently slow operation of the ailerons to bring the sight back on to the target.

"This snaking tends to increase with increase of speed and once it has commenced it is impossible to correct it within the limits of time available during an attack."

Whether this would have proved to be a fatal flaw in actual combat or merely an annoyance to the type's pilots will never be known.

It says a lot about the fortunes of Britain in the war and the role of the Meteor that a large section of the CFE report is devoted to how difficult it would have been to fly in formation. It is impossible to imagine the Germans, desperate to rush their jets into action, bothering to do the same for the Me 262.

NORTH AMERICAN P-51D MUSTANG

ABOVE: Beloved of its pilots, the P-51D was an excellent air superiority fighter, though it was poorly armoured and could be a handful at low level. This is serial number 44-14955 'Dopey Okie' of the 487th Fighter Squadron, part of the 352nd Fighter Group.

LEFT: North American P-51D-5-NA Mustang serial 44-13926 serving with the 375th Fighter Squadron. The famous 'Cadillac of the sky' was America's best regarded fighter of the war. It was capable of flying huge distances and performed exceptionally well at high to medium altitude.

Flown in huge numbers while escorting American bombers, the Mustang is widely accepted as having been the USAAF's most successful air superiority and escort fighter.

In P-51D form its performance was excellent at high altitude. Powered by a Packard-built version of the Rolls-Royce Merlin engine and featuring a bubble canopy, it boasted a good though not sparkling rate of climb and exceptional visibility.

It retained a good measure of agility even above 400mph and was a very stable aircraft with few vices to punish the inattentive. At low altitude and in low speed encounters with enemy aircraft however, its large turn radius became a real disadvantage.

In addition, as a high performance long-range escort, it was lightly built and poorly armoured – rendering it vulnerable to even slight battle damage. Many American pilots using the Mustang for strafing ground targets found that even a light flak hit could be fatal.

In high speed, high altitude encounters, the Mustang was able to reach its full potential and there was little to match it in this, its own stomping ground – as Fw 190 and even Me 262 pilots discovered.

REPUBLIC P-47D THUNDERBOLT

RIGHT: P-47D-30 Thunderbolt 44-32760 'Shorty Miriam' of the 354th Fighter Group. The Thunderbolt was a huge, powerful fighter and in the right circumstances could beat the Messerschmitt Me 262. It gave continual mechanical problems, however, and was less able than the P-51D.
BELOW RIGHT: Like the Hawker Typhoon, the P-47 achieved great success as a fighter-bomber, though it was also a superb fighter. Pictured here is P-47D-25 42-26641 'Hairless Joe' of the 56th Fighter Group.

Faster and higher flying than even a Mustang, the P-47D Thunderbolt was a big, heavy aircraft – the Tempest to the Mustang's Spitfire. As such, it could also soak up more battle damage and could carry a heavier weapons load too.

On paper, the Thunderbolt seemed to have the edge over the Mustang, but pilots told a different story. The Mustang was simply more agile – it handled better and was easier to fly well. Against German fighters, the Thunderbolt seems to have been just as effective at all altitudes. In the end, the Thunderbolt lost out simply because fewer were used in situations where they were likely to enter aerial combat with German fighters.

One source gives the total number of enemy aircraft shot down by the P-47 as 3662 compared to the P-51's 5944. General der Jagdflieger Adolf Galland's Me 262 was shot down by a P-47 Thunderbolt though, not a P-51.

Against the Spitfire, neither the P-47 nor the P-51 could be said to have had a clear advantage. Both were slower, less manoeuvrable at all altitudes and less able to climb at speed – but they had the capacity to keep up with high-flying B-17s and B-24s long after a Spitfire would've had to turn for home.

LOCKHEED P-38L LIGHTNING

FAR LEFT: A Lockheed P-38L Lightning in flight. Thanks to its powerful twin engines, the 'L' could climb at an incredible rate and it boasted cutting edge technology – but it was behind the P-51 and P-47 in manoeuvrability.

LEFT: The P-38L was used by fighter squadrons of the 1st Fighter Group in Europe. Pilot 2nd Lieutenant Jim Hunt of the 27th Fighter Squadron sits atop P-38L 'Maloney's Pony'. The aircraft was never flown by its namesake, 1st Lieutenant Thomas Maloney, because on August 19, 1944, his P-38 (a different one) was forced down on the French coast. While walking along the beach to find help, he trod on a landmine and was badly injured – spending the next three and a half years in and out of hospital.

The oldest of the three piston-engined American fighters featured here, the P-38, had matured by 1945 and had been available in its definitive P-38L form since June 1944.

Its twin engines made it heavy and gave it a very broad wingspan, but since these were set back from the cockpit they also allowed the pilot an excellent view in all directions.

It wasn't astonishingly fast in a straight line but the Lightning could outclimb anything short of an Me 163 rocket-powered interceptor – an incredible accolade for a fighter that had first flown in 1939. Its counter-rotating propellers meant there was no torque effect in flight and enabled the Lightning to turn equally well to the left or the right. In addition, it had cutting edge features such as power boosted ailerons and electrically operated dive flaps.

In the late war combat environment, the P-38L could be said to lack stopping power – being equipped with only one 20mm cannon and a quartet of .50 calibre machine guns in its nose. In addition, the Lightning was complicated and pilots had to manage twice the number of engine controls while watching twice the number of gauges.

It therefore must come last when compared against its American contemporaries.

LOCKHEED P-80A SHOOTING STAR

LEFT: The faster of the two XP-80A Shooting Star prototypes, 44-83021 'Gray Ghost'. While this aircraft was given an all-over pearl grey paint job, the other XP-80A, 'Silver Ghost', was left in bare metal finish for comparative tests. These showed that just painting the Shooting Star had the effect of increasing its top speed. The P-80 was quicker than Gloster's Meteor but still failed to beat the Me 262.

BELOW: Lockheed P-80A-1-LO Shooting Star 44-85004 in flight. The production P-80A was fitted with wingtip fuel tanks which extended its range but resulted in performance-sapping drag.

Just two pre-production YP-80A Shooting Stars saw active service during the Second World War, operating briefly from Lesina airfield in Italy with the 1st Fighter Group. Another two were stationed at RAF Burtonwood in Cheshire for demonstration and test flying.

Powered by a single General Electric J-33-GE-9 jet engine mounted centrally in its fuselage, the Shooting Star was aerodynamically clean and was therefore able to reach an impressive 536mph in level flight at 5000ft – though only when fully painted and without wingtip fuel tanks.

In natural metal finish and with those range extending tanks, performance tests carried out by the USAAF's Flight Test Division showed top speed to be just over 500mph – placing it behind all of its jet-powered contemporaries.

Many postwar comparisons of wartime jets have been overly favourable towards the P-80 and tend to take their figures from later, improved versions.

The aircraft available during the last four months of the war was somewhat less impressive. Without wingtip tanks, its range was that expected of a short-distance high-speed interceptor – 540 miles – yet with them its range improved but its best rate of climb was down to just 3300ft/min.

Armament was six .50 calibre machine guns – the same as that of a Mustang.

LAVOCHKIN LA-7

Based largely on the earlier La-5 fighter and powered by an air-cooled 1850hp ASh-82FNV radial engine, the La-7 incorporated more alloys in place of the original wooden structure. The cockpit got a rollbar, the landing gear was improved and a better gunsight, the PB-1B(V), was installed along with a new VISh-105V-4 propeller and an enlarged spinner to improve streamlining.

Unfortunately, the bigger spinner meant less air reached the engine for cooling so a fan was fitted behind it.

Visibility was excellent and either a pair or trio of 20mm cannon gave good though not exceptional firepower.

The Soviets at the time honestly believed that the La-7 was the best fighter in the world for dogfighting and it was certainly faster and more manoeuvrable than the older marques of Fw 190A that it typically faced on the Eastern Front.

In company such as that discussed here, however, it fails to make the grade. The latest and last Fw 190s, the A-9 and D-9, outperformed it in all areas except in a turn. Small and lightweight, the La-7 had to be flown at low level because it simply couldn't manage at high altitude.

It was available in big numbers though, that the Germans were simply unable to match.

ABOVE: The Russians believed that the Lavochkin La-7 was the world's best piston-engined fighter aircraft in 1945. They were wrong.

LEFT: It boasted a powerful radial engine which gave it a performance advantage over older Luftwaffe types but the La-7 was falling behind as the war ended.

YAKOVLEV YAK-3

The Russians did their best to develop small lightweight fighters that could be produced in huge numbers and this design philosophy had its greatest success in the form of the Yak-3.

Work on it commenced in 1941 but was seriously hampered by first a lack of aluminium and then the German invasion which resulted in design work actually being halted.

As the tide of battle turned, Yakovlev picked up where it had left off and produced the Yak-1M, a lighter, shorter-winged version of the Yak-1. This embodied many technological advances such as a mastless radio antenna, reflector gunsight and better armour. It was meant to have a 1600hp Klimov M-107 V12 engine but this was unavailable and the 1300hp M-105 had to be used instead.

Even with this relatively small powerplant fitted, the redesignated Yak-3 was still 40mph faster than the Yak-9, which despite its name actually entered service first.

The fact that the Yak-3 can be found somewhere towards the bottom of every table associated with this comparison belies its greatest strength – its ability to out-turn both the Bf 109 and the Fw 190 below 20,000ft. Pilots who were new to the Yak-3 found it easy to fly but its true potential was only realised in the hands of an experienced flyer.

Against the best of the Luftwaffe's machines, performing at their best, the Yak-3 would have been found sorely lacking but it was ideal for low-level skirmishing and could face standard German types on a near-equal footing.

RIGHT: A Yak-3 pictured in Poland during 1945 beside the carcass of a Bf 109. Its high power to weight ratio meant that it handled extremely well in the hands of an expert.

YAKOVLEV YAK-9U

The first Yak-9s off the production line were fitted with the same Klimov M-105 as the Yak-3 and being substantially heavier paid a big price in performance. Top speed was just 367mph – about the same as that of a Spitfire Mk.I in 1939.

However, when the Yak-9 was fitted with the Klimov M-107A, which delivered 1650hp, its performance dramatically improved. Like the Yak-3, it offered excellent all round visibility but armament was somewhat lacking – with just a single 20mm cannon firing through its propeller hub and a pair of .50 calibre machine guns mounted in its engine cowling.

Like the La-7 and the Yak-3, the Yak-9U did its best work at low altitude. It was heavy only when compared to the Yak-3 and even with the more powerful M-107A it could still be considered underpowered in this company.

It was manoeuvrable and had better armour than the Yak-3 but it was still no match for the likes of a Fw 190D-9 or a Bf 109K-4 on a good day.

ABOVE: A Yakovlev Yak-9U of the 151st Guard Air Fighter Regiment at Yambol in Bulgaria. The original Yak-9, fitted with a Klimov M-105, was a poor performer, but once it had the Klimov M-107A it joined the front rank of fighters available in 1945.

RIGHT: Visibility from the Yak-9U's cockpit was good and it manoeuvred well at low altitude but its performance was unremarkable compared to its more powerful peers.

BELL P-63A KINGCOBRA

LEFT: Row upon row of P-63 Kingcobras lined up at the Bell factory prior to delivery to the Soviet air force.

BELOW: Pilots of the Soviet 66th Fighter Wing take a break beside their Bell P-63s. More than two-thirds of all Kingcobras built went to the Russians.

The Americans did not think too highly of Bell's Kingcobra. They had thought even less highly of its predecessor, the Airacobra, largely because it had been designed to fly with a turbosupercharger but was put into production without one.

The Soviets, however, who received hundreds of Airacobras from the Americans on a lend-lease basis, rather liked it. Much has been written about the Airacobra's strengths as a ground-attack aircraft, even though the Soviets themselves never regarded it as such and tended to use it for air-to-air interception missions instead.

The Kingcobra saw the turbosupercharger finally installed and the overall design modified to incorporate technological advancements – such as laminar flow wings, a redesigned tail and a four-blade propeller. The first XP-63, a converted XP-39E, was first flown on December 7, 1942.

From the outset, the Soviets were involved in the development process to the extent of supplying personnel to fly the prototypes at Bell's factory.

Overall Kingcobra production ran to 3303 examples and 2397 of them were supplied to the Soviet Union.

No Kingcobra ever saw combat with a USAAF squadron, which is not surprising since the P-63's range was limited and its performance was poor at high altitude – making it useless as an escort fighter.

At low level, however, where the Soviet fighter pilots flew, it was effective. Like the other high performance fighter aircraft flown by the Soviets, its top speed and rate of climb were by no means sparkling but it was highly manoeuvrable below 8000ft.

FOCKE-WULF FW 190A-9

The Fw 190A was the fastest production fighter aircraft in the world when it first appeared in 1941. Once overheating problems with its powerful BMW 801 engine were largely overcome, it joined the Bf 109 as one of the Luftwaffe's two front line fighters.

ABOVE: The Fw 190A-9's BMW 801S (TS) engine was a compromise but still produced a respectable 2000hp. Note the bubble canopy and the broad paddle blades of the VDM-9 propeller on this example.

In 1944, with the streamlining of German aircraft production, unprecedented numbers of Fw 190s were churned out, mostly in A-8 guise. All the while, BMW had been attempting to improve its engine design with little success.

Unfortunately the company had succeeded in producing an engine that had very little development potential. The standard Fw 190 engine was the BMW 801D-2 and the firm's engineers were aiming for a model they called the 801F. This, though, was taking years to perfect – years that Germany didn't have.

Therefore some of its components were fitted to the standard engine as an interim measure. First these were used to create the 801U, which had 1730hp at 2700rpm at sea level, compared to the standard D-2's 1700hp. Then they managed to use more components, creating the 801S or TS, with a much more impressive 2000hp.

It was this engine which was fitted to a largely unmodified Fw 190A-8 airframe to create the type's final form – the Fw 190A-9. The first production model appeared in August 1944 and production continued until the end of the war.

BMW was heavily bombed towards the end of the war, reducing production of the 801S to a snail's pace so fewer than 1000 A-9s were built. In combat, the Fw 190A-9 gave its pilots a greater edge over their Soviet adversaries but the Allies' machines were still markedly superior.

Its performance at high altitude was poor, the Fw 190's rate of turn was never a match for that of the Spitfire and even the aircraft's exceptional roll rate and dive speed was being cancelled out by the raw power of types such as the Spitfire XIV.

Unlike the Spitfire IX, the Fw 190A was largely obsolete by 1944 but the Germans had little choice but to keep on producing it since so many assembly lines had been geared up for it and every fighter was sorely needed.

FOCKE-WULF FW 190D-9

German pilots were largely thrilled by the performance of the Fw 190D-9 – a stretched Fw 190A powered by the Junkers Jumo 213A-1 which could be boosted up to an output of 2000hp with MW-50 injection.

The 'long nose' D-9 lost some of the Fw 190A's handling and manoeuvrability as the trade-off for its increased speed however.

ABOVE: The Fw 190D-9 was regarded by those who flew it and those that flew against it as a development of the Fw 190A. In fact, it was simply Focke-Wulf's attempt to provide an alternative engine for the Fw 190 airframe in case the supply of BMW units was disrupted. This example, WNr. 210051, has just rolled off the production line at Bremen-Neuenlanderfeld. It was later delivered to III./JG 54

RIGHT: An early production Fw 190D-9 stands out in the snow prior to delivery to III./JG 54, the first unit to operate the type, in September 1944. In combat, the D-9 was fast with MW-50, particularly in a dive. Its performance surpassed that of the Fw 190A types but Allied types such as the Mustang still eclipsed it.

Focke-Wulf designer Kurt Tank never intended the D-9 to be an advanced version of the 190 design and was on record as saying that the airframe simply needed an alternative powerplant since BMW's factories were being so heavily targeted by Allied bombing.

There has been some suggestion that without water-methanol injection, the D-9's top speed was around 360mph. The Soviets who tested examples they captured intact but without MW-50 were certainly deeply unimpressed with its performance.

The long nose restricted forward and downward visibility, which became a problem because the aircraft had a high wing loading – its wings were the same as those used on the A-8 – and therefore needed a fast landing and stalled easily. Having to put the aircraft down fast and being unable to see where you were going was a bad combination.

Even so, German pilots still considered the D-9 easier to land and take off in than any Bf 109 variant due to its wide-track landing gear.

Armament was a pair of wing-mounted 20mm cannon and two .50 calibre machine guns in the engine cowl – not outstanding but still sufficient, particularly against lightly armoured opponents such as the Soviet types.

FOCKE-WULF TA 152H

The Ta 152 had a tortuous history. It was intended from the outset to replace the Fw 190 completely – and was certainly not a development of the Fw 190D – but production compromises meant the finished product much more closely resembled a 190 than designer Kurt Tank would have liked.

To add insult to injury, the long-proposed basic fighter version of the Ta 152 was cancelled or delayed and the only model to actually see combat, and then only in tiny numbers, was the high altitude 'H' version.

Powered by the long-delayed but finally sorted supercharged Junkers Jumo 213E-1 engine, the 152 was the fastest piston-engined aircraft to see combat during the war by a considerable margin. It also had a decent rate of climb, the highest ceiling of any piston-engined fighter of the war and a remarkable wingspan of 47ft 4½in.

Even its armament was good – two 20mm cannon in the wings and a single 30mm cannon in the nose – though in practice problems were encountered with jamming. There was no chance of development work to

resolve the issue since by this stage the factories that built the Ta 152H had already been overrun by Soviet troops.

Precisely how manoeuvrable the production Ta 152H-1 is is largely based on speculation. Its surviving pilots have defended its reputation to the hilt – standing by their claim that it was better than almost anything else in the sky by the end of the war.

However, there have been no flying examples available since the end of the war and even while the type was briefly in service it was prone to sudden and mysterious failures which on a couple of occasions resulted in the death of the pilot.

It seems to have enjoyed mixed fortunes in combat against the excellent Hawker Tempest V and somewhat more success against Yak-3s but it never faced a Mustang or Thunderbolt in their high altitude area of operations, as far as is known. If it had done, it might have faced them on at least an equal footing.

LEFT: Focke-Wulf Ta 152H WNr. 110003 of JG 301 as it appeared having been captured by the Allies and shipped to America with the Foreign Equipment number 112. The abilities of the Ta 152H remain difficult to assess since so few were made. On paper it was, perhaps, the best piston-engined fighter of the war.

MESSERSCHMITT BF 109K-4

ABOVE: Messerschmitt Bf 109K-4 WNr. 330130 at a Messerschmitt factory during the autumn of 1944. In all round performance the K-4 surpassed the final development of its great rival, the Fw 190A-9, but still suffered from its antiquated narrow track undercarriage and small wings.
LEFT: The ultimate development of the Messerschmitt Bf 109 to actually reach front line service was the K-4. It was a remarkable upgrade of the type but was often let down by shoddy workmanship and sabotage. This one is WNr. 330230 'White 17' of 9./JG 77 at Neuruppin in November 1944.

The final production version of the long-suffering Bf 109 design was the K-4. The first production examples of the type, conceived in the mid-1930s as a lightweight highly manoeuvrable fighter, flew in 1937, making it easily the oldest type here.

The Bf 109 that saw a vast increase in production alongside the Fw 190A-8 was the Bf 109G-6 and later versions were produced in progressively smaller numbers. Shortly before the war's end, Willy Messerschmitt had been preparing his company to wind up production of the 109 in preparation for a wholesale switch to the Me 262 and its projected successors.

The K-4 was an attempt to give the basic design a cleanup using all the available technological advances to produce something close to the ultimate Bf 109. It was also a move intended to remove the need for the bewildering variety of sub-variants spawned as part of the Bf 109G series.

Further K series 109s were projected beyond the K-4 but none made it to production.

The K-4's cockpit canopy was 'bulged' to provide improved visibility and a powerful Daimler-Benz DB 605D engine was installed, producing 1800hp

during takeoff, rising to an incredible 2000hp with MW-50. This in an aircraft that was lighter than any of the lightweight Soviet designs.

At its best, the Bf 109K-4's performance figures were nothing short of astounding. Its boosted top speed of 440mph put it in the same league as the Spitfire XIV and P-51 Mustang, and a climb rate of 4500ft/min was among the very best.

Armament was a problem, however. The K-4's standard load was a 30mm MK 108 firing through the propeller hub and a pair of MG 131 .50 calibre machine guns mounted in the engine cowling. There were difficulties in getting the MK 108 to work properly in this configuration though which meant that the gun jammed easily if attempts were made to fire it while manoeuvring.

In practice, many Bf 109K-4s reached the front line without their MW-50 kits fitted or with some other defect whether as a result of deliberate sabotage or simply poor craftsmanship on the part of the forced labourers who built many of their components. The type was therefore seldom able to reach its dazzling full potential in combat.

MESSERSCHMITT ME 262A-1A

The Me 262 was the first operational jet fighter anywhere in the world when it equipped Erprobungskommando 262 and then KG(J) 51 in May-June 1944 and began to enter combat against Allied aircraft.

Some American writers such as Robert F Dorr have attempted to advance the claim of the Bell P-59A Airacomet to being the first operational jet fighter – since it entered 'service' in late 1943, but in practice this was little more than part of the development process.

The Me 262 was a high performance combat machine that could outrun anything short of a rocket-powered Me 163, was armed with four 30mm cannon and potentially R4M air-to-air rockets – making it the most heavily armed aircraft here – and could handle sufficiently well to make good use of its other virtues.

Its design was futuristic – those swept-back wings were revolutionary – and a lengthy period of development before it entered even service testing meant many, though not all, of its early foibles had been worked out and eliminated.

In combat it was by no means indestructible and its engines had only a very limited operational lifespan before they needed to be removed and overhauled. Its nosewheel was notoriously weak, acceleration was slow, landing speed was high and the aircraft was so fast in combat that pilots unfamiliar with jets – in other words most of its pilots – struggled to hit their targets.

But still, the Me 262 was a deadly opponent for any Allied fighter. It could be outmanoeuvred by a Spitfire but it was very difficult to catch. Even its cruising speed, 460mph, was above anything the Allies could match except in a dive.

It has been endlessly opined that had the Me 262 been built in much larger numbers – or fractionally sooner – the war might have had a different outcome, but in reality it was at the very edge of what was technologically possible for 1945 and its engines were the source of its worst problems. They simply could not be made good enough fast enough.

ABOVE: The Me 262 took years to develop but the end result, when its engines had been freshly reconditioned and everything was working correctly, was spectacular. Pictured here is Me 262A-1a 'White 4' of JG 7 at Achmer in Germany towards the end of 1944.

ABOVE: The first jet fighter to begin combat operations anywhere in the world, the Me 262, was an engineering masterpiece and remains a design icon. Not only that, it was also an excellent fighter. One of the best known Me 262s, the unpainted WNr. 111711, was surrendered to the Americans by Messerschmitt company pilot Hans Fay at Rhein-Main airfield on March 30, 1945.

MESSERSCHMITT ME 163B-1

The first rocket-powered aircraft in the world was the tailless Ente or 'duck' – a glider designed by Alexander Lippisch powered by an engine produced by rocket pioneers Max Valier and Friedrich Sander at the behest of car company publicist Fritz von Opel.

After Opel left Germany in 1929 and Valier was killed in 1930, Lippisch went to work for the DFS – the German glider research organisation. Here he produced several revolutionary tailless designs and in 1940 these were fitted with a powerful liquid rocket engine designed by Hellmuth Walter, the HWK 109-509, and the Messerschmitt Me 163 was created.

The tiny lightweight interceptor had two 'fuel' tanks, one filled with a methanol, hydrazine hydrate and water mixture known as C-Stoff and the other with a high test peroxide known as T-Stoff. When combined, these volatile liquids produced a powerful jet or sometimes a catastrophic explosion.

This was enough for just seven and a half minutes of powered flight, although during that time the aircraft could reach a speed of nearly 600mph and an altitude of nearly 40,000ft. This performance put every other Second World War aircraft in the shade but it was also the Me 163's undoing as a fighter.

It was armed with a pair of 30mm MK 108 cannon – sufficient to destroy any aerial target, bomber or fighter, with only a couple of hits – but the Komet closed so rapidly on its target and the cannon were so slow-firing and short-ranged that it was almost impossible for the pilot to hit anything.

There was usually only enough time and fuel for a couple of passes at enemy bombers before the Me 163 was forced to begin its unpowered glide back to base – often at the mercy of Allied fighters.

For all its years in development, the deaths of several of its pilots and the huge efforts required to maintain it in service, the Me 163 is believed to have achieved only nine aerial victories.

RIGHT: Filled with volatile explosive chemicals that provided enough thrust for only seven and a half minutes of powered flight and lacking even a proper undercarriage once it had been glided back to the airfield, the Me 163 was as much a danger to its pilots as it was to the enemy.

HEINKEL HE 162A-2

More so than the Me 163 – which had actually been in development when the Third Reich was at its peak – the Heinkel He 162 was a product of desperation.

Its design was largely the result of experience with the Me 262. It was powered by a single jet mounted above the fuselage so that when it crashed the precious BMW 003 engine had a better chance of survival and the major structural elements were made mostly out of wood.

An ejection seat was fitted but this was ineffective at low altitude. Design work was started by Heinkel as the P.1073 in July 1944 and submitted as the company's attempt to meet an RLM requirement for a cheap jet that was easy to build and easy for a novice to fly, a people's fighter, or Volksjäger, two months later. Once it was declared successful on September 23, 1944, the Heinkel design was modified and rushed into production. The first test flight took place on December 6, and efforts to bring it into front line service were being made as the war ended.

The He 162 had a hidden problem however. The design should have used Tego film plywood glue – which was in common use with other German aircraft types – but the factory that made it at Wuppertal was destroyed in an RAF bombing raid and an alternative was needed to ensure He 162 production could go ahead.

The replacement glue, unbeknownst to Heinkel, had a gradual corrosive effect on wood and the He 162s that were produced began to suffer from mysterious structural failures. It didn't help that the BMW 003 wasn't ready for service either and was prone to flameouts.

When the He 162 was working properly and not falling apart in the sky, pilots regarded it as an excellent aircraft with light controls that was stable at high speed. While its speed couldn't match that of the Me 262, or even the Meteor F.3, it could out-climb either of them.

Its armament of two MG 151/20 autocannon was relatively light but the small aircraft simply wasn't up to housing the twin MK 108s originally projected.

Given more time and better glue, the He 162 might conceivably have been a contender but in the event it was a non-starter.

ABOVE: Most photographs fail to capture just how small and light the He 162 was – this image of a captured one taking off at Muroc Flight Test Base, California, shows the test pilot, Bob Hoover, looking surprising large in relation to the machine.

LEFT: The very first He 162 V1, WNr. 20001. When it remained in one piece, the He 162 was a fine fighter aircraft, yet it still matched the speed and hitting power of the Me 262.

So which was the best?

From among the 20 aircraft examined here, there are some obvious dropouts when it comes to deciding which was best. The British Hawker Tempest V was a better fighter than the Typhoon, so the latter can be safely ruled out.

The same applies to the Focke-Wulf Ta 152 and both of the Fw 190A types. The A-9 and the D-9 can be ditched. Similarly, the Me 262 would have been the better fighter even if the He 162 could have been made to work flawlessly so the notorious Volksjäger has got to go. The Me 163 was too fast and its endurance too brief to be an effective fighter so it can also be taken out of contention.

The slowest of the American types was the P-38 Lightning. It climbed well but was surpassed as a dogfighter, therefore it too has to go.

Though they were good at low-level fighting they were certainly not superior to their contemporaries so all four of the Soviet types can be excluded too.

This leaves a top 10 of the Tempest V, Spitfire IX and XIV, Meteor F.3, P-47 Thunderbolt, P-51 Mustang, P-80 Shooting Star, Me 262A-1a, Ta 152 and Bf 109K.

The non-operational Meteor F.3 and P-80 can probably be ruled out due to ongoing development issues, the Bf 109K could not be said to have surpassed the Ta 152 in performance, the P-47 Thunderbolt was less manoeuvrable than the P-51 and the Spitfire IX lacked the raw speed to keep up with the new German jets, so a reasonable top five would be the Tempest V, Spitfire XIV, P-51 Mustang, Me 262A-1a and Ta 152.

Here the narrowing down gets more difficult. The Ta 152 was designed as a high altitude fighter and relied heavily on its complex engine to give it its amazing turn of speed. Its guns were prone to jamming and its reputation rests on only a handful of accounts by decidedly partisan witnesses. It ought therefore to be excluded.

The Tempest V was fast and deadly but it lacked performance at high altitude and straight line speed. Would it have been able to best a Spitfire XIV in a dogfight? Maybe, maybe not.

The choice really comes down to three machines – the Spitfire XIV, the P-51 Mustang and the Me 262A-1a. All three were potent dogfighters, loved by their pilots and feared by their enemies. The P-51 was the best aircraft in the world for its particular role – escorting bombers over long distances at high altitude – but was it the best fighter of the three finalists?

It lacked the speed of either the Spitfire or the Messerschmitt and its rate of climb was significantly below that of the other two. Its manoeuvrability was excellent but it did not surpass that of the Spitfire.

The Me 262 represented the future of air combat. It could outrun almost anything and its armament was second to none – yet it had serious problems in operational service.

Built by dedicated German engineers rather than slaves, flown in numbers from well-defended airfields and kept well supplied with fuel and fresh engines, it would undoubtedly have had the edge over the Spitfire, but in reality Germany's war situation coupled with its own design flaws served to handicap the world's first truly successful jet fighter.

In the final analysis, the winner has to be the British Supermarine Spitfire XIV. It was faster than any other piston engine aircraft bar the Ta 152, its manoeuvrability was outstanding, it could perform exceptionally at any altitude and its rate of climb was stupendous. Its short range made it unsuitable for escort missions but in a straight fight it was simply very hard to beat.

After the war, former Luftwaffe General of Fighters Adolf Galland said: "The best thing about the Spitfire XIV was that there were so few of them."

CLAIMED TOP SPEED

1.	Me 163B-1	596mph
2.	Me 262A-1a	540mph
3.	P-80A Shooting Star	536mph
4.	Meteor F.3	528mph
5.	He 162A-2	522mph
6.	Ta 152H	462mph
7.	Spitfire Mk.XIV	447mph
8.	P-47 Thunderbolt	443mph
9.	Bf 109K-4	440mph
10.	P-51 Mustang	437mph
11.	Tempest V	432mph
12.	Fw 190D-9	430mph
13.	Yak-9U	417mph
14.	Fw 190A-9	414mph
15.	P-38L Lightning	414mph
16.	Typhoon 1b	412mph
17.	La-7	411mph
18.	P-63 Kingcobra	410mph
19.	Spitfire LF.IX	409mph
20.	Yak-3	407mph

RATE OF CLIMB

1.	Me 163B-1	31,000ft/min
2.	P-38L Lightning	4750ft/min
3.	Tempest V	4700ft/min
4.	Spitfire Mk.XIV	4700ft/min
5.	He 162A-2	4615ft/min
6.	Bf 109K-4	4500ft/min
7.	Spitfire LF.IX	4470ft/min
8.	P-80A Shooting Star	4100ft/min
9.	Meteor F.3	3980ft/min
10.	Ta 152H-1	3937ft/min
11.	Me 262A-1a	3900ft/min
12.	Yak-3	3645ft/min
13.	Fw 190D-9	3300ft/min
14.	Yak-9U	3280ft/min
15.	P-47D Thunderbolt	3260ft/min
16.	P-51D Mustang	3200ft/min
17.	La-7	3095ft/min
18.	Typhoon 1b	2740ft/min
19.	P-63A Kingcobra	2500ft/min
20.	Fw 190A-9	2350ft/min

WINGSPAN

1.	P-38L Lightning	52ft
2.	Ta 152H-1	47ft 4½in
3.	Meteor F.3	43ft
4.	Typhoon 1b	41ft 7in
5.	Me 262A-1a	41ft 6in
6.	Tempest V	41ft
7.	P-47D Thunderbolt	40ft 9in
8.	P-80A Shooting Star	38ft 9in
9.	P-63A Kingcobra	38ft 4in
10.	P-51D Mustang	37ft
11.	Spitfire Mk.XIV	36ft 10in
12.	Spitfire LF.IX	36ft 8in
13.	Fw 190A-9	34ft 5in
14.	Fw 190D-9	34ft 5in
15.	Bf 109K-4	32ft 9½in
16.	La-7	32ft 2in
17.	Yak-9U	31ft 11in
18.	Yak-3	30ft 2in
19.	Me 163B-1	30ft 7in
20.	He 162A-2	23ft 7in

CEILING

1.	Ta 152H-1	49,540ft
2.	Meteor F.3	46,000ft
3.	P-80A Shooting Star	45,000ft
4.	P-38L Lightning	44,000ft
5.	Spitfire Mk.XIV	43,500ft
6.	P-47D Thunderbolt	43,000ft
7.	P-63A Kingcobra	43,000ft
8.	Spitfire LF.IX	42,500ft
9.	P-51D Mustang	41,900ft
10.	Bf 109K-4	41,000ft
11.	Me 163B-1	39,700ft
12.	He 162A-2	39,400ft
13.	Fw 190D-9	39,370ft
14.	Me 262A-1a	37,565ft
15.	Tempest V	36,500ft
16.	Fw 190A-9	35,443ft
17.	Typhoon 1b	35,200ft
18.	Yak-3	35,000ft
19.	Yak-9U	35,000ft
20.	La-7	34,285ft

RANGE (without drop tanks)

1.	P-51D Mustang	950 miles
2.	P-47D Thunderbolt	800 miles
3.	Ta 152H-1	745 miles
4.	Tempest V	740 miles
5.	Me 262A-1a	646 miles
6.	He 162A-2	602 miles
7.	Fw 190A-9	569 miles
8.	P-80A Shooting Star	540 miles
9.	Fw 190D-9	520 miles
10.	Typhoon 1b	510 miles
11.	Meteor F.3	504 miles
12.	Spitfire Mk.XIV	460 miles
13.	P-38L Lightning	450 miles
14.	P-63A Kingcobra	450 miles
15.	Spitfire LF.IX	434 miles
16.	Yak-9U	420 miles
17.	La-7	413 miles
18.	Yak-3	405 miles
19.	Bf 109K-4	350 miles
20.	Me 163B-1	25 miles

EMPTY WEIGHT

1.	P-38L Lightning	12,800lb
2.	Meteor F.3	10,517lb
3.	P-47D Thunderbolt	10,000lb
4.	Tempest V	9250lb
5.	Typhoon 1b	8840lb
6.	Ta 152H-1	8640lb
7.	P-80A Shooting Star	8420lb
8.	Me 262A-1a	8366lb
9.	Fw 190D-9	7694lb
10.	P-51D Mustang	7635lb
11.	Fw 190A-9	7055lb
12.	P-63A Kingcobra	6800lb
13.	Spitfire Mk.XIV	6578lb
14.	Spitfire LF.IX	6518lb
15.	La-7	5743lb
16.	Yak-9U	5526lb
17.	Yak-3	4640lb
18.	Bf 109K-4	4343lb
19.	Me 163B-1	4200lb
20.	He 162A-2	3660lb

WHEN WEE WILLIE RAN OUT OF LUCK

APRIL 8, 1945: BOEING B-17G 42-31333 IS DESTROYED

One of the iconic images of the American daylight bombing campaign is a photograph showing a B-17 Flying Fortress with one wing blown off, plummeting to its doom on April 8, 1945. But which Fortress was it, where had it been and who was on board?

The 302nd Boeing B-17G to roll off the production line at Boeing Plant 2, King County, Washington, was serial number 42-31333. It was the second aircraft of the fourth production block of B-17Gs and was therefore one of a hundred B-17G-15-BOs.

Like all the early B-17Gs, it was painted up in camouflage colours before being flown to United Airlines' completion and modification centre at Cheyenne, Wyoming, on October 22, 1943.

From here, 42-31333 was flown to Grand Island Army Airfield in Nebraska, a journey east of some 360 miles, on November 3. Six days later, it was transferred to Memphis and on December 20, 1943, it arrived at USAAF Station 121, aka RAF Bassingbourn in Cambridgeshire.

Coded LG-W and referred to in reports as 'aircraft #333', 42-31333 was assigned to the 322nd Bombardment Squadron of the 91st Bombardment Group (Heavy) 'The Ragged Irregulars' and was immediately prepared for its operational debut.

The first pilot to take 42-31333 into action was 2nd Lt Robert L Gough. The mission, on Christmas Eve, 1943, was an attack on German installations under construction south of Andres, near Calais, in France. Gough and his crew took off at 11.12am along with seven other B-17 crews, hit the target area with sixteen 300lb bombs from 21,000ft at 1.41pm and returned home safely at 4.36pm.

Results could not be observed due to poor visibility and no enemy fighters were encountered but flak over the target was intense. 42-31333 came through unscathed, though one of the other B-17s suffered minor damage.

The next mission for Aircraft #333 saw a different pilot take the controls – 2nd Lt Paul D Jessop. This time it was a New Year's Eve raid on the Bordeaux-Merignac Aerodrome, five miles west of Bordeaux in France. The base was home to the Luftwaffe's Kampfgeschwader 40, operating anti-shipping Focke-Wulf Fw 200Cs and Junkers Ju 88s.

This time 42-31333's payload was 21 M47 incendiaries. Heavy cloud cover over Bordeaux-Merignac, however, resulted in the raid being diverted to Cognac-Chateaubernard, also used by KG 40 and its Fw 200Cs. The airfield was hit from 18,000ft and the results were reported as 'good'.

This time, however, the B-17s were met by 15 to 25 German aircraft, including Messerschmitt Bf 109s, Focke-Wulf Fw 190s and Junkers Ju 88s. None of the bombers were lost but of the seven aircraft from the 322nd involved, six were damaged including #333.

From this point on 42-31333 became Jessop's regular ship and he named it 'Wee Willie', having a cartoon image of a baby standing atop a bomb painted on the side by line mechanic and nose artist extraordinaire Sgt Anthony 'Tony' Starcer – the same man who painted the 'Memphis Belle's' famous telephone girl.

PICTURES ABOVE: Three photographs taken by the automatic bomb strike camera of a Boeing B-17 show the final 18 seconds of 42-31333 Wee Willie on April 8, 1945, over Stendal, Saxony-Anhalt, Germany, after it was hit by an 88mm flak burst. In the first, far left, Willie's' port wing has already sheared off and is spinning over its tail, gouting flames. The second photograph, frequently used to show the horrors faced by American air crews during the daylight bombing campaign over Germany, shows the aircraft during the final seconds of its death dive. All nine crew members are still inside. In the last photograph, Wee Willie has exploded. Fragments of debris, wings, tail and fuselage fall burning to the ground.

ABOVE: The first regular crew of B-17G-15-BO 42-31333 Wee Willie. They are, back row from left, co-pilot 1st Lt John A Moeller, navigator 2nd Lt Harry Lerner, waist gunner SSGT Robert Kelley, ball turret gunner SSGT Sidney D Martin, bombardier Lt Joe Gagliano, pilot 1st Lt Paul D Jessop. Front row from left, waist gunner SSGT Robert C Elroy, radio operator SSGT Berchel L Shope, flight engineer/top turret gunner SSGT Walden P Southworth and tail gunner SSGT Joe Zastinchik.

More missions followed on January 7 and 21, 1944, Jessop having flown a different B-17 on January 14 while Willie was undergoing repairs and maintenance.

He flew Willie once again on January 24 before being promoted to 1st Lieutenant on January 26. He next flew Willie on January 30 but during the following mission, to Wilhelmshaven in Germany on February 3, 1944, Willie suffered major flak damage. Bombing altitude was 29,500ft but nevertheless Willie suffered a bad hit. Waist gunner Sergeant Henry F Osowski was wounded and the aircraft was out of commission for more than two weeks while repairs were carried out.

It was to be the last time that Jessop would fly 42-31333. That May he was promoted to captain, completed the last of the 25 missions he and his crew were required to undertake, and went home to the US. Wee Willie now passed from one pilot's hands to the next, a total of 37 men including Gough and Jessop taking it into action with dozens of different crewmen occupying the various positions inside the fuselage.

After brief stints with lieutenants Clarence N Pingel, Edward Robertson and Bernard W Hayen, Wee Willie's second long-term pilot was Lieutenant Edward L Mooney.

Mooney had joined the 322nd on April 28, 1944, and his first mission, on the 29th, saw him flying as a co-pilot

"It was the third mission to Troyes, France, where Mooney commanded his own crew in combat as the pilot."

for the first of two 'check rides' with pilot 2nd Lieutenant Edward Waters over Berlin.

Mooney's second mission to Lyon, France, saw him once again in the co-pilot's seat as the marginally more experienced pilot 1st Lieutenant Lester W Duggan commanded Mooney's crew.

It was the third mission to Troyes, France, where Mooney commanded his own crew in combat as the pilot.

Mooney was eager to get his 25 missions done. His crew's tail gunner, John F Coyne, said Mooney "offered our services for every available fill-in" because his wife Eileen was pregnant and he "wanted to be home for the grand occasion".

It is equally possible that he simply wanted to get himself and his men home and out of danger – every time they climbed into a B-17 they had about a one in five chance of not making it back.

In the end, he managed all 25 and 12 more – toward the end, 35 missions were required and Mooney did 37 (two being aborted with no credit given) – in roughly 12 weeks.

In doing so, he and his crew flew in numerous B-17s, including Fifinella twice, The Bloody Bucket once, Boston Bombshell twice, Heavenly Body once, Lassie Come Home three times, The Liberty Belle once, Red Alert once,

Bachelor's Bride once, Man O War II once, My Baby twice, Superstitious Aloysius three times, Texas Chubby five times, Chowhound once – and Wee Willie 13 times.

Every Fortress that Mooney flew was eventually shot down – none survived the war.

Mooney's first acquaintance with Wee Willie, came on May 20, 1944, when elements of the 322nd were sent to join a bombing run on Villacoublay airfield in northern France, which was being used by fighter units of Luftflotte 3. Willie suffered minor damage, with holes in the nose and waist.

Mooney next flew Willie to Berlin on May 24 but despite heavy enemy opposition the aircraft suffered only one flak hit.

May 25 saw him flying to Nancy-Easey, France, to bomb a target without flak or fighter attacks taking place.

On June 3, he flew Willie against coastal gun emplacements at Hardelot in the Calais area – part of the pre-D-Day tactics of convincing the Germans that the invasion would arrive there rather than in Normandy.

Next, on D-Day itself, June 6, 1944, Willie bombed a radar station close to La Riviere. This was part of the Gold Beach landing area – where at 7.25am, 13 minutes after the B-17 attack, British troops began to wade ashore.

D-Day +1, June 7, saw Willie and Mooney in action again, this time attacking the Ju 88C fighters of V./KG 40 based at Kerlin-Bastard on the Brest peninsula. There was flak over the target but no fighters.

On June 8, Willie took minor flak damage to its nose during a raid on a railway bridge over the Loire river, about six miles east of Tours but otherwise came through unscathed.

June 11, 12, 13, 15 and 18 saw still more raids on airfields and an oil refinery in Hamburg. June 19 was Mooney's final mission with Wee Willie, an attack on the KG 40 aerodrome at Merignac in Bordeaux.

Good results were observed, the runway having been rendered unusable with 100lb bombs.

Thus ended Mooney's 'one month with Willie' tour.

The frenetic activity of June had taken its toll on the bomber however, and it did not fly again until June 28, and during that mission, to attack a railway bridge over the Oise canal at Anizy Le Chateau, eight miles south-west of Loan, pilot Lt Louis M Walton was forced to turn back due to mechanical problems with two of its engines.

More repairs followed and it was not until July 8 that Willie was back in the air, this time with a third long-term pilot in the hot seat – Lt Roy A Hammer. He had the aircraft for just seven missions in 20 days but during that time he and his crew attacked the Junkers aircraft factory, Messerschmitt's Augsburg facility and the hydrogen peroxide plant at the Peenemünde research facility.

Another pilot, John M Hamilton, then flew Willie for a single mission to attack Lechfeld where pilots were being trained to fly Germany's first operational jet and rocket fighters. Hammer returned on July 24 for a ground support mission against German troop formations south of St Lo ahead of Operation Cobra – the breakout from the Normandy beachhead.

His association with Willie ended after a mission on July 28 and five more pilots took Willie up for a handful of missions: lieutenants Dale N Brant, Thomas P Burne, Russel H Brown, Howard Mitchell and William H Trent.

Lt Louis G Starks flew the aircraft for six missions in a row from August 24 to September 8 but it would be one of his predecessors, from the five, who would go on to become the most prolific Willie pilot of them all by a considerable margin – William H Trent.

After a single mission attacking a heavy gun position on the Brest peninsula on August 11, 1944, Trent returned to Willie on September 19, 1944, for an attack on the rail marshalling yards at Hamm, Germany, and again on September 25 for a rail on the Frankfurt rail yards. During this mission Trent's tail gunner S/Sgt Dennis J Moore was hit in the left eye by a piece of flak debris and needed three stitches.

Trent was promoted from second to first lieutenant the same month and on October 9 he flew Willie during an attack on the ball bearing factory at Schweinfurt. Five days later, he took Willie out over Cologne, then it was Brunswick's turn on October 22 and the oil plant in Hamburg's dockyard area on October 25. More than a month after its first visit, 42-31333 returned to Hamm's rail yards, though contrails from other aircraft got in the way and necessitated bombing from 28,900ft.

ABOVE: Boeing B-17G 42-32095 LG-L Ack Ack Annie was a contemporary of Wee Willie flying with the 322nd Bombardment Squadron. The pair flew together on more than 60 missions and Ack Ack Annie was there on April 8, 1945, when Willie was destroyed.

LEFT: Two men gaze into the forward crew access hatch of Wee Willie at Bassingbourn in Cambridgeshire. The photograph is undated. LIBRARY OF CONGRESS

BELOW: The four bomb markings on the nose of 42-31333 indicate that this photograph was probably taken between January 21 and January 24, 1944. It seems likely that it was taken to commemorate the nose art newly painted on to the aircraft by mechanic Anthony 'Tony' Starcer.

ABOVE: An automatic bomb strike camera image showing just that – bombs hitting the synthetic oil production facility at Merseburg during the raid on November 2, 1944. It was during this attack that four former pilots of Wee Willie were killed and a fifth was taken prisoner.

TOP RIGHT: Another contemporary of Wee Willie with the 322nd was 43-38901 LG-T Star Dust. It was also flying nearby when Willie was fatally damaged on April 8.

ABOVE RIGHT: Lt Edward L Mooney was the second longest serving pilot of Wee Willie, in terms of missions flown. He took the aircraft into action over Normandy before, during and after the D-Day landings.

STURMBOCK ATTACK

The aircraft's greatest challenge to date came with a mission to the Leuna oil refinery at Merseberg on November 2, 1944, with Trent again at the controls.

The 322nd provided 13 of the 693 B-17s sent to attack the target and they were part of the high squadron of the bombing group. Former Willie pilot Roy A Hammer, now a captain, was flying the leading aircraft, 44-8208 My Baby II.

The target was hit as planned and the formation turned around to return westwards. As they were passing Hamburg the B-17s were bounced by a formation of between 50 and 75 enemy aircraft. Many of these were Fw 190 Sturmbock bomber killers but there were also Me 163 interceptors and Me 262 jets involved in the attack.

The Sturmbocks, heavily armoured and fitted with 30mm cannon, moved in on the B-17s in formation, line abreast, and hit them at close range. The effect was devastating but not quite as devastating as the Germans would have liked.

According to the official 322nd Bombardment Squadron report: "After the first pass the attack was continued by individual aircraft and formations up to five aircraft from all directions. The attacks covered a period of about 20-25 minutes. Friendly fighters were engaged at the time by large formations of enemy aircraft including a few Me 163s and Me 262s.

"The group lost 13 aircraft to flak and fighter attacks, the worst loss suffered to date. Of these the 322nd lost six ships. Captain Hammer's aircraft #208 was last seen off to the left of the formation apparently under control but with

fire observed in the radio room and behind #3 engine due to enemy action.

"Lt Burne in aircraft #212 flying on Captain Hammer's left wing was observed peeling off from the formation, losing altitude but apparently under control with no visible damage. Lt Russel H Brown in aircraft #298 in the number three position of the high element was last seen lagging about 1000ft behind the formation under control and with no apparent damage.

"Lt Hare flying number three of the low element in aircraft #083 was last seen under control but with his left wing on fire and under persistent attack by six to eight Fw 190s. Lt Brant in the flying spare #202 was lost at the time of the enemy aircraft attack but no observations were made of the circumstances.

"Lt Hamilton, flying aircraft #102 in the number four position of the low element, was last observed under control but losing altitude rapidly and burning fiercely in both wings at the number two and number four engines.

"The tail gunner S/Sgt Wayne W Ritchie, ball turret gunner, S/Sgt Thomas R Giordano, and S/Sgt Joseph M Wirtz Jr, on Lt Sparkman's crew, distinguished themselves during the attack by continuing to fire their guns in spite of severe damage to their aircraft and wounds sustained by them."

On a single mission, five former Wee Willie pilots had been lost – Captain Hammer and lieutenants Burne, Brown, Brant and Hamilton. Hammer and seven of his crew were taken prisoner when My Baby II crashed at Micheln, Germany. The ninth man, Emile Freeman, was killed.

Tom Burne and four of his crew died when 43-38212 Gal O'My Dreams had its intercom shot out and bomb bay set on fire by the German fighters. It crashed at Gross Oesingen and the four survivors became PoWs.

Russel Brown and five of his crew died and their aircraft, 44-6298 White Cargo crashed at Neugattersleben. The three survivors were captured. Dale Brant managed to get out of his aircraft, 43-38202 Miss Slipstream, over Marbitz, near Halle, but he and his navigator John F Gustavson were shot dead near the crash site. His other seven crew members were taken prisoner.

Hamilton, his co-pilot, the tail gunner and a waist gunner aboard 42-98012 Cannon Ball Too were killed. The other five crewmen managed to jump from the stricken aircraft and were taken prisoner. The aircraft crashed at Haideburger.

Despite being hit by a Me 163 during the attack, Wee Willie, Trent and his crew made it back to Bassingbourn in one piece. Three days later they were back in the air and heading for the rail marshalling yards at Frankfurt. The mission seemed to go as planned but when the 322nd's aircraft returned and photographs of the bombing run were analysed it was found that they had actually dropped their bombs over the western edge of Offenbach, a town five miles east of the target.

Another raid on November 9 was even further off target due to faulty navigational gear. Trent and the Willie crew, among 12 aircraft allocated to the raid from the 322nd, were meant to hit a fortress four miles south east of Metz in support of American ground forces. Instead, they ended up dropping their bombs six and a half miles away.

Eventually, after three unsuccessful runs at the target, the B-17s, including Wee Willie, were forced to land at a captured airfield in France for refuelling before they could return home.

A third failure followed on November 16. It was another raid in support of ground forces, this time fighting in the Aachen area. There was little flak and radio beacons were functioning properly for guidance but there was heavy cloud over the target and little was achieved by the 322nd.

There was another attack on the Merseburg oil plant on November 21 but this time the 322nd's objective was the flak battery protecting it. Very low cloud forced the B-17s down to 19,500ft and on the way back from the target Willie was forced to make another unscheduled stop on the continent, this time due to mechanical failure. Trent put it down on an airfield in Belgium for repairs.

Five days later, Willie was part of a group attacking a railway viaduct at Altenbeken and on November 27 Trent flew it on a mission to attack a bridge at a railway marshalling at Offenburg. Cloud cover was a problem again, however, and the pilots decided to make their bombing run entirely on instruments. When the photos were later

examined, it was found that the bombs had been dropped two and a half miles away from the target.

Trent ended a month of almost nonstop action with another raid on Merseburg at the controls of Wee Willie on November 29.

An attempt to bomb the Soest railway marshalling yard near Kassel on December 4 was another failure due to poor weather conditions. Neither Wee Willie nor Lt Trent took part in a raid on Berlin the following day – the first attack on Berlin by the 322nd since June. However, another ex-Willie pilot did fly the mission: Howard Mitchell in his now regular aircraft, the unnamed 43-38693.

After the mission, the official report stated: "Anti-aircraft fire was accurate and consisted of both barrage and tracking fire. Our aircraft #693, Lt Mitchell pilot, was last observed at 1058 hours with number one prop windmilling. Six chutes reported."

In fact, only five men survived. Mitchell and three of his crew were killed.

Wee Willie was flown by Lt Robert L Schuck on December 9 for a mission against the railway marshalling yards at Stuttgart but Trent was back in command on Christmas Eve, 1944. This time Willie was to attack the airfield at Merzhausen near Frankfurt where the Fw 190A-8/R6s and new Fw 190D-9s of I./JG 2 were based. A total of 198 B-17s joined the attack in five waves.

According to the 322nd report: "Visual sighting was done and good results obtained on the hangar line. On return, persistent fog at base forced our aircraft to land at Bury St Edmunds."

> "Wee Willie was flown by Lt Robert L Schuck on December 9 for a mission against the railway marshalling yards at Stuttgart but Trent was back in command on Christmas Eve, 1944."

BOTTOM LEFT: Two of Wee Willie's pilots appear in this badly faded photograph. Lt William H Trent is seated in the aircraft's cockpit while Captain Roy A Hammer is in the front row on the right. Also pictured are, back row, radio operator S/Sgt Emile Freeman, the only member of Hammer's crew killed when his B-17, My Baby II, was shot down over Merseburg on November 2, 1944; Hammer's engineer S/Sgt William Nagy and Sgt John Baird. Beside Hammer on the front row is his navigator Lt Raphael Czepkiewicz. When the photograph was taken Trent was Hammer's co-pilot. It is possible that the aircraft shown is in fact Wee Willie during Hammer's tenure in July 1944. LIBRARY OF CONGRESS

BELOW: The only known photograph of 42-31333 Wee Willie in flight before the photographs taken during its destruction. USAF

BOTTOM: An unidentified later crew of Wee Willie.

From a German perspective, the 'good results' were anything but. I./JG 2 was taken completely by surprise. All five waves of bombers hit the airfield and turned it into a cratered wasteland. Most of the station buildings on the north side were destroyed too, though only two German personnel were killed and only one Fw 190 was destroyed. It took until December 31 to make the airstrip usable again.

Before then, on December 28, Trent flew Wee Willie to attack the railway bridge at Remagen over the Rhine. Another mission, to hit a German communications centre at Wittlich, followed on December 29 – it was Trent's last with Willie and the last of his operational tour.

THE NEXT GENERATION

With almost all of Willie's previous pilots now dead or gone home, a new generation took over sporadically. First to take the helm was Lt James L Ashlock Jr for another attack on a communications centre, this time at Bitburg on New Year's Eve. The raid was relatively successful but no results could be observed due to heavy cloud cover.

December 14 had seen the arrival with the 322nd of new pilot Lt Robert E Fuller, from Hollywood, California, and his first mission was to bomb Cologne on January 3, 1945. Wee Willie took part in the uneventful mission but was flown by another newcomer as of December 4, Lt Robert Marlow. Lt Edward E Chase had joined the unit in the same intake as Fuller and he flew Willie for the first and only time on January 5, also against Cologne.

Lt Ashlock flew Willie again on January 10 during a mission to bomb Ostheim aerodrome, home to elements of JG 11, and Lt Arthur Ernst took a turn flying Willie on January 14 for an attack on the Deutsch bridge over the Rhine at Cologne. It was Ashlock again on January 15 and 20 for bombing runs on rail yards at Ingolstadt and a bridge over the Rhine at Ludwigshaven respectively.

Lt Harold L Reinhart flew Willie on January 21 – more marshalling yards, this time at Aschaffenburg – and Lt Fuller finally took his first turn on February 1 to hit still more rail yards at Mannheim.

The rest of February saw five more unfamiliar faces flying Wee Willie for brief periods – Robert W Roach, Marvin L Pearson, Wayne F Swegle, Robert H Miller and Nelson D Van Blarcom.

From February 14, 1945, to February 21, Swegle flew Willie for four missions in a row. The first of these would have seen Willie bombing Dresden – the city already burning from a night of incendiary attacks by the RAF – however, a diversion to avoid an unexpected front of bad weather saw the 322nd's aircraft diverted to bomb Prague instead.

On the way home, the squadron encountered heavy flak over Munster and seven aircraft suffered damage. B-17G #027, with Fuller at the controls, was the worst hit, with Fuller himself being wounded.

Rather than attempt to reach Bassingbourn, Fuller turned his aircraft in the direction of Advanced Landing Ground A-83, Denain in northern France. After jettisoning the ball turret, Fuller made a belly landing and was taken to hospital.

Swegle's other missions with Willie, including another four in early March 1945, were uneventful, with little or no damage taken to any 322nd aircraft, including Wee Willie.

After March 7, Willie was taken off the roster until March 19, when it was sent back into action with yet another pilot, Lt Leroy B Hansen, against the Bohlen synthetic oil plant. Lt Gerald G Kranch flew Willie for two missions, on March 22 and 23, then it was Joseph J Troccoli's turn for a single mission on March 24.

Having finally been passed fit for service once again, Fuller's first mission back in action after his injury was on March 30, 1945, flying Wee Willie once again. The objective was the shipyards at Bremen and the 322nd encountered heavy flak, though Willie came through unscathed and was back in action again the following day with Fuller taking it on a raid over a locomotive depot at Halle.

Several missions in early April were scrubbed so Willie's first outing of the month was to the airfield at Reinsehlen on April 4. No enemy opposition was encountered but then cloud cover was so thick that no positive identification of the target could be made and the 322nd brought their bombs back to Bassingbourn. Fuller flew Willie again on April 7 against airfields at Fassberg and Kohlenbissen, the group achieving "excellent results".

RAID ON STENDAL

It was business as usual the following day, April 8, 1945, when Fuller flew Wee Willie as part of a 73-bomber raid on the locomotive repair shops at Stendal in Saxony-Anhalt, Germany. The mission was carried out using H2X 'Mickey set' ground search radar to identify the target – although the lead and high squadrons, the latter including Wee Willie, could actually see it anyway.

The mission was a great success, the 322nd's official report noting: "The high squadron was furnished by the 322nd, led by Lt Johnson. Strike photographs for the high squadron's bombs show an excellent concentration of hits covering the aiming point.

"Almost the entire concentration lies within a 1000ft circle over the MPI. Meagre to moderate tracking AA fire on the bomb run which was extremely accurate resulted in minor damage to 13 aircraft and major damage to four in the group. The high and lead squadrons each lost one aircraft in the target area from flak damage."

The aircraft lost from the lead squadron, the 401st, was B-17G-50-BO 42-102504 Times A-Wastin' flown by Lt Peter Pastras. Its demise was witnessed by Lt Mike Fodroci, a navigator aboard another B-17. He saw the four gun batteries on the ground tracking bursts of flak through the lead formation, getting closer and closer to Times

RIGHT: Another automatic bomb strike camera shot, this time showing bombs falling on the rail yards at Stendal on April 8, 1945. Just minutes later, Wee Willie was destroyed.

BELOW: Another unidentified crew with Willie. The number of mission markings on the fuselage, around 105, tends to indicate that the pilot might be Lt Wayne F Swegle, who flew the aircraft on eight occasions around this time.

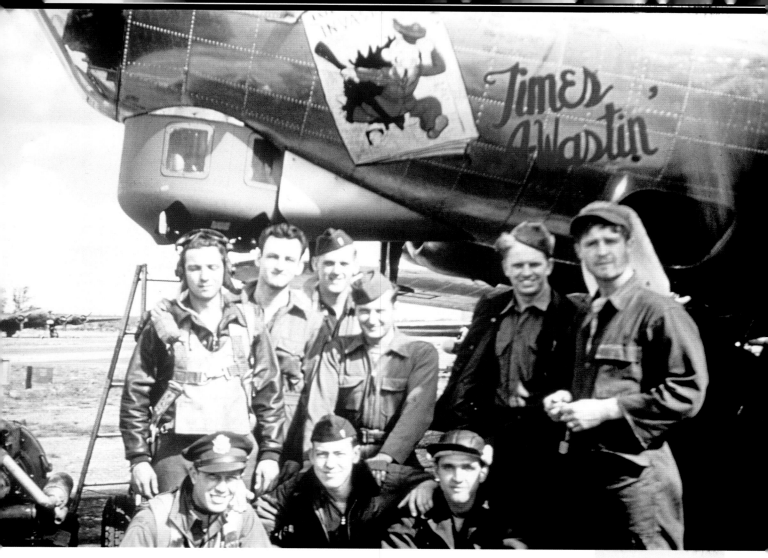

A-Wastin' until the fourth one went directly into the aircraft's still-open bomb bay.

In his report he states: "The pilot must have been killed instantly; for the ship pulled up and veered to the right, climbing directly over our ship. Captain Shelby put our ship into a dive so steep that I was thrown up against the astro hatch of the ceiling in the nose – seems I hung there for a brief second or two.

"I also observed that a bad fire was burning on the aircraft's forward bomb bay area and that the co-pilot was trying to climb out of the small window with his back pack on. Somehow, we saw three chutes emerge from #504 as she spun toward the earth."

Times A-Wastin's co-pilot, Bob Morris, was killed when the B-17 exploded in mid-air, along with all but two of its crew, engineer Lyle Jones and radio operator Bob A Smith, who were taken prisoner on the ground.

The aircraft lost from the high squadron was 42-31333 Wee Willie. In the Missing Air Crew Report S/Sgt George Little, a gunner aboard a 401st B-17, states: "I observed 42-31333 receive a direct flak hit approximately between the bomb bay and the number two engine. The aircraft immediately started a vertical dive. The aircraft fuselage was on fire and when it had dropped approximately 5000ft the left wing fell off.

"It continued down and when the fuselage was about 3000ft from the ground it exploded, and then exploded again when it hit the ground. I saw no crew members leave the aircraft or parachutes."

> **"Times A-Wastin's co-pilot, Bob Morris, was killed when the B-17 exploded in mid-air, along with all but two of its crew, engineer Lyle Jones and radio operator Bob A Smith, who were taken prisoner on the ground."**

There was another witness to Wee Willie's end, however, that was able to offer an even more accurate account of what happened. About a third of the B-17s flying on any given mission were equipped with bomb strike cameras. These were fitted under the floor in the radio room and the lens cone was exposed to the elements.

The cameras were automatically operated from 'bombs away' until they ran out of film or automatically stopped after a predetermined number of exposures. They took an exposure every six seconds, with the mechanism then winding the film on, ready for the next shot.

In this way, the success or failure of a mission could sometimes be determined by examining the photographs.

The automatic camera on another B-17, flying beside or below Wee Willie, captured the aircraft's violent final 18 seconds in three photographs.

Shortly before the last of the three, Willie was torn apart by an explosion that ripped right through the fuselage and blew Lt Robert E Fuller clear out of the cockpit. Somehow, he managed to get his parachute open and survived the descent. The remainder of his crew were all killed.

Although he is recorded as having been taken prisoner, Fuller's final fate remains unknown and in some sources he is listed simply as 'killed in action' alongside his crew.

Wee Willie had completed 127 missions and was destroyed on its 128th. ●

ABOVE: B-17G-50-BO 42-102504 Times A-Wastin' was blown apart by a direct flak hit at around the same time as Wee Willie over Stendal. This colour image shows an earlier Times A-Wastin' crew.

WORLD'S FASTEST MESSERSCHMITT

APRIL 9, 1945: HANS-GUIDO MUTKE'S CONTROVERSIAL DIVE

Whatever might be said about its other abilities and frailties, there is no denying that the Messerschmitt Me 262 jet fighter was fast. Extremely fast. Little was known for certain about the sound barrier in 1945, but did one German pilot manage to push his Me 262 through it?

ABOVE: Swiss ground crew attempt to tow Hans-Guido Mutke's Me 262A-1a/R1, 'White 3' WNr. 500071, after he landed near Zurich on April 25, 1945. Presumably they have taken heed of the printed notice on the forward landing gear door not to tow the aircraft by its nosewheel. BUNDESARCHIV

TOP: Towards the end of his life, former Luftwaffe pilot Hans-Guido Mutke claimed that during the Second World War he had flown his Messerschmitt Me 262 faster than the speed of sound. Pictured here during the 1960s, Mutke, who stood 6ft 2in tall, became a gynaecologist after returning to Germany.

For every famous pilot who flew the Me 262 in the last days of the war there are a dozen more whom history has all but forgotten.

Fähnrich Hans-Guido Mutke looked certain to be just such an unremembered and uncelebrated pilot.

Born in Neisse, Germany, on March 25, 1921, he was called up to join the war effort as a medical student after pilot training he joined Nachtjagdgeschwader 1 in 1942, flying Messerschmitt Bf 110s and Dornier 217s against British bombers.

Then, in March of 1945, he was transferred to 10./EJG 2 (Ergänzungsjagdgeschwader 2 or 'Operational Fighter Training Group 2') at Lechfeld for retraining on the Me 262 since his experience with twin-engine fighters made him an ideal candidate.

On April 9, Mutke was ordered to carry out a training mission at high altitude and therefore climbed to just over 36,000ft – close to the Me 262's ceiling of 37,565ft. He was at this near-maximum altitude when he overheard a flight controller warning that a P-51 Mustang was about to intercept one of his fellow trainees and decided to fly down to help.

He pushed his Me 262 'White 9' over into a steep 40-50° left bank with both engines on full power and plunged downwards.

In just a few seconds, the aircraft began to shudder violently.

Mutke himself recalled: "The airspeed indicator was stuck in the red danger zone, which is over 1100kph. I noticed that rivets began popping out of the tops of the wings. The aircraft began vibrating and shaking wildly, banging my head against the sides of the cockpit.

"I moved the stick wildly around the cockpit. For a brief moment, the aircraft responded to controls again, then went back out of control. The aircraft still did not respond to pressure on the stick so I changed the incidence of the tailplane.

"The speed dropped to 500kph, the aircraft stopped shaking and I regained control. After diving about three miles I was able to return to base. On the runway the mechanics were very surprised by the appearance of the aircraft, which looks as though it had been shaken by the hand of a giant."

In another interview, Mutke stated: "What happened had never happened to another pilot as I entered a very dangerous realm without knowing it. I had no idea what was happening. I thought there was something wrong with the aircraft."

The mechanics may have been bewildered by the state of Mutke's jet fighter but his superiors were not impressed.

He said: "When I landed, the commander was furious and demanded to know what I had done with the aircraft, and demanded to know if I had gone above the red mark of 950km.

"I said, 'Of course not. You know, this might be a Monday production'. That means it was made the day after the workers had been drinking."

Mutke soon discovered that the comrade to whose aid he had been rushing got shot down anyway, but had managed to parachute to safety.

And that might have been the end of the story.

Two weeks later, on April 23, Mutke was ordered to go to Fürstenfeldbruck to join 7./JG 7 but the following day American tanks advanced to within 30 miles of the airfield and the unit was transferred to Bad Aibling. On the same day the unit's leader, the famous ace Major Heinz Bär, left to join Adolf Galland's 'squadron of aces' JV 44.

At the last minute, with almost everyone already en route, it was realised that one particularly well dispersed Me 262 had been forgotten about – WNr. 500071 'White 3' which was sitting under cover in woodland just over a mile from the airfield.

Since Mutke was available, he was ordered to collect it and fly it to join his new comrades at Bad Aibling.

When he got out on to the airfield he discovered that the only personnel in sight were a trio of soldiers who had no idea how to service a Me 262.

Mutke later recalled: "I didn't even know how long the Me 262 had been standing there and if it was filled up with fuel or not.

"I called the three soldiers, but all the efforts to start the aircraft were in vain. So we decided to try it again next morning. On the morning of April 25, we succeeded in starting the Messerschmitt. It was a high risk, because I didn't know where the aircraft had come from and how long it had been standing there.

"We found out that the fuel tanks were almost empty. We towed it to the petrol station and in order to reduce the time of filling the fuel tanks, the pump attendant put two fuel hoses into it, one in each of the two fuel tanks."

Just as the fuel was flowing, Mutke looked up and saw 25-40 B-26 Marauders approaching the airfield. He ordered the attendant to pull out the hoses, fired up the aircraft's twin engines and took off. The bombers, seeing him become airborne, flew into a bank of cloud and by the time he had gained enough altitude to give chase he could see no sign of them.

Checking his fuel, he saw that he did not have enough to reach Bad Aibling and resolved to fly to Lake Constance and ditch in it instead.

When he reached it, he decided to attempt a landing over the border in Switzerland. However, he had no idea whereabouts in Switzerland he could put the aircraft down. Reaching the southern shore of the lake, his fuel gauge showed zero.

He flew over the airfield to alert the Swiss to his presence before being escorted down by four Swiss fighters. Mutke was taken prisoner and his aircraft was handed over to the Swiss military for testing before being put in storage.

From October 1945, Mutke was treated as an interned civilian and returned to his medical studies. In later years he moved to Argentina and then Bolivia, working as a pilot for civilian airlines flying DC-3s.

A move back to Germany followed and Mutke took up a position as a gynaecologist in Munich.

In 1957, the Swiss authorities handed Me 262 WNr. 500071 over to the Deutsches Museum in Munich.

During a conference to mark the 50th anniversary of jet powered flight in 1989, Mutke mentioned his experiences of April 9, 1945, to some of the experts present and they discussed with him the possibility that he might in fact have broken the sound barrier some two years earlier than Chuck Yeager – who officially became the first man to go supersonic on October 14, 1947.

The precise details of Mutke's flight, the suitability or otherwise of the Me 262 for passing through the sound barrier, the accuracy of its in-flight instruments, and the technical difficulties of proving or definitively disproving the pilot's story have occupied the minds of Me 262 enthusiasts and the aircraft's detractors ever since.

Those who support his claim – he died on April 8, 2004, donating his body to anatomist Gunther von Hagens – cite a handbook on the Me 262 written by the USAAF in January 1946 based on tests of captured aircraft.

This states: "At speeds of 950 to 1000kph the airflow around the aircraft reaches the speed of sound, and it is reported that the control surfaces no longer affect the direction of flight. It is also reported that once the speed of sound is exceeded, this condition disappears and normal control is restored."

Computer simulations carried out at Munich Technical University in 1999 concluded that the Me 262 might have been able to go supersonic.

Professor Otto Wagner told Reuters, which was reporting on Mutke's claims in 2001: "I don't want to exclude the possibility but I can imagine he may also have been just below the speed of sound and felt the buffeting, but did not go above Mach 1."

In addition, engineers recreating the Me 262 at the time in the US, using modern engines in a replica airframe, said they believed Mutke might have been right. Jim Byron of the Me 262 Project said: "We met with Herr Mutke and having listened to his story, we believe he could have accomplished this in the severe dive and engine flameout."

Wartime flight tests by Messerschmitt engineers determined that the Me 262 would become uncontrollable beyond Mach 0.86, leading to an ever steepening dive that could not be corrected by the pilot. Higher speeds would then result until the airframe came apart due to high G loads.

Some believe that Mutke's changing the tailplane incidence enabled him to overcome the steepening dive and level out to regain control briefly at just above supersonic speed.

Sceptics have pointed to the unreliability of German measuring equipment during the later stages of the war and compressibility in pitot tubes that resulted in inaccurate readings close to the speed of sound.

Also counting against the Me 262 was its fuselage, designed without knowledge of the area rule, which would have resulted in very high drag at transonic speeds. Nevertheless, it is acknowledged that engine thrust combined with the pull of gravity during a steep dive might have supplied sufficient force to push the Me 262 through the sound barrier and into supersonic flight.

In all likelihood, while the air passing over Mutke's aircraft might have exceeded Mach 1, his jet probably did not. However, it will never be known for certain just how fast he really went. ●

BELOW: When Mutke landed in Switzerland, his aircraft was carefully examined by Swiss engineers and photographed from every conceivable angle. As an R1, WNr. 500071 was equipped to fire salvos of R4M rockets, although it wasn't fitted with any when Mutke flew it on April 25, 1945.

LEFT: A rear view of Mutke's Me 262 as engineers tinker with an access panel on its nose.

BELOW: Another view of WNr. 500071 under tow. The aircraft was involved in the second controversial episode for which Hans-Guido Mutke is primarily remembered.

CANADIANS AGAINST THE KOMET

APRIL 10, 1945: LEUTNANT FRIEDRICH KELB ACHIEVES THE FINAL ROCKET FIGHTER VICTORY OF THE WAR

ABOVE: Veteran Messerschmitt Me 163B Komet rocket fighter pilot Leutnant Friedrich 'Fritz' Kelb of I./JG 400 in the cockpit of his aircraft. Kelb was sent up to attack the Allied bomber formation targeting rail yards near Leipzig on April 10, 1945, using a new weapon over which he had only indirect control. The SG 500 Jägerfaust was fitted in the aircraft's wings and triggered automatically by a daylight sensor.

As the Allies advanced into Germany, Bomber Command continued to target German rail infrastructure. On April 10, it was the turn of the marshalling yards at Engelsdorf and Mochau near Leipzig. The mission was almost routine but one of the defenders the bombers faced when they got there most definitely was not.

It was planned that two waves would strike the rail yards – one during the early evening and one that night.

In the first wave were 134 Lancaster bombers – 110 from 6 (RCAF) Group's 419, 424, 427, 428, 429, 431, 433 and 434 Squadrons and another 24 from 8 (Pathfinder) Group – plus 90 Halifaxes from 408, 415, 420, 425, 426 and 432 Squadrons and six Mosquitos of 105 Squadron.

Having taken off from their bases in England between about 2.30pm and 3pm, the bombers linked up with their escort, RAF Mustang IIIs, and had reached their target by about 6pm. The skies were blue with patchy cloud.

In the meantime, one Halifax from 408 Squadron had become lost and turned for home, while another four Halifaxes and two Lancasters suffered mechanical trouble and went back to base early, running on three engines.

There was heavy flak as the bombers prepared to release their loads at between 15,500 and 19,000ft and several aircraft were hit – including Lancaster I PB903, BM-F, of 433 Squadron, flown by Flying Officer Robert Grisdale. He feathered the starboard inner engine after it took damage.

A 425 Squadron Halifax had a hole measuring 2sq ft blasted through the wireless operator's compartment, wrecking the oxygen system. Then the Mosquitos dropped their target indicator flares.

An air gunner with 433 Squadron, Cameron Clare Campbell, wrote in his diary: "This was a good raid but we were towards the rear of the formation and took a dreadful pounding from slipstreams all the way to the target.

"There was heavy predicted flak close to the target. With predicted flak, the Germans would fire a burst and from observing the blast could make a correction on the next shot which would be closer, then make a correction on the second burst and usually the third burst had your number on it.

"The secret was to change your height or heading after the first blast. Just as we were about to drop our bombs, I heard Chris ask the bomb-aimer who was flying F Freddy because it was on fire. Just as Plaskett answered him telling him it was Grisdale's crew, the bombs and the plane blew up. I never saw the explosion as it was slightly ahead of us and to the right but we felt the blast and saw the debris as we passed."

According to the official RCAF report: "This Lancaster was hit by flak, the starboard inner was seen to be feathered. Then a small explosion was seen, the aircraft flipped onto its back and spiralled to the ground. No parachutes were seen."

It was at this point that several crews saw small dark shapes flitting among their aircraft and were quick to identify them as Messerschmitt Me 163B-1 Komet rocket-propelled point interceptors.

The pilot of 415 Squadron Halifax VII RG447 'S', Flying Officer R Jupp, spotted an enemy fighter at 6.02pm at 16,500ft, 4500ft off the port bow. The Halifax's mid upper gunner told Jupp: "Corkscrew starboard" and opened fire with the Me 163 some 2400ft away. The rear gunner joined in at 2100ft and the Me 163 reportedly broke away.

At around the same time, 6.02pm, the crew of 425 Squadron Halifax NP937 'T' saw a Me 163 attacking a Lancaster bomber. They reported seeing flames coming from the Lanc's rear turret and no combat manoeuvres being undertaken by the bomber. NP937's mid-upper gunner fired at the Me 163 and reportedly saw it stall, roll onto its back and go into a steep dive.

That Lancaster was ME315 'LQ-K' of 405 Squadron – a Lancaster III. The pilot was Squadron Leader C H Mussels. The official report on what happened stated: "In the target area, immediately following release of target indicators, Lancaster aircraft 'K' ME315 was attacked by an enemy fighter Me 163. The attacking aircraft approached from the rear and above, and with one burst completely shot away the rear turret, rudder and elevator.

"Damage was also caused to the H2S set and mid-upper turret. The rear gunner, Flight Lieutenant Mellstrum, was in his turret when the attack commenced and is believed killed. This officer is missing, no further information available.

"A number of Mustangs who were acting as fighter escort moved in closer to the disabled aircraft and covered it until it reached the front lines. The pilot, due to the fact that he had only partial control of the aircraft, ordered the crew, except for the mid-upper gunner, to bale out over RAF station Woodbridge.

"Had not the mid-upper gunner been injured the whole crew would have baled out. The pilot was successful in making a reasonable landing at RAF station Woodbridge. All members of this crew, with the exception of the rear gunner, are back at this unit."

One of the RAF Mustang pilots, Flying Officer Johnny 'Slops' Haslope of 165 Squadron, claimed to have destroyed the Me 163 during the attack. His report stated: "I was flying as Green 1 when at approx. 6.05pm I noticed a bomber begin to smoke and something appear to fly off it. This resolved itself into a Me 163 which climbed vertically at great speed.

"I reported the aircraft and dropped my overload tanks and gave chase at full throttle. The Me 163 turned towards me and I had a shot at him in a right-hand turn, range about 900 yards and 30 degrees defection, but observed no strikes.

"The Me 163 then spiralled into a vertical dive which I followed, firing several bursts of about 2-3 seconds observing strikes on four occasions on the wing roots and several small pieces came off.

"These strikes were observed by Flying Officer Rae flying Green 2, Flying Officer Lewin, Green 3 and Flight Lieutenant Kelly 64 Squadron. I overshot rapidly at 3000ft and had to pull up to avoid collision, wrinkling the wings as I did so.

"The Me 163 continued on down and was observed by Squadron Leader Potocki of 315 Squadron and Flying Officer Wacnik of 306 Squadron to hit the ground and explode near an airfield believed to be either Brandis or Manstorf.

"I turned away from the aerodrome and climbed back with Green 2 to rejoin my squadron, followed by 40mm flak from the aerodrome."

It is believed that his Mustang III, KH557 SK-Z, was so damaged by his power dive in following the German aircraft that it never flew again.

Precise records are lacking but it is believed that three Me 163B-1s from 1./JG 400 had been sent up to attack the bombers, one of them flown by Lt Friedrich 'Fritz' Kelb of 1/JG 400. He took off from Brandis airfield near Leipzig with the express purpose of field-testing a new weapon. His aircraft was one of three Me 163s to have been equipped with the SG 500 Jägerfaust weapon and was the only one to see action. This was also the last time that any Me 163s would see action.

The SG 500 was designed and patented in 1944 by Oberleutnant Gustav Korff and consisted of a number of rifled steel tubes, each loaded with a single projectile and mounted vertically in the carrier aircraft.

The single shot tubes were linked to an optical sensor mounted on the upper portion of the carrier aircraft which when it sensed the substantial difference in light caused by flying underneath a bomber, into its shadow, fired the tubes automatically.

The tubes themselves were ejected beneath the aircraft as the projectiles flew upwards, cancelling out any hazardous recoil and simply leaving a series of holes in the carrier aircraft. A 20mm version of the weapon was tested on a

ABOVE: Lancasters flying in large formation during daylight was a rare sight for most of the war – but the attack on railway marshalling yards near Leipzing on April 10 took place just after 6pm. Sunset would have been at around 7.45pm. This switch to daylight bombing made the Allied aircraft a viable target for the Me 163 point defence interceptors of I./JG 400.

BELOW LEFT: The small size and unusual shape of the Me 163B-1 rocket fighter are evident in this photo showing 2./JG 400's Unteroffizier Rolf Glogner, pictured right, and his machine. Glogner proved that the Me 163 could be effective in the right circumstances by shooting down a de Havilland Mosquito on March 16, 1945. After the disbandment of JG 400, he served with Leutnant Kelb in JG 7 on the Eastern Front flying Me 262s.

BELOW: This still from a propaganda film shot between August 21 and September 9, 1944, shows Me 163s on the apron at I./JG 400's base at Brandis airfield, near Leipzig.

LEFT: Lancasters of 405 Squadron, like this one, were pathfinders for the main bomber force on April 10. During the attack, two bombers were lost but the only 405 Squadron machine to suffer heavy combat damage, Lancaster III ME315 'LQ-K', made it home, albeit without its tail gunner. Several witnesses saw ME315's tail section being hit by a Me 163.

TOP: An Avro Lancaster bomber belonging to 433 Squadron. The Canadian unit was based at RAF Skipton-on-Swale in North Yorkshire and flew Handley Page Halifaxes for over a year before re-equipping with Lancasters for the last three months of the war. On April 10, 433 Squadron's Lancaster I PB903, BM-F, flown by Flying Officer Robert Grisdale was shot down over the unit's rail yard target.

ABOVE: A I./JG 400 Me 163B under full rocket power over Brandis, near Leipzig, in 1944. The unit became operational at the airfield in July 1944 and remained there until its dissolution a fortnight before the war's end.

BELOW: North American Mustang IIIs of 315 Squadron in Europe in the spring of 1945. The unit's Squadron Leader Wladyslaw Potocki witnessed a Me 163 attacked by Flying Officer Johnny 'Slops' Haslope of 165 Squadron hit the ground and explode on April 10, 1945.

Fw 190 before the production 50mm version was built for the Me 163.

On the Me 163, four tubes were fitted to each wing, with the optical sensor being installed in the port wing were there was already a suitable access panel.

Signals officer with 2./JG 400 Feldwebel Hans Hoever saw what happened when Kelb took the weapon into combat: "I watched Kelb attack a formation of about 150 Lancasters that were bombing Leipzig and the city's outskirts on April 10. I had just finished my shift and was standing on the observation tower of the fighter control command post next to the Würzburg radar when I heard over the loudspeaker that Leutnant Kelb was about to take off with his special aircraft.

"I heard the rocket motor and saw Kelb climb above the trees at the end of the runway south of where I was standing. I followed him with the aid of the long-range flak telescope and saw him head towards the lead aircraft of the bomber formation which was flying at a height of about 8000m.

"I thought he wanted to ram it but just at the moment he passed about 100m below the aircraft, the bomber exploded in a cloud of smoke and flames. I had never before seen a bomber so easily destroyed as that attack by Leutnant Kelb.

"Just after the bomber exploded I noticed that the escort fighters had spotted Kelb. My first thought was that he had enough fuel left, at least enough for 15 seconds, to reignite his engine. I was pleased to see the motor spring to life just

as the fighters swarmed down to attack him and Kelb shoot through them to a height 2000m above them.

"My telescope allowed me to follow the ensuing fight. With his fuel spent, Kelb turned and dived past a fighter that was close to him with such a speed that the fighter was not aware of what had happened."

A German report on the use of the Jägerfaust on April 10, made on April 12, stated: "The first and also the last operational trial of the Jägerfaust was made over Leipzig on April 10, 1945. At about 6pm a strong formation of enemy bombers appeared over the city. A Me 163B with 'vertical armament' went into action.

"The aircraft came unheeded below the enemy machines. The armament was immediately discharged. A bomber at once fell out of the sky like a burning torch, none of the crew being able to make their escape. Two other aircraft were so badly damaged that they also crashed after flying over our airfield. Our aircraft was able to draw away still unobserved by the enemy, and was only located and attacked by Mustang and Thunderbolt fighters when it had arrived back over our airfield.

"The anti-aircraft defences were able to keep the enemy aircraft at a distance while a smooth landing was made with no damage to our aircraft. These were the last successes obtained with the Me 163B."

AFTERMATH

Kelb was killed in action less than three weeks later, on April 30. After the disbandment of JG 400, he joined I./JG 7 flying the Me 262. During a fighter sweep he was apparently attacked by a pair of fighters from the 358th Fighter Group flown by Lieutenant Joseph Richlitzky and Captain James H Hall, each claiming a Me 262 damaged. Another version of events suggests that he was hit by flak near the Focke-Wulf facility at Cottbus.

Every crewman aboard Grisdale's Lancaster I PB903, BM-F, was killed and their remains were buried in Berlin War Cemetery. Another bomber went down during the same raid, Halifax BIII NA185, 6U-B, which was reportedly hit by bombs from another aircraft. All of its crew were killed too.

Nothing of the tail gunner of Lancaster III ME315, LQ-K, of 405 Squadron, Flight Lieutenant Melborn Leslie Mellstrum, remained in his turret when the crippled aircraft arrived back at Woodbridge, but he had not disappeared completely as a surprising number of men did during the war.

A British prisoner of war, Gunner Robert David Williams of the 11th (HAC) Regiment, Royal Horse Artillery reported on June 24, 1945, that he had been at Stalag IVG at Engelsdorf during April 1945, when a chaplain had asked him to join a funeral service for two British servicemen – one of them another PoW killed during an air raid, and the other an airman whose body had been found by the Germans.

After he was liberated, he told the British military authorities: "The burial took place in the evening of April 13 at

> ## "Every crewman aboard Grisdale's Lancaster I PB903, BM-F, was killed and their remains were buried in Berlin War Cemetery."

the cemetery of the Luthren Evangelical Church at Engelsdorf about 10km east of Leipzig.

"The bearers and all the burial party were from Lager 29. The men were under the command of Lance Sergeant Frank Cole. They slow-marched from outside the mortuary to the grave. The coffins were draped with the Union Flag. They were lowered into the grave simultaneously by two different parties.

"After the service the men saluted. The Germans were unable to supply the usual firing party as the Americans were just outside Leipzig and the guns could be heard constantly. We ourselves were evacuated by the Germans at 3am the following day."

Williams asked after the airman's identity following the service and several hours later was told that it was Melborn Leslie Mellstrum.

To this day, it is unclear precisely which aircraft Kelb hit with his novel upwards firing weapon. If he was alone, then it would make sense that Lancaster ME315 was badly damaged by him. If there were indeed two other Me 163s with him, the flak hit on Lancaster PB903, Grisdale's machine, may in fact have been the result of his SG 500 – the effects of which would have been very like a flak strike.

The machine that blew Mellstrum from his turret and was then followed to its destruction by Haslope's Mustang might then have been one of Kelb's comrades, rather than Kelb himself.

It is a mystery that is unlikely to ever be satisfactorily resolved. ●

ABOVE: This low quality shot purportedly shows the underside of a Me 163 wing fitted with SG 500 firing gear. The white block with the vertical row of four holes in it gives more visible evidence of the positioning of the unusual weapon.

LEFT MIDDLE: The wreckage of a Me 163 modified to fire the 50mm SG 500 weapon. The only visible evidence of this is on the machine's port wing. A series of small black holes runs in a straight line through the centre of the white Balkenkreuz from front to back. With the weapon installed, the tips of four metal tubes would have been visible protruding from the holes. When the SG 500 was fired, the tubes were ejected from the bottom of the wing, while the projectile shot upwards, leaving just the holes, four in each wing.

BELOW: Veteran assault glider pilot Hauptmann Wilhelm Fulda was the commander of I./JG 400 on April 10, 1945. The unit was disbanded just nine days later.

ABOVE: Flight Lieutenant Melborn Leslie Mellstrum was the tail gunner in 405 Squadron Lancaster III ME315 'LQ-K' when it suffered severe damage during a Me 163 attack. His turret was torn open and his body fell to the ground. It was recovered by the Germans and buried three days later by a party of British PoWs.

ABOVE: Gun camera footage of a Me 163 in flight and under attack. The distinctive 'bat wing' shape was enough to strike fear into the hearts of bomber crews wherever it appeared. Though the type is believed to have been responsible for destroying only 16 Allied aircraft, 12 of them were four-engined bombers.

THE GRASSHOPPER THAT KILLED A STORK

APRIL 11, 1945: PIPER L-4H V FIESELER FI 156 STORCH

One of the oddest air-to-air actions of the war took place on April 11. Often wrongly cited as the 'last dogfight' in the European theatre, it nevertheless spoke volumes for the courage of US airborne artillery spotters.

American tanks of the 5th Armored Division were rolling across central Germany in the direction of Berlin by April 11, 1945, and on the front line was the 71st Armored Field Artillery Battalion.

Equipped with M7 self-propelled 105mm howitzers and M4 Sherman tanks, the unit had been driving east and south along the Weser river before crossing at Hamlin and continuing to push east.

According to the official history of the battalion, Fire Mission: The Story of the 71st: "The old familiar tactics of bypassing heavy resistance by using secondary roads and passing through only small villages were put to use again.

"Sixty and 70 mile marches were standard operations during the passing of those lightning fast days. The deeper we drove into the Reich the longer our supply lines were stretched and the more difficult the job of service battery became."

And on April 11: "That day German air activity increased over the column. All sizes and types either roared or limped past. Our ack-ack would pull off to the side of the road at the slightest pause."

Since landing at Utah beach on July 28, 52 days after D-Day, the 71st's progress had been guided by spotter pilots flying ahead over enemy territory. Equipped with tiny two-seat 65hp Piper L-4 Grasshoppers, the spotters flew long hours in often hazardous conditions.

One of the 71st's most experienced Grasshopper pilots was 24-year-old Merritt Duane Francies of Wenatchee, Washington. Known as Duane, or sometimes 'Doc' because he had taken some pre-med courses at college and was often called upon to give first aid for minor injuries, Francies had been with the 71st from the start of the European campaign.

He flew an L-4H called Miss Me!? He said: "I named my plane Miss Me!? Because I wanted the Germans to do that, the reason for the exclamation point, but I also wanted someone back home to 'miss me', so there was the question mark."

ABOVE: Pilot Lieutenant Duane Francies, left, and observer Lieutenant William Martin in front of Piper L-4J 44-80699, serial number 12965, G-54 – one of three L-4s used by observers for the 71st. Another, J-54, was named Miss Me!? by Francies.

RIGHT: Lieutenant William Martin, left, and Lieutenant Duane Francies with the Fieseler Storch they forced down on April 11, 1945.

April 11 saw Francies and his observer Lieutenant William Martin flying ahead of the 5th Armored about 100 miles west of Berlin. Not far from the 5th's advancing vehicles, on a side road, they noticed a German motorcycle and sidecar speeding along. Moving in to get a closer look, they then saw a Fieseler Fi 156 Storch observation aircraft flying at about 700ft above some trees.

Abandoning the motorcycle outfit, Francies and Martin decided that they needed to do something about the Storch, and fast, before it had a chance to report on the 5th's positions.

Afterwards, Francies wrote: "The Storch had an inverted eight Argus engine. It was also a fabric job and faster and larger than the Miss Me!?. It spotted us and we radioed: 'We are about to give combat.'

"But we had the advantage of altitude and dove, blasting away with our Colt .45s, trying to force the German plane into the fire of waiting tanks of the 5th. Instead, the German began circling."

Flying slightly above and across the German aircraft, Francies and Martin had opened their aircraft's side doors and emptied their pistols into the Storch. They saw hits on its windscreen, fuel tank and right wing. Francies then gripped the Grasshopper's control column between his knees while he reloaded. He wrote: "The two planes were so close I could see the Germans' eyeballs, as big as eggs, as we peppered them."

Trying to avoid the American aircraft that dogged its every move, the Storch went into a low turn – too low – and its right wing tip struck the ground. It span around, cartwheeling, its right wing and undercarriage coming apart, before finally coming to rest right side up.

Francies set down close by and he and Martin ran to the wreck. The German crew had stumbled, dazed, from their machine. When they saw the Americans approaching, the pilot jumped behind a pile of sugar beet to hide and the observer dropped to the ground, defeated.

Seeing that the observer had been hit in the foot, Francies ran over and went to help. He pulled off the man's boot and a .45 bullet fell out. Martin, his gun now also reloaded, fired a warning shot and the pilot came out with his hands up.

Francies took the pilot's uniform insignia and a German flag they found inside the Storch. He wrote: "I never found out their names. They could have been important, for all I know. We turned them over to our tankers about 15 minutes later, after the injured man thanked me many times for bandaging his foot. I think they thought we would shoot them."

GRASSHOPPER v STORCH

	Piper L-4 Grasshopper	Fieseler Fi 156 Storch
Crew:	2	2
Length:	22ft 5in	32ft 6in
Wingspan:	35ft 3in	46ft 9in
Height:	6ft 8in	10ft
Empty weight:	765lb	1900lb
Loaded weight:	1220lb	2780lb
Powerplant:	1 x Continental A-65-8 air-cooled four-cylinder, 65hp	1 x Argus As 10 air-cooled inverted V8, 240hp
Maximum speed:	87mph	109mph
Range:	220 miles	240 miles
Service ceiling:	11,500ft	15,090ft
Rate of climb:	450ft/min	945ft/min

ABOVE: One of the lightest aircraft to see action during the war, the Piper L-4's diminutive size made it a difficult target to hit and meant it used fuel only sparingly – allowing it to remain aloft to extended periods. PETE MARKHAM

Not long after their aerial victory, Francies and Martin were scouting ahead of the 5th when elements of the division reached the Elbe. They flew over the river and landed on the other side, only to be approached by a group of Soviet soldiers wearing grey greatcoats and riding steppe ponies.

The Russians backed off when they saw the Grasshopper's white star insignia but were not friendly and 10 minutes late the Americans got back in their aircraft and flew back to the 71st. They had not realised that they were supposed to remain on the 'American' side of the Elbe.

When the war ended, Francies had twice been recommended for the Distinguished Flying Cross but had not received it. Years passed and the recommendations were forgotten about. Francies served during the Korean War before becoming a commercial pilot. In 1966, historian Cornelius Ryan wrote about his exploits in his book The Last Battle. A US senator, Harry Jackson, pressed for Francies' achievements to be recognised and finally, the following year, Francies got his DFC. ●

BELOW: The Fieseler Storch is a physically larger, tougher and more powerful aircraft than the Piper L-4 but only 3000 or so were built, compared to 20,000 L-4s. TONY HISGETT

PISTON ENGINE ZENITH

Focke-Wulf's Ta 152 fighter had such a long and tortuous development that it barely entered service in time to see the end of the war. Nevertheless, it was flown in combat and its most notable success was in the hands of Oberfeldwebel Willi Reschke against arguably the most powerful British fighter then in service – the Hawker Tempest V.

APRIL 14, 1945: OBERFELDWEBEL WILLI RESCHKE DESTROYS A HAWKER TEMPEST V

ABOVE: Oberfeldwebel Willi Reschke flew Ta 152H-1 WNr. 150168 on April 14, 1945, when he shot down the Hawker Tempest V, SN141, of New Zealander W/O Owen James Mitchell. Reschke was one of only a handful of pilots ever to fly the type.

The Ta 152 was the ultimate development of the Focke-Wulf Fw 190 and had come about as the result of a compromise.

When it became clear that the Fw 190's BMW 801 engine could not be improved any further, company chief designer Kurt Tank set out to create a replacement fighter that built on the strengths of the existing one but with a better power plant.

He had intended to build an all-new fighter, the Ta 153, but was forced instead to put one together using as many existing Fw 190 parts as possible to avoid disrupting production lines.

Three different engines, all still in development themselves, were selected as candidates for the new Ta 152 fighter in late 1942. The Jumo 213A-powered design was the Ta 152A, the Jumo 213E design the Ta 152B and later the Daimler-Benz DB 603 L the Ta 152C.

In every case, the Ta 152 took the basic Fw 190A-8 airframe and lengthened the forward fuselage to accommodate the new engine and an engine mounted MK 108 cannon. The wing was moved forwards to adjust the centre of gravity and the rear fuselage was lengthened with the fitting of a 0.5m section into it.

The undercarriage was the same as the A-8's but with larger 740 by 210mm wheels. The wings were slightly enlarged to a span of 11m, from the Fw 190A's 10.5m, by inserting an extra 0.5m section into each one. This was so

that the larger wheels could be moved outboard by 0.25m each for propeller clearance.

While the standard Ta 152 fighter was being worked on, Tank decided to pit the design against Messerschmitt's proposed Bf 109H high-altitude fighter as the Ta 152H. When the Bf 109H proved to be a disaster, Tank's competing design was approved.

Problems with engine development meant that none of the Ta 152A, B and C standard fighters reached production, but the H did.

The Ta 152H had the same A-8 airframe alternations as the standard fighter designs but the fuselage centre section was designed as a pressurized chamber with a volume of about one cubic metre, sealed with DHK 880 paste. The sliding cockpit canopy was sealed with a tube partly filled with foam rubber.

In addition, wingspan was increased to 14.4m (47ft 3in) from the standard Fw 190A's 10.5m (34ft 5in).

TA 152H INTO SERVICE

The war situation was deteriorating rapidly, but sufficient testing had been done for the Ta 152H to enter full production in late November 1944, just 11 months after the first prototypes had been ordered.

Neuhausen, near Cottbus in Brandenburg, on the far eastern edge of Germany, was chosen as the Ta 152 production centre and work began slowly. While the facilities were available for mass production, the materials and components were not. There were continuous delays at the factory as missing parts were tracked down for the first run of Ta 152H-0 aircraft.

Focke-Wulf chief test pilot Hans Sander flew the first machine off the production line, WNr. 150 001 CW+CA, on November 24, 1944. The second machine was first flown on November 29 and the third on December 3. A total of 21 H-0s had been completed by the end of December. These had no wing fuel tanks or MW 50/GM 1 boost.

Production was in full swing during January but on January 16, a group of 40 USAAF Lightnings and Mustangs attacked the airfield at Neuhausen, where the new Ta 152s had been gathered prior to delivery to III./JG 301, the first unit intended to operate them. Fourteen brand new 152s were completely destroyed and another was damaged.

The Ta 152C programme was forging ahead but was still in the prototype stage of development by the end of January 1945. Another 20 Ta 152s, H-0s and H-1s, would be completed that month and three more in February before production ceased, giving a total of 44 production machines, plus 11 prototype/experimental airframes.

Pilots from the Erprobungskommando Ta 152 test unit at Rechlin had been flying the aircraft since November 2, 1944, but the first unit to operate it was III./JG 301. The Gruppe was withdrawn from front line operations to begin conversion to the type on January 27, 1945. Four days earlier, the order had been given to redesignate the test unit as Stabsstaffel JG 301 but in practice the Erprobungskommando took no part in front line activities.

III./JG 301 pilots were taken to Neuhausen by truck in the early hours on January 27 and when they arrived were presented with 12 Ta 152s parked in three rows of four. After a technical briefing lasting half an hour they flew the aircraft to nearby Alteno. One of those pilots was Oberfeldwebel Willi Reschke. He recalled: "The first unpredictable surprises occurred during practice flights over the airfield in the Ta 152, when aircraft from other Staffeln were encountered. Such encounters often proved problematic, for the outline of the Ta 152 was virtually unknown to German pilots.

"In such encounters pilots also reacted very differently. The vast majority immediately displayed defensive reactions or offensive intentions, but there were also pilots who reacted to the encounter with panic and tried to flee to safety. The pilots of the Ta 152 had to deal with these reactions until the end of the war."

He said the Ta 152 gave a sense of "tremendous power" and gave impressive acceleration. It was also able to perform well above 30,000ft, where the Fw 190A-8 would be losing power and behaving sluggishly.

After the initial 12 had been transferred, III./JG 301 received a further four Ta 152s over the next two months but none thereafter. It therefore only had 16 in total, though

it had been planned that it would receive 35. The first was lost on February 1 when Unteroffizier Hermann Dürr's machine entered a flat spin and crashed near Alteno.

As the conversion continued into the middle of February, all of III./JG 301's pilots flew the Ta 152, while also continuing offensive operations with the unit's Fw 190A-8s and A-9s. On February 19, III./JG 301 was forced to abandon Alteno as Soviet forces advanced towards it, relocating to Sachau west of Berlin.

STAB./JG 301 IN COMBAT

It was while based at Sachau that the Ta 152 nearly made its first 'kill' – a Boeing B-17 Flying Fortress claimed shot down by III./JG 301's Oberfeldwebel Josef 'Jupp' Keil. In fact, no B-17s were lost that day, though some were damaged.

"Their first mission from this new home, on the same day of the move, was to attack American forces that had just overrun Stendal."

Another Ta 152 was destroyed after stalling too close to the ground during the unit's first few days at Sachau, killing pilot Oberfähnrich Jonny Wiegeshoff.

Keil tried again on March 1, this time claiming a North American P-51 Mustang shot down. This seems more likely, since the US 8th Air Force lost seven Mustangs that day.

On March 2, 1945, during a mission to escort Fw 190A-8 and A-9 Sturmbocks attacking an American bomber formation, a unit of Bf 109s attacked III./JG 301's Ta 152s and forced them to take evasive action – aborting the mission.

ABOVE: Another shot of Ta 152H-1 WNr. 150067 showing the type's elongated fuselage. It was captured by the Americans in flyable condition at Erfurt-North on April 15, 1945. It is believed to have been selected for conversion to Ta 152H-10 standard – a high-altitude reconnaissance version originally designated Ta 152E-2.

RIGHT: The aircraft flown by Oberfeldwebel Willi Reschke during his combat with 486 Squadron Tempest Vs, WNr. 150168, after its capture by the British.

On March 13, the remaining Ta 152s were formed up into a Stabsschwarm (staff flight) at Stendal, away from their comrades at Sachau. They moved again on April 10, this time to Neustadt-Glewe air base – hidden by woodland in a secluded area.

Their first mission from this new home, on the same day of the move, was to attack American forces that had just overrun Stendal. While providing top cover for this mission, Oberfeldwebel Keil claimed an American P-47 as a 'probable' kill in his Ta 152, though this has proven hard to verify.

By April 14, Soviet forces had crossed the River Oder and were advancing on Berlin. In the late afternoon, two Hawker Tempests were spotted attacking the railway line from Ludwigslust to Schwerin and three Ta 152s were sent up to intercept them – flown by Oberfeldwebel Sepp Sattler, Oberfeldwebel Willi Reschke and Oberstleutnant Fritz Auffhammer.

Reschke, who flew Ta 152H-1 WNr. 150168, wrote in his autobiography: "As our takeoff was in the same general direction as the railway line, we reached the Tempests' attack area shortly after leaving the airfield. I was flying as number three in the formation, and as we reached the area where the Tempests were I saw Sattler's Ta 152 go down for no apparent reason. Now it was two against two, and the low-level battle began.

"As I approached my opponent pulled up from a low-level attack and I attacked from out of a left-hand turn. Both pilots realised that this was a fight to the finish, and from the outset both used every tactical and piloting ploy in an attempt to gain an advantage. At that height neither could afford to make a mistake, and for the first time I was to see what the Ta 152 could really do.

"Twisting and turning, never more than 50m above the ground, I closed the range on the Tempest. At no time did I get the feeling that my machine had reached the limit of its performance. The Tempest pilot quite understandably had to undertake risky manoeuvres to avoid a fatal burst from my guns. As my Ta 152 closed in on the Tempest, I could see that it was on the verge of rolling the other way: an indication that it could not turn any tighter.

"The first burst from my guns struck the Tempest in the rear fuselage and tail. The Tempest pilot reacted immediately by flicking his aircraft into a right-hand turn, which increased my advantage even further. There was no escape for the Tempest now. I pressed the firing buttons again, but my guns remained silent. Recharging them did no good: my guns refused to fire a single shot.

"I can't remember whom and what I cursed at that moment. Luckily the Tempest pilot was unaware of my bad luck, for he had already had a sample. He continued to twist and turn, and I positioned my Ta 152 so that he always had a view of my machine's belly.

"Then came the moment when the Tempest went into a high-speed stall: it rolled left and crashed into a wood. This combat was certainly unique, having been played out at heights which were often just 10m above the trees and rooftops.

"Throughout I never had the feeling that my Ta 152 had reached its performance limit, instead it reacted to the slightest control input, even though we were practically at ground level. Oberstleutnant Auffhammer also gain the upper hand against his Tempest, but in the end the enemy succeeded in escaping to the west.

"As the combat had taken place just a few kilometres from the airfield, in the late afternoon we drove out to the scene and discovered that Oberfeldwebel Sattler's Ta 152 and my Tempest had crashed within 500m of each other. The treetops had absorbed some of the force of the crash and the Tempest looked like it had made a forced landing.

"The damage inflicted by my cannon shells was clearly visible on the tail and rear fuselage and the pilot was still strapped in the cockpit. It turned out that he was a New Zealander, Warrant Officer Owen James Mitchell of 486 Squadron, Royal Air Force. The next day the two fallen pilots were buried with military honours in the Neustadt-Glewe cemetery."

WHAT 486 SQUADRON SAW

W/O Mitchell had in fact been flying one of four, not two, Tempest Vs on April 14 in the Ludwigslust area. The section was led by the 122 Wing Leader, Wing Commander Richard Edgar Peter Brooker, Pink 1, and consisted of 486 Squadron pilots W/O William John 'Bill' Shaw, Pink 2, F/O Sydney John 'Sid' Short, Pink 3, and Mitchell, a new pilot with the squadron, who was Pink 4.

They had taken off from Advanced Landing Ground B-112, at Hopsten, Westphalia, Germany, at 6.25pm and later split up into two sections of two – Brooker and Shaw, and Short and Mitchell. At 7.30pm, the former pair saw a lone Fw 190 and shot it down after a brief battle.

Short and Mitchell had been strafing ground targets when they were set upon by three other fighters. While Mitchell, flying Tempest V SN141 SA-U, was shot down and killed, Short, in NV651 SA-R, claimed to have damaged one of his attackers – which he believed to have been a Bf 109E.

Short's official report of the combat states: "I was flying Pink 3 on an armed recce of the Perleberg-Ludwigslust area and together with my No. 2 W/O Mitchell was pulling up from attacking Met north of Ludwigslust when we saw two Me 109s at 1000ft and another four 109s at about 3000ft. The two 109s were coming in to attack us from port rear-quarter.

"I called up and advised my No. 2 and instructed him to drop his tanks. I broke port but could not quite get onto the tail of the leading 109, who started turning with me. A climbing turning match ensued and after three turns I was able to give the 109 a burst with about 45° off. The 109 flew through and I observed four strikes after of the cockpit.

"I was unable to observe further results because I had one 109 on my tail and another positioning to attack. The last I saw of my No. 2 was from 6000ft, when I saw him turning at deck level with some 109s. Cine camera used. I claim one Me 109 damaged."

Meanwhile, Shaw and Brooker were not far away. Shaw, who was flying Tempest V NV753 SA-J, reported: "I was flying Pink 2 and while diving to attack Met on a road about 10 miles east of Ludwigslust I saw a single Fw 190 flying east at deck level. I reported this to Pink 1 who ordered me to follow him in to attack.

"The 190 broke when we were out of range and as I could see that my No. 1 would be unable to attack I dropped my tanks and climbed for height. As the enemy aircraft straightened out east I dived on it passing my No. 1. This time the 190 broke rather later and again to port and I was able to pull my bead through until he disappeared beneath my nose.

ABOVE: Oberfeldwebel Josef 'Jupp' Keil was the first pilot to shoot down an enemy aircraft with a Ta 152.

ABOVE: Ta 152H pilot Oberfeldwebel Sepp Sattler was killed when his aircraft crashed shortly before his comrades engaged in combat with a pair of RAF Hawker Tempests. The cause of his aircraft's crash was never discovered.

ABOVE: Oberfeldwebel Willi Reschke was awarded the Knight's Cross on April 20, 1945, six days after his combat over Ludwigslust.

"It was a full deflection shot and I opened fire when I judged I had two radii deflection on him. I fired a long burst and then broke upwards to observe the results. As the 190 came in sight again I saw the flash of a strike just forward of the cockpit.

"An instant later flames appeared from the port side and, enveloped in flames, the 190 went down in a gradual straight dive to the deck. I saw it crash in a field and explode. Cine camera used. I claim one Fw 190 destroyed."

It is almost certain that the 'Me 109' damaged by Short was a Ta 152. It is also very likely that the Fw 190 claimed by Shaw was Oberfeldwebel Sattler's Ta 152.

Though he was a relative newcomer to 486 Squadron and front line combat, having been posted to the unit in early March 1945, Mitchell was not a rookie pilot. He joined the RNZAF in 1942 straight from university, where he had been an engineering undergraduate, and transferred to England where he completed his training.

He then flew with various Operational Training Units as both pilot and instructor and had racked up 700 hours before he converted to the Hawker Tempest V in early 1945.

AFTERMATH

More than two years after his death, in September 1947, Owen James Mitchell's body was recovered by the Missing Research and Enquiry Unit. The official report stated: "We visited the area (now in the Russian Zone) and found Body No. 1. This body was found to be clothed in khaki battledress and had New Zealand marked on the shoulder. The socks were RAF blue and the boots RAF

escape type flying boots. On a handkerchief found in the pocket I found the name Pettitt in print letters, about a quarter inch high on the hem."

The body was reinterred at the British Military Cemetery in Heerstrasse, Berlin.

Reschke continued flying the Ta 152 for only 10 more days after shooting down Mitchell. On April 21, 1945, the Stabsschwarm's Ta 152s encountered their first Yak-9s during a mission to cover Fw 190As flying fighter-bomber missions against Soviet targets on the eastern side of Berlin. Oberfeldwebel Keil claimed two of them shot down.

It was Reschke's turn three days later. On April 24, he found himself facing a group of Yak-9s. He recalled: "Having never encountered Russian fighters before, I was unfamiliar with their tactics, but figured that if I got in trouble I could still climb up into the clouds. The Russians held their tight formation, consequently I was a first unable to turn as tightly as I would have liked.

"I soon went from being in front of the enemy fighters to behind them, further proof of the Ta 152's manoeuvrability. Only after I shot down the number four aircraft did the Russian formation split up, and each tried to get me on his own.

"Only one of the Russians had the will to carry on, however, and the other two withdrew. The remaining pilot was probably the leader of this small fighter unit, but his Yak-9 was hopelessly inferior to my Ta 152. In the end he went down trailing smoke."

This was the last known flight of the Ta 152 in service and the British captured his machine shortly afterwards. ●

"It was a full deflection shot and I opened fire when I judged I had two radii deflection on him. I fired a long burst and then broke upwards to observe the results."

ABOVE: The leader of 122 Wing, Wing Commander Peter Brooker, was flying with three 486 Squadron pilots during an armed reconnaissance mission on April 14 when his men were involved in air-to-air combat with Ta 152s of Stab./JG 301.

BELOW LEFT: A Tempest V of 486 Squadron, NV763 SA-Z, in flight during 1945, though after hostilities had ended. Gerald Trevor Roberts via John Roberts

BELOW: A group of 486 Squadron RNZAF pilots in conversation with their commanding officer at Advanced Landing Ground B60 in Belgium. The man who appears sixth from left, with his eyes shadowed by his cap, is Pilot Officer Sid Short, who was flying with Warrant Officer Owen Mitchell when he was shot down by Willi Reschke.

TWO SHOTS TO THE HEAD

APRIL 16, 1945: THE MURDER OF CAPTAIN CHESTER E 'COGGIE' COGGESHALL JR

It was a strafing mission much like any other. Tudor Red flight of the 343rd Fighter Group were shooting up the airfield at Ainring near the Austrian border at around 3.45pm and each of the four P-51 pilots claimed a Focke-Wulf destroyed on the ground. Then things went badly wrong for Red Leader…

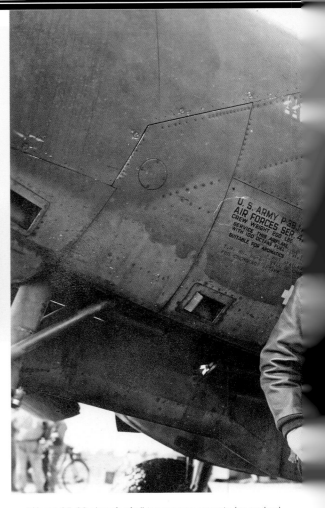

ABOVE RIGHT: Pilot Chester E Coggeshall Jr during his days as a P-38 pilot early in the war.

BELOW RIGHT: Captain Chester E Coggeshall of the 343rd Fighter Squadron, 55th Fighter Group.

BELOW: Lt Coggeshall, as he then was, wears his nickname emblazoned on both his headgear and his case.

The 343rd were having a field day. During one of their regular freelance strafing missions they had stumbled upon a large selection of German aircraft parked out in the open and were doing their best to fill them full of holes.

The attack turned out to be not quite the turkey shoot that the Americans were expecting, however. Tudor Red flight was Red Leader Captain Chester E 'Coggie' Coggeshall Jr in P-51D 44-15608 CY-T 'Cape Cod Express', with 2nd Lieutenant George A Apple in 44-15735 as Red 2, 1st Lieutenant Walter Strauch in 44-72362 CY-B as Red 3 and 2nd Lieutenant Jack A Bevington in CY-L as Red 4.

Strauch reported of the combat: "I was flying Tudor Red 3 on the mission of April 16. We passed over Ainring aerodrome in the vicinity of Salzburg.

"About 25-30 aircraft of all types were seen to be parked around the field. Red Leader, Captain Coggeshall, decided to attack the field, so we came in to the field out of the hills to the south of it, making our pass from south to north.

"I saw Red Leader and his wingman, Lt Apple, firing at 190s. I picked a Focke-Wulf Fw 189 and my wingman, Lt Bevington, chose another 190. I got a good concentration of hits on my target and saw it burst into flame.

"When we pulled up off the field I saw Capt Coggeshall in a shallow dive attempting a crash landing. Since I had also been hit by flak we did not attempt any further attacks on the field. However, on looking back over the field after Capt Coggeshall had gone in, I could see that there were four distinct fires burning."

In the Missing Air Crew Report filed on Coggeshall, he reported: "We drove down to strafe an airfield west of Salzburg and when we pulled up to about 1000ft I noticed Red Leader Capt Coggeshall, making a very gentle turn to the left and losing altitude.

"I immediately started over toward him and noticed his airplane was covered with oil, and about this time he made a fast belly landing, dug a wing in and cartwheeled. I went back to investigate and saw where the plane had hit a small brick building. There was no fire but the airplane was completely demolished."

Strauch's wingman, Lt Bevington, reported: "When we came across the field from out of the south, I was trailing behind the rest of the flight.

"I picked out a Fw 190 for my target and fired a short burst at it. The strikes were pretty well concentrated about the engine and nose of the aircraft. It had begun to smoke badly when I passed over it. I did not get a chance to look back at it since the flak was pretty heavy and our flight leader, Capt Coggeshall, had been hit and was attempting a crash landing."

Bevington also contributed to Coggeshall's MACR. He wrote: "We went down to strafe an aerodrome just west of Salzburg. I was last man across the airfield and after pulling up I noticed Capt Coggeshall's ship smoking. He started to pull up, then went into a slow turn, losing altitude.

"Just before hitting the ground he straightened the ship up and attempted to belly land at high speed. His right wing dug in, after sliding three quarters of the way across an open field, and he cart-wheeled through a small building at the opposite end of the field. Although the ship did not burn it was completely demolished."

Coggeshall had crash-landed at Sillersdorf, Germany, just over three miles west of Freilassing. When his shattered Mustang came to rest, he was conscious and struggled to extract himself from the cockpit. Four French PoWs, who had been working in the fields nearby, ran over to help, along with a German civilian.

Fighting to remain conscious, Coggeshall asked them: "Friend or foe?" They told him: "Friend."

Not long after the crash, however, Freilassing policeman Joseph Lohmeir received a telephone call about it and drove to the scene in an armoured car. When he arrived, he found the meadow with the wrecked aircraft lying in it. Fifty metres away from that, Coggeshall was lying on a stretcher on the ground and standing beside it were the four PoWs and the German civilian.

Lohmeir asked the men for the pilot's papers and they handed them to him along with a box, a map, some flight manuals, a small dictionary, a booklet and a number of other small items.

He then asked them to help him take Coggeshall to the nearest farmhouse. Lohmeir said later: "At the railroad station we put down the stretcher and then I saw exactly that one eye was swollen. I think the right eye and somewhere on his side there was a wound and he didn't say anything."

He asked the Frenchmen if the pilot had been conscious and they said he had been for a short time, describing the encounter.

Lohmeir asked the farmer's wife for some water and Coggeshall took a small sip but then coughed and some blood came out of his mouth. After calling for the

local ambulance and being told that it was unavailable, Lohmeir put the stretcher, with Coggeshall strapped to it, on top of the armoured car and drove him to the police station at Freilassing.

When he arrived there, he was told to take the American to the temporary military post inside the local school house. He got back in the car and drove the short distance over, followed by a growing crowd of 20-30 curious civilians.

Lohmeir tried to report to the company commander, Leutnant Karl Böhm, but got acting Hauptfeldwebel Ludwig Suldinger instead. After Suldinger had confirmed that Coggeshall was in fact still alive, he had a call placed to the nearest Luftwaffe station at Ainring four miles away – the same one Coggeshall had been shooting up less than an hour earlier.

He then went and got four civilian recruits from inside the school house to help him carry the wounded pilot inside. They got him down from the car and Suldinger ordered them to carry him up to the dispensary on the first floor of the building.

At that moment the town mayor, August Kobus, jumped in front of the stretcher bearers and blocked the entrance by stretching out his arms and legs. He told them: "In this house this man will not be carried." Suldinger told his men to get on with it, ignoring Kobus, but the mayor repeated: "This man will not be carried in here."

Kobus, 45, had joined the Germany Army when he was just 13 and served until 1918 when he suffered a severe head injury and lost his right hand. Now he was both the mayor of Freilassing and the town's Nazi party leader or 'ortsgruppenleiter'. He wore a brown uniform with

TOP: When he was shot down on April 16, 1945, Capt Coggeshall was flying his usual P-51D Mustang, 44-15608 CY-T 'Cape Cod Express'.

ABOVE: Flying as Red 2 to Coggeshall's Red Leader on April 16 was 2nd Lt George A Apple. He was shot down and killed the following day.

LEFT: Tudor Red Flight's Red 3 was 1st Lt Walter Strauch, who was soon after promoted to captain.

ABOVE: Red 4 on April 16 was 2nd Lt Jack A Bevington. Along with Strauch, he filled out the Missing Air Crew Report for Coggeshall.

peaked cap and red swastika armband. He also carried a holstered .32 pistol.

Suldinger got angry with Kobus but then Lt Böhm, arrived. He spoke with the mayor then a car arrived with Böhm's superior, a captain, and Böhm reported to him. The captain told Böhm to sort out the matter of the American airman himself and then left. Kobus put his arm around Böhm's shoulder and had words with him in private.

Suldinger took the opportunity to inspect Coggeshall, who had been lying on the ground on his stretcher in the meantime. Suldinger said: "I observed that he had a wound on the left side and one on the right side. Some blood on his head. One eye was swollen and the other eye was open and looking around vividly. I had the impression that he was not wounded dangerously."

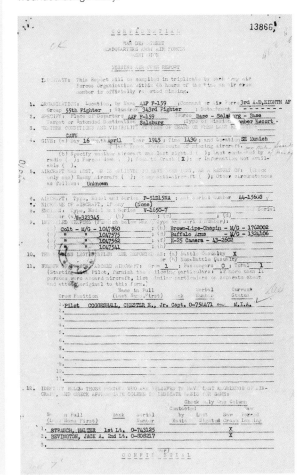

RIGHT: The front page of Capt Coggeshall's MACR.

The mayor told the soldiers that the American could not stay in the town and that he would have to go elsewhere. When asked where, he said: "Oh, some place, I will go along."

He got on his bicycle and began riding away down the street. Böhm directed his junior platoon commander, Lt Rudiger von Massow, 22, to have Coggeshall put back on the armoured car. Once the pilot was secured, von Massow and three of his men got into the armoured car and set off after Kobus. The last Suldinger saw of Coggeshall, he was reaching up and adjusting a pillow or cushion that had been put under his head by von Massow.

A preacher, Markus Westenthaner, saw this unlikely convoy heading down the road at about 5.45pm: "I saw a soldier in a foreign uniform on the car. He was lying flat on the vehicle. He had long black hair which was hanging down. He was a tall man. I presume he was wounded because his face showed some pain."

A Polish man working in a meadow nearby also saw them: "I was at my work. It was about 5.45 or 6 o'clock in the evening I saw the Burgomeister when he was driving down the road on a bicycle. He went into the woods and shortly after the armoured car came down."

The mayor, the soldiers and Coggeshall had entered Pfarrau, a wooded area near the church and cemetery of Freilassing. Von Massow later said he felt intimidated by Kobus and followed his orders. Kobus leaned his bike up against a tree.

In a statement made a month later, Kobus said: "The American airman was removed from the vehicle. I then approached this airman, who was lying on a stretcher, and from a distance of 4m shot him twice in the head with a pistol. The American pilot screamed after I fired the first shot at him. I silenced him with the second shot.

"Lt Von Massow and the three German soldiers from the 7th Panzer Reconnaissance Company were present during the time that I murdered this American pilot."

Less than 15 minutes later, Coggeshall's corpse had been loaded back on to the armoured car and driven back into town.

Kobus then had the captain's still warm body, soaked with sweat, taken to the local mortuary. When it arrived the undertaker saw that a coal sack had been placed on the head. Kobus told the man: "I bring you a dead American and we have to bury him immediately."

When he was told that there was no coffin or grave immediately available, Kobus replied: "It is not necessary to have a coffin, just bury him like that."

Then a German soldier came in and said he had to remove Coggeshall's uniform, his shoes and a bandage that was on his head. Once he was finished, the body was only clad in underwear. The mortuary owner's wife removed Coggeshall's captain's insignia from his uniform and kept it as a souvenir.

When the coal sack was removed, it revealed a bullet wound to the airman's forehead. The soldier told the wife that "it was a shot of mercy" without bothering to explain further.

A grave was dug at 9.45am the following day in the Freilassing cemetery by undertaker Johann Mitiska. That evening, at 6.45pm, Kobus summoned Mitiska to his office and told him he suspected that he had been telling people that he, Kobus, had shot the American. He angrily told Mitiska: "The only choice I had was whether to shoot or hang him." Then he threatened to kill the undertaker if he talked about the body to anyone.

Nine days later, on April 25, Freilassing was hit by 44 Douglas A-26 Invaders of the USAAF's 416th Bombardment group. Their target, from 10,000-13,000ft, was an ordnance depot north of the town.

They dropped 132 100lb fragmentation bombs with "excellent results", encountering no flak. According to the official report of the mission "buildings and installations in the depot area were severely damaged, roads and railroad tracks were cut. Many fires were also kindled".

The town was devastated and there was further damage when the RAF also bombed the town that night. Whatever the truth, the townspeople firmly believed that they were being deliberately targeted because of what the mayor had done to Coggeshall.

Another nine days later, on May 4, Freilassing shopkeeper Alois Denk saw Kobus on the armoured car and approached him. He asked the mayor: "Why did you shoot this American?" Kobus replied that he hadn't, it was von Massow. Denk told him: "You tell a lie, you did shoot him. Why did you do it?" Kobus answered: "I had to fulfil the order of the Kreisleiter."

Kobus later claimed he had been told "that these pilots and these crews of the enemy's bombers and enemy strafing planes are to be treated and considered not as soldiers, but as murderers". Other mayors from the area later verified that they had been gathered together by the Kreisleiter of Berchtesgarden, Bernhard Stredele, some weeks earlier and told to "liquidate" any Allied airmen who came into their area.

The direct order to shoot Coggeshall, Kobus said, had been given to him by Stredele via telephone on the day of the incident.

A war crimes investigating team arrived in Freilassing on May 10, 1945, and Coggeshall's body was disinterred. It was positively identified by his friend, Captain Frederick E Pickens, and August Kobus was arrested.

He was tried before a general military court at Ludwigsburg, Germany, on a charge of violation of the laws of war on November 13-14, 1945, and was found guilty. He sentenced to death by firing squad but this was changed to death by hanging on February 6, 1946.

Stredele was also tried, on February 25, 1946, found guilty and sentenced to death. This was commuted to life imprisonment because the only real evidence of him giving the order to kill Coggeshall was Kobus' testimony, which the presiding military panel had found particularly compelling and convincing.

Both Rudiger von Massow and Karl Böhm were also charged with war crimes but were acquitted.

Coggeshall's body was sent back to the US, arriving in New York, where his US Navy pilot instructor brother arranged for his burial. His grave is at Long Island Cemetery, Framlingdale, New York. ●

> **"He was tried before a general military court at Ludwigsburg, Germany, on a charge of violation of the laws of war on November 13-14, 1945."**

SPITFIRES O

350 (BELGIAN) SQUADRON'S MAGNIFICEN

RIGHT: The leader of 350 Squadron's Red Section on April 20, 1945, and the mission leader, was Spanish Flight Lieutenant Robert 'Roberto' Muls. VIA SERGE BONGE

EVEN IN COMBAT

Seven Spitfires were engaged in a fight to the death with Focke-Wulf Fw 190s on April 20, 1945, on the western fringes of Berlin. The young RAF men came out on top but one of their number failed to return…

It was approaching sunset on April 20, 1945, as seven 350 (Belgian) Squadron Supermarine Spitfire Mk.XIVs flew northwards on a fighter sweep around the western fringes of Berlin.

The Rolls-Royce Griffon-engined single-seaters passed Nauen at gone 7.20pm and continued northwards in the direction of Neuruppin. Smoke still lingered in the air following Eighth Air Force B-17 bombing raids on rail marshalling yards at both locations earlier in the day.

Not too far away, on the opposite side of Berlin, Russian units had crossed the River Oder and were advancing on the city. The following day, April 21, the German capital would be hit by Soviet artillery fire for the first time.

Within the centre of the city itself, in the Führerbunker, beside and beneath the Reichs Chancery, Hitler was making his final decision to stay in Berlin to the last – when his staff realised that the window of opportunity to escape by air or by road was rapidly closing.

THE SEVEN

The Spitfires flew in formation in two sections. Red section, and the mission, were being led by a 25-year-old Spaniard – Flight Lieutenant Robert 'Roberto' Muls in SM825 MN-M.

Muls, from Barcelona, joined the Belgian section of the RAF on June 10, 1942, before undergoing extensive training. After converting to the Spitfire in March 1944, he was posted to 350 Squadron, his first front line unit, on May 30, 1944. At the outset of the April 20 sweep, he had just one shared aerial victory – a Fw 190 shot down 15 days earlier over Aschendorf.

Red 2 was Belgian Pilot Officer Emile Pauwels, 24, in NH697 MN-K. He had been in Belgium when it finally capitulated to the Nazis on May 28, 1940, but escaped to England on May 15, 1942. After training, he joined 350 Squadron on July 27, 1944. On March 2, 1945, he was credited with damaging a Bf 109.

The third member of Muls' section, 25-year-old Flight Lieutenant David Howorth, was from Bolton, Lancashire, and flew RM618 MN-P. He became a sergeant in the RAF Reserve on July 27, 1940, and became a flying officer exactly a year later. He had no combat victories.

Lastly, Red 4 was 22-year-old Warrant Officer Jacques 'Pichon' Groensteen (Pichon meaning young pigeon) who had fled Belgium as a refugee on May 20, 1940. He joined the Belgian Aircrew Receiving Centre

in September 1941 and after training was posted to 350 Squadron on December 23, 1942. He then transferred to 349 Squadron on June 15, 1943, and more training followed until he was finally returned to 350 Squadron on January 10, 1945.

On March 2, 1945, he claimed a Bf 109 shot down in the Rheine-Munster area. On April 20 he was at the controls of NH686 MN-V.

Yellow section was led by Pilot Officer Desmond 'Des' Watkins, 23, from Llwyn-y-pia in the Rhondda Valley, south Wales, flying RB155 MN-C. Already an experienced pilot, Watkins had participated in the first Spitfire sortie over Germany with Squadron Leader Geoffrey Page and others on April 26, 1944. He had destroyed several enemy aircraft on the ground but had no air-to-air victories.

His No. 2 was Flight Sergeant Andre Kicq, 21, in RM733 MN-J. Like Pauwels, he escaped occupied Belgium in 1942, before joining the RAF Volunteer Reserve in July 1942. Fully trained as pilot by August 1943, he was posted to 350 Squadron in July 1944. On April 17, 1945, he had achieved his first aerial victory by shooting down a Fw 190 south of Hamburg.

Seventh, Yellow 3, was 26-year-old Pilot Officer Marcel Doncq flying NH693 MN-J. Of all the men, he had perhaps had the longest journey to reach the seat of his Spitfire XIV. He had been in the Belgian Army when war broke out and was captured by the Germans with his unit at Lombardsijde.

Escaping Belgium into France on April 16, 1941, he worked his way south across the whole of the occupied country, crossing into neutral Spain on April 25. Arrested near Barcelona by fascists, however, he was put in prison and languished in various cells for nearly a year.

BELOW: A Spitfire Mk.XIV of 350 (Belgian) Squadron in 1944 – the following year noses of the unit's fighters were painted black and the tail stripes were removed.

ABOVE: Pilot Officer Emile Pauwels had escaped occupied Belgium in 1942 and signed up for the RAF as soon as he was able. During the combat on April 20 he stuck with Flt Lt David Howorth. VIA SERGE BONGE

Liberated on February 7, 1942, he reached Gibraltar on February 11, 1942. He was transferred to England on March 11, 1942, and he joined the RAF Volunteer Reserve. He was next sent to Canada for training and first flew solo in a Tiger Moth on March 4, 1943.

A year later he was back in Britain and had converted to the Spitfire. He joined 350 Squadron on June 12, 1944. By April 20, however, he had achieved no victories.

THE BATTLE

The seven Spitfires had set off from Advanced Landing Ground B.118 Celle in Lower Saxony, Germany, at 7.04pm with perhaps an hour and a half of daylight still remaining. Celle, 175 miles from Berlin and formerly home to a Luftwaffe flying school, had only been captured from the Germans, largely intact, nine days earlier.

Half an hour later, the RAF aircraft had reached their target area and were flying in a north-easterly direction at

RIGHT: Warrant Officer Jacques 'Pichon' Groensteen at the controls of his battered Spitfire. VIA SERGE BONGE

9000ft when Howorth saw something and within seconds all hell had broken loose.

According to his combat report: "When in the Nauen area I saw four Fw 190s going in the opposite direction, south, below, but owing to the R/T being in use was unable to report them for the moment."

When he was finally able to report his sighting, Muls ordered Yellow section to attack.

Watkins reported: "Yellow 2 immediately went down and I was on the point of doing so when I noticed two Fw 190s coming towards me and my No. 3 slightly below us. I selected the one on the port side and made a sharp turn to port and gave a quick burst as the enemy aircraft was overshooting me.

"I observed strikes on starboard mainplane. The enemy aircraft then rolled on its back and in the process caught a long burst in its belly. The enemy aircraft turned into a tight spiral and spun towards the ground when I saw it blow up."

Yellow 3, Doncq, wrote: "Yellow 2, F/Sgt Kicq, went down and we were about to follow him when we noticed two more coming towards us on a reciprocal course and slightly below. Yellow leader and I went in to the attack – the leader taking the enemy aircraft on his port side and I selected the other one.

"As soon as the enemy aircraft which I identified as a Fw 190 saw me, it made a sharp turn to starboard and jettisoned its auxiliary tank. I turned to port and opening full throttle followed it as it started climbing very steeply. It then went on its back making a half roll during which time I had closed to within 200 yards. I fired twice a two second burst and the enemy aircraft blew up."

As for the diving Yellow 2, Kicq reported: "Red 1 reported enemy aircraft at 3 o'clock. I turned to starboard and caught sight of two Fw 190s some 3000ft below me proceeding on a south westerly course. I continued to turn and dived down on them.

"As soon as the enemy aircraft observed that I was chasing them, they dropped their auxiliary tanks and dived onto the deck. They were in line abreast at 30 yards interval some 300 yards from me. Every time I closed in, the one on the port side turned to port, followed three or four seconds afterwards by the other one.

"While turning after them I fired many short bursts and observed strikes on the fuselage of the starboard enemy aircraft. I then climbed and waited until they were again in formation below me and I resumed the chase once more. That happened four times. On the fourth occasion they split up and I dived from 4000ft on one of them and fired line astern from 250 yards for a second. The enemy aircraft again turned to port but crashed into a tree."

Howorth, Red 3, wrote: "I was about to follow Yellow section when I saw a Fw 190 coming down on me from above. I pulled to one side skidding and he overshot me. I turned in and gave him a two second burst at about 100 yards closing and climbing slightly and turning starboard. I saw strikes on the engine and cockpit. I broke away to avoid the debris.

"The pilot of the Fw 190 left the cockpit but no parachute was seen to open. I was at about 8000ft. There being no more enemy aircraft I climbed above cloud (about 12,000ft) and rejoined the rest of the squadron."

The leader, Muls, reported: "Red 3 reported two enemy aircraft below flying south-west, and at the same time I saw a gaggle of eight enemy aircraft about a mile to starboard flying slightly below. Yellow section went down to attack when I saw a Fw 190 climbing towards me.

> **"I pulled to one side skidding and he overshot me. I turned in and gave him a two second burst at about 100 yards closing and climbing slightly and turning starboard. I saw strikes on the engine and cockpit."**

"While the enemy aircraft was turning towards me I opened fire at about 500 yards continuing to fire head on. The enemy aircraft was also firing but I was not touched. We closed to 50 yards or less when the enemy aircraft dived down. At that moment I observed an explosion followed by a trail of smoke on the enemy aircraft's starboard wing root.

"I dived to port and saw the enemy aircraft diving steeply down but did not follow on account of other enemy aircraft being around."

Suddenly, it was all over. During the skirmishes, Pauwels had stuck with Howorth and confirmed his victory, but of 'Pichon' Groensteen there was no sign. He had last been seen

TOP: Flight Lieutenant David Howorth, from Bolton, Lancashire, became a sergeant in the RAF Reserve on July 27, 1940. He had no previous combat victories when he set off on the fighter sweep over the western fringes of Berlin on April 20. As of 2013 he was living in Queensland, Australia. VIA SERGE BONGE

ABOVE: Pilots of 350 Squadron at ease in the grass behind a lineup of their Spitfires. The aircraft nearest the camera, RB155 was being flown by Des Watkins when he shot down a Focke-Wulf Fw 190 over Berlin. VIA SERGE BONGE diving in to attack the Fw 190s but nothing had been heard from him since. After the six remaining pilots touched down back at Celle, Red section at 8.20pm and Yellow at 8.37pm, Groensteen was posted as missing.

CRASH SITE

It would be 55 years before Groensteen was seen again. In 1999, a team of German aviation historians searching for the crash site of a B-24 bomber that went down near Berlin during the summer of 1944 were told about a promising woodland debris field comprising hundreds of metal parts.

The team investigated and immediately found aluminium wreckage that indicated the site of a plane crash. There were so many pieces that the Germans at first thought that they had found the bomber. However, they soon found parts painted in colours only used in the manufacturing of British aircraft.

Part of a canopy frame was then discovered with bits of Plexiglas still stuck in it and it became evident that this was the last resting place of a Spitfire. Further finds included a rear view mirror and pieces of the engine stamped with the Rolls-Royce logo. Guns and ammunition were found too – indicating that this was not a reconnaissance version of the Spitfire and that it therefore could not have crashed near Berlin before 1945.

An initial theory was that this was a Russian operated Lend-Lease Spitfire but this was discounted when a brass plate was found indicating that this was a Griffon 61 engine – the Russians never received Griffons. It was now clear to the team whose Spitfire they had found.

Researching the time and date of Jacques Groensteen's crash, they uncovered an account from the official records of IV./JG 51 Mölders. Oberfeldwebel

Heinz Marquardt of 15./JG 51, an ace with more than 100 victories, had been flying a Fw 190D-9 south of Berlin on the evening of April 20, 1945, escorting some Fw 190 fighter-bombers on their way to attack Soviet ground units to the west of the city.

On his way back, Marquardt was radioed by a comrade to say that he was being attacked by four Spitfires. Marquardt flew to the rescue but had been flying too high. As he dived down, he saw a flash on the ground and assumed that his comrade had already been killed, but to his surprise he received a second communication from his comrade to say that one of the Spitfires had "touched the wires and crashed". The battle on April 20 had taken place near two radio transmitting stations.

Bones were also found at the crash site, along with goggles and the dial of a wristwatch – the hands of which had marked it at 7.35 through the force of the impact. The investigators determined that the crash had happened at high speed, with the Spitfire flying east, and the debris field covered an area measuring 160 by 60m. Much of the debris was just bent up pieces of metal but around 200 pieces could be positively identified and based on this evidence it was conclusively proven that the wreck was that of Jacques Groensteen's Spitfire Mk.XIVc.

In 2003, after 58 years, what remained of Jacques Groensteen was put into a small coffin, draped with the Belgian flag, and flown back to Belgium. The coffin was met by the Belgian Defence Minister Andre Flahaut and then transferred, with full military honours, to the cemetery at Evere, Brussels. A funeral was held on April 8, 2003, and Groensteen was finally laid to rest among other fallen Belgian pilots of the Second World War. ●

> *"The investigators determined that the crash had happened at high speed, with the Spitfire flying east, and the debris field covered an area measuring 160 by 60m."*

MN O V NH686

BELOW: Jacques Groensteen was just 22 years old when his Spitfire, flying flat out at extremely low altitude as he chased a fleeing Fw 190, hit an obstacle on the ground and crashed. His remains lay undiscovered at the wooded crash site until investigators found them in 1999 and he was laid to rest in 2003 with full military honours. VIA SERGE BONGE

ABOVE: Despite being the youngest of the seven Spitfire pilots from 350 Squadron flying over the edge of Berlin on April 20, 1945, Flight Sergeant Andre Kicq, 21, was the only one to have previously downed a Focke-Wulf Fw 190 single handed. VIA SERGE BONGE

RIGHT: Pilot Officer Marcel Doncq, left, with Robert Muls, right, and another pilot. Doncq, a former soldier with the Belgian Army, had escaped the Germans and fled to Spain, only to be captured by fascists. He was eventually liberated and made his way to Britain and joined the RAF to carry on the fight. VIA SERGE BONGE

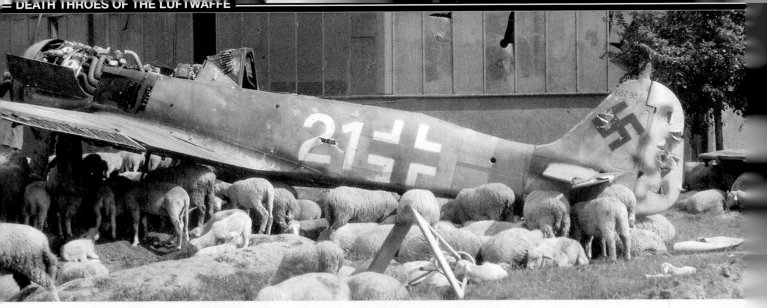

DEATH THROES OF THE LUFTWAFFE

APRIL 24, 1945: GERMAN AIR OPERATIONS TWO WEEKS FROM THE WAR'S END

The German air force continued to fight hard against the Soviets and Western Allies in the final weeks and days of the Second World War, despite a severe lack of fuel and overwhelming enemy air superiority. April 24, 1945, was a good example of a typical day of German air operations in the closing stages of the conflict.

BY ANDREW ARTHY

TOP: Abandoned Fw 190A-8 WNr. 682989 'White 21 + -', formerly of 5./JG 301, but pictured here wrecked and captured by the Allies in 1945. On April 24, 1945, the Luftwaffe was still able to field hundreds of Fw 190s, Bf 109s and other fighters. Just two weeks later, the war was over.

While many postwar sources give a general impression that the Luftwaffe was little more than a disorganised rabble by this time, in fact it was still functioning as effectively as the circumstances allowed.

April 24, 1945, saw at least 800 daytime sorties flown by the various operational Luftwaffe commands, and impressive successes were claimed (see table, opposite page). Of course this came at a cost of German aircraft and pilots, and the German figures paled in comparison with the British, American and Soviet figures (the Western Allies reported a total of 2747 sorties on the Western Front alone).

While some of the more exotic German aircraft were in action on April 24, including He 162, Me 262 and Ar 234 jets, the majority of missions flown were by the standard, long-serving Focke-Wulf Fw 190 and Messerschmitt Bf 109 fighters and fighter-bombers.

At this point the Luftwaffe was almost entirely devoted to army support, as the inexorable Soviet advance on Berlin continued. It had been launched on April 16, 1945, and eight days later the German capital was close to being in their hands.

At 5.15am on April 24 the Soviets began a new barrage of German positions, supported by bombers and ground-attack aircraft. Meanwhile, on the northern flank of the Western Front the British drove towards Hamburg against generally ineffective resistance, and to the south the Americans and French pushed towards Austria and the Czechoslovakian border.

Given the importance and significance of the German capital, inevitably the main focus of Luftwaffe efforts was there.

At this time there was a dramatic restructuring of the Luftwaffe command chain. With Germany almost cut in half by the Soviet and American advances, on April 21 the Luftwaffe was divided into northern and southern commands.

The northern formation, Luftflotte Reich, took charge of all units based in northern Germany, Denmark, Norway, and in the lingering pockets of resistance along the Baltic coast, while the southern formation, Luftflotte 6, took charge of units based in southern Germany, Czechoslovakia, Austria, northern Italy, and Yugoslavia.

Despite the command changes, the subordinate units continued to fight to the extent that the fuel situation allowed, with reserves on most fronts horrendously low.

LUFTWAFFE DAYTIME SORTIES, APRIL 24, 1945

UNIT	FIGHTERS	FIGHTER BOMBERS	GROUND ATTACK	ANTI-TANK	RECCE	TOTAL	AERIAL VICTORIES	TANKS DTRYED	VEHICLES DTRYED
Luftflotte Reich									
Lw.Kdo. Kurland	2+	-	?	-	?	2+	?	?	?
Lw.Kdo. Ostpreussen	?	?	?	?	?	?	?	?	?
Lw.Kdo. Nordost	218	51	86	?	43	398	35	2	68
K.G.d.Lw. in Norwegen	-	-	-	-	-	-	-	-	-
14. Flieger-Division	17+	?	?	-	?	17+	3	?	?
15. Flieger-Division	18+	?	?	-	?	18+	1	?	?
Miscellaneous	2+	?	?	-	1+	3+	?	?	?
Total	**257**	**51**	**86**	**?**	**44+**	**438**	**39**	**2**	**68**
Luftflotte 6									
Southern Reich	(91+16 Me 262s)	?	?		107	9	?	7+	
VIII. Fliegerkorps	100	?	70	30	44	244	13	15	148
Luftflotte 4	4+	?	2+	?	?	6+	?	1+	?
K.G.d.Lw. in Italien	-	-	-	-	1+	1+	-	-	-
Total	**211+**	**?**	**72+**	**30**	**45+**	**358**	**22**	**16+**	**155+**
Grand Total	**468**	**51**	**158**	**30**	**89**	**796**	**61**	**18+**	**223+**

BATTLE FOR BERLIN

Due to the Allied advances, on April 24 the Germans could only provide support to the Berlin fighting from the area of Luftflotte Reich to the north. Luftwaffe units located within range of the city were ordered to participate, and were urged to focus on the area north-east of Berlin, where the Soviet 1st Belorussian Front was attacking near Oranienburg.

The sun rose over Berlin at around 6am, and one of the first German units to arrive over the capital was the Stab of Jagdgeschwader 301, which was equipped with the new Focke-Wulf Ta 152 fighter. Oberfeldwebel Walter Loos, an ace at 22, took off as the sun came up, and soon became embroiled in a battle in poor visibility with Soviet fighters over the German capital.

He reported the destruction of two LaGG-9s, although secondary sources suggest that they were Yak-9s, before returning to base at 7.05am. There have also been suggestions that Loos never actually claimed any victories in the Ta 152.

As Walter Loos and his Stab JG 301 comrades duelled with enemy fighters, II./JG 301 operated its Fw 190As as fighter-bombers, carrying out low-level attacks on Soviet ground targets.

Remarkably, small detachments of German aircraft were still based in the heart of Berlin itself, despite the encroaching Soviets, constant smoke haze, and the regular presence of enemy fighters over the Reich capital. One such detachment was that of I./JG 11 at the magnificent and sprawling Tempelhof airfield, located directly south of the city centre.

This detachment found itself much too close to the frontline on the morning of April 24, as the airfield came under fire from tanks and artillery. This forced a transfer to Gatow on the western outskirts of the city; a suggestion that I./JG 11 operate from the Ost-West-Achse in the centre of the city had been rejected as impossible.

All remaining serviceable Fw 190s were ordered to take off from Tempelhof at 8am, and after flying a bombing and strafing mission and tangling with Yak-9s, the pilots landed at their new base. Oberleutnant Richard Franz was head of the Kommando, and was the last to leave the badly cratered field as Soviet shells landed around him.

He later recalled the situation: "Our further operations, all of which were directed by a Luftwaffe command post in the 'Führerbunker', targeted tanks and troops in urban areas.

"During these missions we had to deal with a far superior number of Russian fighters which hung as a fighter umbrella throughout the day over the city, which at this point was already practically encircled."

In the afternoon the Gatow detachment flew escort for Fw 190 ground-attack aircraft and 10 to 15 of the ever-present Yaks were encountered, with veteran Hans-Gerd Wennekers downing one of them, and Herbert Drühe getting another, his 15th victory of the war.

However, two I./JG 11 pilots were lost in combat in the Tempelhof area. Another of the dwindling detachment was posted missing as a result of aerial combat during a transfer flight from Gatow out of the beleaguered city.

Meanwhile, the rest of I./JG 11 was based in rather more comfortable circumstances, at Rechlin-Lärz to the north-west of Berlin. From there it flew over the city on at least three occasions, beginning at 5.40am. Entries in logbooks note regular encounters with Yak-9s from the Soviet air umbrella.

Emphasising the desperation of the situation was an escort mission flown in the late afternoon. Contact had been made with Yak-9s over the German capital, but as it returned the Gruppe was disastrously ambushed by 130 Squadron Spitfire XIVs near its base.

BELOW: An aerial view of Berlin Tempelhof airport, circa 1948. This was where a detachment of Jagdgeschwader 11 was based until the morning of April 24, 1945. At that point, advancing Soviet troops got too close to the airfield, forcing a hasty evacuation. USAF

BOTTOM: Surrendered German aircraft at Flensburg, May 1945. At the end of the war many of the Luftflotte Reich units flew from all over northern Germany and the Baltic coast to land at Flensburg and other airfields in Schleswig-Holstein. This was where many of the Courland Fw 190s ended up. In this photo can be seen numerous Fw 190s and a solitary Bf 109. IWM CL 3307

ABOVE: Surrendered line-up of Fw 190s from SG 2 and II./JG 6 at Mimoň-Hradčány in Czechoslovakia (German name Kummer am See) at the end of the war. CRAIG BUSBY

ABOVE RIGHT: Some of the Luftwaffe defenders of Courland, 1945. General der Flieger Kurt Pflugbeil, commander of the Luftwaffe in the pocket, meets with his Jagdgeschwader 54 unit leaders. To the left in the photo is Gerhard Thyben, the most successful German pilot during the Courland air fighting. THYBEN

RIGHT: Me 262A-1a/U3 WNr. 500539 'White 33 +', probably of 1./NAGr 6 at Lechfeld in 1945 or 1946. The aircraft had been test flown by Flugkapitän Oeller at Eger on March 16, 1945, and was subsequently flown to Lechfeld. JAMES V CROW

Flight Lieutenant P E Sibeth claimed one Fw 190 destroyed and a Bf 109 damaged, Flying Officer C E Mertens claimed a Fw 190 damaged and Flight Lieutenant William North Stowe claimed another Fw 190 destroyed on his own, plus a Bf 109 destroyed shared with Flight Lieutenant W Bruce.

Paul Berndt was one of the German pilots on the receiving end: "Back at Rechlin I lowered the flaps and landing gear for landing when I was warned by the Bodenstelle: 'Indians over our garden fence!' I looked back and saw a Spitfire with a red nose directly behind me.

"The guy hit me with the full load – shot up my flap motor, undercarriage motor, and all of this in the curve at 250kph. It was not possible to climb and gain height to bail out, and belly-landing was also out of the question because the undercarriage legs no longer retracted.

"My wingman, Oberleutnant Spangenberg – a former Zerstörer pilot – although barely hit – quickly flew away from the airfield, and returned home later with his parachute under his arm."

Berndt managed to land safely, but his Fw 190 was in a bad way: "Our ground personnel counted 65 hits in my aircraft."

This I./JG 11 mission, with its encounter with two different Allied air forces, shows just how difficult the situation now was for the Luftwaffe. The pilots were not safe anywhere.

Just as important as the fighters were the Fw 190 fighter-bombers, which were also very active over Berlin on April 24, 1945. Their high speed and ability to carry a variety of weapons loads made them invaluable, providing the most effective daylight support available to the Luftwaffe at this time.

Schlachtgeschwader 1 was heavily involved in the battle for Berlin, with the II. Gruppe active from Tutow (110 miles north of the city), and the III. Gruppe based a little further south, at Neubrandenburg.

"Its 17 Fw 190D-9s were engaged by eight Yak-3s north of Spandau and in a sharp combat managed to down three Soviets for no losses."

In the early afternoon III./SG 1 took off to fly a mission, its Fw 190F-8s and F-9s carrying AB 250 bomblet containers and the newly introduced Panzerblitz anti-tank rockets; 12 of the latter being carried on under-wing racks.

This load gave a single Fw 190 much potency against a variety of possible targets. This particular III./SG 1 mission targeted Soviet columns south of Eberswalde, a town to the north of Berlin, and strafing attacks were also carried out with the two 20mm cannon and two 13mm machine-guns.

At 3.35pm it was the turn of Hauptmann Heinrich Heins' II./SG 1. Leutnant Friedrich Schreck was one of the pilots involved, a former Stuka flyer and veteran of 162 missions. On this occasion he reported his AB 250 and four underwing SD 70 bombs falling on a vehicle column in the area of Velten, also to the north of Berlin. II./SG 1 took off from Tutow again with its Fw 190s towards dusk, once more using the AB 250 bomblet containers, which were excellent against soft targets.

In the morning a unit hitherto operating on the Western Front turned its attention eastwards: I./Jagdgeschwader 26. The Gruppe, which had last flown against the Soviets during a brief period of Eastern Front service in 1943, was also thrown into the fighting over the salient at Oranienburg, and intended to attack Soviet truck convoys.

Its 17 Fw 190D-9s were engaged by eight Yak-3s north of Spandau and in a sharp combat managed to down three Soviets for no losses.

A refuelling stop was made at Rechlin-Lärz, but this resulted in the unit's aircraft being grounded for some time due to the presence of Tempests over the airfield. They eventually made it back to Sülte (50 miles west of Rechlin) towards dark. Parts of II./JG 26 also transferred to Rechlin during the day, but details of any operations flown by that Gruppe to Berlin are unknown.

Several famous Luftwaffe units had been reduced to shadows of their former selves, and some of the remnants were thrown into the battle of Berlin. Jagdgeschwader 2 'Richthofen', long one of the most feared Luftwaffe fighter units on the Western Front, had despatched a battle group of Fw 190D-9s from the III. Gruppe to the north of the German capital, while the rest of the unit was disbanded in the south of the country.

On this day the JG 2 battle group was instructed to join the fight north-east of Berlin. Also receiving those orders was the Schwerin-based II. Gruppe of Jagdgeschwader 27. Mid-afternoon saw 10 Bf 109s from that unit successfully strafe trucks and anti-aircraft positions in the Oranienburg area, and a LaGG-3 was also downed by Feldwebel Walter Saynisch.

BELOW: He 162s being readied for take-off, including 'White 21 +'. HANS BERGER

Eight Fw 190D-9s of the III./JG 2 detachment were active, clashing during the day with 20 Soviet aircraft south-east of Oranienburg. Jagdgeschwader 4 was another of the Luftwaffe fighter units active over Berlin and Oranienburg on this day, reporting one pilot shot down in combat there, and another shot down and killed in combat at Küstrin, to the east of the city.

Attempts were made by Luftwaffe reconnaissance units to determine the ground situation along the Elbe River to the west of Berlin. Flying an Me 262, the 25-year-old South African Staffelkapitän of 1./NAGr 1, Hauptmann Friedrich Dünkel, reconnoitred the river between Magdeburg and Wittenberg, this being the sector of the American Ninth Army. Dünkel, a nine-victory ace and Ritterkreuz-holder, was born in Lüderitzbucht, German south-west Africa – he survived the war and died in Laaiplek, South Africa, in 1984.

His unit was also based at Rechlin, once the main Luftwaffe testing ground but now a major operational base.

Many other German air units were involved in the Battle for Berlin on this day, with the above providing just a small sample of the air action there on April 24, 1945. However, the Luftwaffe operations flown to Berlin could have little real impact on the course of the land fighting: the result of the battle for the German capital was now a foregone conclusion.

NORTH-EASTERN GERMANY

Not too far from Berlin was another important sector of the Eastern Front, north-eastern Germany, where the Soviets were steadily advancing along the Baltic coast. It was here that the German Jagdwaffe enjoyed some of its best hunting in the final months of the war, as highly experienced units with the most modern Bf 109 and Fw 190 variants took a heavy toll on Soviet bombers and fighters.

Two of the most successful units operating under Luftflottenkommando Nordost were Jagdgeschwader 3 and the IV. Gruppe of Jagdgeschwader 51.

IV./Jagdgeschwader 51 had a long and proud history, and in 1945 found itself in the fortunate position of having a formidable core of excellent, successful and experienced fighter pilots (see table, right). On April 24, the Gruppe was based at Schmoldow, close to the Baltic coast, and it was from there that it began its operations for the day at 11.40am, when some Fw 190A-8s and D-9s undertook a sweep to the Prenzlau area.

Happily for the fighter pilots opposition was encountered, and Unteroffizier Brünoth was able to down an Il-2 for his third victory of the war. The aircraft then landed at their forward base, Prenzlau, roughly 60 miles south-south-east of Schmoldow. Mid-afternoon a pair of reconnaissance Bf 109s were escorted to the front from Prenzlau, and there was combat with eight La-7s and 12 Yak-3s.

In the evening the 13. Staffel flew a sweep east of Prenzlau, before heading back to Schmoldow, a safe distance behind the ever-encroaching front. The unit's best success for the day actually came during a transfer flight, as Fahnenjunker Oberfeldwebel Heinz Marquardt and Unteroffizier Willy Herpertz brought a pair of Fw 190D-9s forward to Prenzlau.

The Kommandeur, Günther Josten, wrote in his diary: "Meanwhile, we have received some 190D-9s and get a tremendous number of victories. Oberfeldwebel Marquardt downed four Yak-3s during the transfer flight."

Herpertz also accounted for a Pe-2, but things did not all go the way of IV./JG 51, with a Soviet bombing raid on Prenzlau hitting two aircraft (including the Dora-9 of Heinz Radlauer).

Major Werner Schroer was a true veteran of the Jagdwaffe, having served with various fighter units since the heady days of the Battle of Britain. At this late stage of the war he was the Kommodore of Jagdgeschwader 3, based at Pasewalk. Flying a Dora-9 adorned with the double chevron marking befitting his rank, the Kommodore reported the destruction of a Yak-3 and a Yak-9 soon after midday in the Greifswald area on the Baltic coast during a scramble.

IV./JAGDGESCHWADER 51 ACES

PILOT	VICTORIES
Kommandeur Oblt. Günther Josten	178
Fhj.-Ofw. Heinz Marquardt	121
Staffelkapitän Lt. Bernhard Vechtel	108
Staffelkapitän Oblt. Toni Lindner	73
Staffelkapitän Lt. Kurt Tanzer	43
Ofw. Helmut Heinze	23
Uffz. Elmar Arensmayer	16
Uffz. Heinz Radlauer	15
Total	**577**

Not too far away, at Prenzlau, and equipped with a mix of Fw 190As and D-9s was Oberleutnant Oskar Romm's IV. Gruppe of Jagdgeschwader 3.

Oscar 'Ossi' Romm had an equally eventful, but quite unfortunate day: "My last combat mission was on April 24, 1945, to the south of Stettin, when with my wing man I attacked a formation of Russian 'Stormovik' ground-attack aircraft.

"I selected full emergency power and with our superior speed we went right through the Russian fighter escort without difficulty. I was just about to open fire on one of the Ilyushins when my cooling gills suddenly opened automatically and the oil and coolant temperature gauges showed that the engine was overheating.

"Either my engine had been hit by enemy fire or it had suffered a failure. I broke off the action by rolling over on to my back and pulling away in a steep dive. The Russian fighters endeavouring to follow were soon left behind and abandoned the chase."

Romm flew for as long as his engine ran towards German lines, and when it finally seized he was able to make a very rough crash-landing near friendly troops. He suffered severe injuries, and this marked the end of his war.

Similarly, 14./JG 3 veteran Oskar Bösch fell victim on this day to a head-on collision with one of four Yak-9 fighters he

TOP: A view of the cement bridge crossing the Danube River at Dillingen. This photograph was taken on June 1, 1945.
THE 12TH ARMORED DIVISION MEMORIAL MUSEUM

ABOVE: Soldiers of the 12th Armored Division guarding the newly captured Dillingen bridge over the Danube River, April 22, 1945.
THE 12TH ARMORED DIVISION MEMORIAL MUSEUM

ABOVE RIGHT: The approach to the bridge over the Danube River at Dillingen, with the 12th Armored Division sign next to the road, May 5, 1945.
THE 12TH ARMORED DIVISION MEMORIAL MUSEUM

engaged following a scramble from Prenzlau: "I opened fire at him; seconds later I collided with my attacker!

"How I managed to parachute from the wreckage, I'll never know. I landed in the Russian front line surrounded by hundreds of Red Army soldiers. With their weapons pointed at me and their hateful looks, I realised that these were my final moments.

"Luckily, a political commissar intervened to question me. I was limping badly, but got no sympathy from my captors who were content to push me along towards their trenches. On the way, I saw a large piece of metal which I recognized as part of the undercarriage from my plane and other debris from the Russian fighter."

The Yak-3 he downed in rather dramatic circumstances counted as his 18th and final victory of the war. Meanwhile, the III. Gruppe of Jagdgeschwader 3 was enjoying tremendous success, claiming the destruction of 18 Soviet aircraft on the 24th.

Jagdgeschwader 4 also operated on the north-eastern front, and carried out a ground-attack mission with AB 250 bomblet containers in the area of Woldegk-Neustrelitz. A pilot from II.(Sturm)/JG 4 recalled the effectiveness of the AB 250: "The enormous shrapnel effect of these fragmentation bombs was ideal for combating the infantry riding on the tanks' hulls."

During this operation Unteroffizier Adolf Neuhoff of 5.(Sturm)/JG 4 fell victim to a LaGG-3, but returned to his unit in a drunken state the next morning, much to the relief of his comrades.

COURLAND, NORWAY AND THE BALTIC OUTPOSTS

Various pockets of German troops held out against the Soviets along the Baltic coast, but air action there was on a much smaller scale due to a crippling lack of fuel. A large German presence remained cut off in the Courland pocket in Latvia, but some shipping escort missions by Fw 190s of Jagdgeschwader 54 were the extent of Luftwaffe sorties there on April 24.

Despite JG 54's efforts, the 1923 ton German vessel *Huelva* was torpedoed and sunk by Soviet aircraft eight miles off Libau harbour.

Further west along the Baltic coast, Jagdgeschwader 51 had elements based at Junkertroylhof, near Danzig in West Prussia, where the Soviet noose was very much tightening. The III. Gruppe had only 12 aircraft on strength on April 23,

and as a result an order was issued for 24 Bf 109s to be flown from Garz to Junkertroylhof on the 24th.

While most of the pilots made the ferry flight successfully, the designated flight leader, 28-year-old Hauptmann Waldemar Wagler, took off late and decided to desert to Sweden, landing there at 4.45pm. Also based in East Prussia was short-range reconnaissance unit 2./NAGr 4 with a handful of Bf 109s, but no details are known about operations by the two Prussia-based units on this day.

The Luftwaffe in Norway could still count on the fighters of Jagdgeschwader 5, as well as some Me 410 heavy fighters, night-fighters, various reconnaissance and maritime units, and the bombers of specialist anti-shipping unit Kampfgeschwader 26, although on April 24 the Luftwaffe operational command in Norway reported no German air activity in the region.

NORTH-WEST GERMANY

With German attention drawn to the east, the British continued their steady drive through northern Germany towards Hamburg. However, north-west Germany saw little operational Luftwaffe activity on April 24.

The I. and II. Gruppen of Jagdgeschwader 1 had recently begun conversion to the remarkable He 162, the so-called 'Volksjäger'. The jet was very potent, but also very unforgiving on its pilots, as events of April 24 would prove.

Conversion was undertaken in sleepy northern Germany. At Leck the I. Gruppe of Jagdgeschwader 1 had been operational since April 19, flying sweeps and scrambles against British fighter-bombers. However, practise operations were still being flown, with Leutnant Gerhard Hanf, Staffelführer of 2./JG 1, undertaking a Schwarmeinsatz around midday. Later in the afternoon Leutnant Hanf scrambled from Leck, but did not chance upon the enemy.

Meanwhile, II./JG 1 was undertaking its conversion training at Warnemünde, and April 24 marked a tragic day. The very experienced Kommandeur, Hauptmann Paul-Heinrich Dähne, undertook his first He 162 flight in the afternoon.

His pilots felt that he lacked confidence, and had delayed his He 162 debut for as long as possible. During manoeuvres at an altitude of 500 metres he suffered serious problems, and probably tried to bail out using the ejection seat, but failed to first jettison his cockpit canopy. A witness on the ground recalled: "He started to turn, and the aircraft began to skid. I then saw the aircraft somersault.

"Small pieces of glass shone in the sun, and a trail of white smoke came from the turbine. The He 162 began to lose height. It fell like a dead leaf and crashed in the marsh at the mouth of the Warne."

Despite the loss of the Kommandeur, other II. Gruppe pilots made successful flights in the He 162 on April 24.

AGAINST THE AMERICANS IN SOUTHERN GERMANY

There were still Luftwaffe forces available to oppose the French and Americans in the south of Germany, but lack of fuel was also a serious problem on that front.

Several bridges over the Danube near Ulm had been captured by the Americans, and significant attempts were made to reconnoitre and attack them with jets and piston-engine aircraft. Dillingen was a focal point on April 24, as elements of EJG 1, JG 27, 53 and 300 were all sent on fighter-bomber operations against targets in that area.

Reconnaissance units were also to focus on potential American crossing places over the Danube, and Oberfeldwebel Nitschke of 1.(F)/100 flew a mission from Lechfeld during the afternoon to visually reconnoitre the state of Danube bridges between Ulm and Ingolstadt. He landed at München-Riem in his Arado Ar 234.

JG 300 started its day very early, as 11 Fw 190s dispersed in a forest near an Autobahn six miles south of their München-Neubiberg base began taxiing at 4am. One aircraft was damaged in a collision in the dark with a Kübelwagen, and then the pilots discovered that there were only six of the special Flam C 250 Wasserballon bombs available for the 17 Fw 190s and Bf 109s of JG 300 and JG 53 assigned to this mission.

The Wasserballon was a 250kg incendiary bomb comprising 30% gasoline and 70% crude oil. When detonated, it created a fireball 15-20m in diameter which would burn for 10-15 seconds.

Further problems soon followed, as six-victory ace Oberleutnant Fritz Wegner later recalled: "Although planned to take place at dawn, the sortie was delayed because the specially modified bombs had not yet arrived.

"At 6.10am I therefore took off after a considerable delay at the head of eight Focke-Wulfs, as the others had got bogged down in the ruts and the mud. While we were still forming up over the airfield, four of my Fw 190s broke off their climb and turned back to land. Things were getting better and better.

"A few minutes later, as we were flying over the front lines on course for the Donau, two more 190s suddenly turned back without the slightest radio message so that my wingman and I were now flying what was no more than an armed reconnaissance sortie. Despite losing my comrades, I was more determined than ever to observe what advances the enemy had made in the vicinity of the Dillingen bridge and to attack any interesting targets.

"I was not even able to do this. During my first strafing pass the enemy flak put up a barrage the likes of which I had never before encountered and it was impossible to evade such dense fire. I was at a height of around 100m as my 190 was hit and caught fire instantly."

He managed to bail out and parachuted to safety. Fritz Wegner had fallen victim to the M16 half-tracks of Battery 'C', 441st Anti-Aircraft Artillery AW Battalion, which reported the shooting down and capture of a German pilot soon after 7.15am.

A second JG 300 operation to the Danube bridges began at 6.55am, involving four Fw 190A-8s and a pair of Fw 190D-9s. A pilot returning to base early after his aircraft was damaged by 'friendly' anti-aircraft fire was wounded in a bad crash-landing near the airfield, but those who made it to the target and carried out the attack claimed two trucks and four armoured vehicles destroyed.

This was JG 300's final operation against the Dillingen bridge.

In the evening JG 53 returned to Dillingen, with Bf 109s taking off from Kleinkarolinenfeld. It would seem that they

were engaged by Republic P-47 Thunderbolts of the 526th FS/86th FG, which reported the destruction of two Bf 109s in that area at the relevant time. I. and III./JG 27 were also active against the Danube bridgeheads, with 19 sorties undertaken for the loss of three Bf 109s.

Less significant, but a fascinating little episode nonetheless, was the destruction of a Bücker 181 liaison aircraft by a II./JG 300 pilot at Holzkirchen. This German-built aircraft had appeared over II./JG 300's base on previous afternoons, and some pilots from the Gruppe were convinced that it was crewed by Americans.

Oberleutnant Karl Rusack of the 5. Staffel had been on readiness on the evening of April 24, and took off in his Fw 190 to shoot it down on the edge of the airfield. This was his second and most unusual aerial victory of the war, as he later recalled: "It was not a glorious victory, in fact probably the 'worst' as far as my war was concerned but no less effective."

There were also some 'Reich defence' operations on April 24, although they were on a scale nothing like what had occurred 12 or even six months before. On two occasions, mid-morning and mid-afternoon, Me 262s of Generalleutnant Adolf Galland's Jagdverband 44, the so-called 'squadron of aces' based at München-Riem, engaged American medium bombers, claiming two Marauders shot down and three probably shot down.

However, these victories came at a cost, including an unidentified Oberfähnrich in the morning, and the tragic loss of revered fighter leader Oberst Günther Lützow in the afternoon. His remains are still to be recovered, but it is believed that he crashed near Donauworth.

In the southern area the Luftwaffe reported a total of 91 fighter and ground-attack sorties, along with 16 sorties by Me 262s. Nine aerial victories were claimed in this area, and good results were achieved against Allied tanks and vehicles.

However, more indicative of the situation was the fact that Jagdgeschwader 53 Kommodore Oberstleutnant Helmut Bennemann issued his final order of the day to his unit on April 24, paying tribute to the many JG 53 men lost during the war, and concluding with: "A 'Horridoh' and farewell to you all".

CONCLUSION

This article provides only a glimpse into Luftwaffe operations on April 24, 1945; there was simply not enough space to feature all the units still active on that date, and their fascinating and often risky undertakings.

Although the Reich had been divided in two, the Luftwaffe command structure continued to function, issuing orders to operational units and receiving reports of the successes achieved. Pilots and aircrew continued to take-off on missions, suffer the loss of comrades, and attack enemy air and ground targets, even though they knew in their hearts that the war was lost.

Certainly the idea that the Luftwaffe was non-existent at this stage of the war is incorrect: battered and outnumbered, yes, but still a fighting force. ●

> *"Despite JG 54's efforts, the 1923 ton German vessel Huelva was torpedoed and sunk by Soviet aircraft eight miles off Libau harbour."*

BELOW LEFT: Adolf Galland, left, and Günther Lützow, right on an airfield in southern Italy. On April 24, 1945, these two senior Jagdwaffe figures were serving together in Jagdverband 44, an Me 262-equipped fighter unit based at München-Riem, southern Germany.

BELOW: Oberst Günther Lützow was one of the most respected officers in the Jagdwaffe, but on April 24, 1945, he lost his life during a mission over southern Germany. He had led several Me 262s of Jagdverband 44 against American B-26 Marauder medium bombers, but never returned to base. His loss was greatly mourned, and his crash site has never been found.

THE RINGMASTER'S GRAND FINALE

APRIL 26, 1945: JV 44 AND ADOLF GALLAND'S LAST BATTLE

ABOVE: Göring and Galland examine a document together. Galland, 19 years Göring's junior, fell out of favour when it became clear that the Luftwaffe's fighter force was fighting a losing battle against the numerically far superior Allies.

RIGHT: After his sacking as General der Jagdflieger by Reichsmarschall Hermann Göring, Adolf Galland was placed under virtual house arrest, his car was seized and his future looked bleak – until his powerful connections gave him one last chance – the opportunity to lead a unit on the front line flying the new Messerschmitt Me 262 jet fighter.

One of the Luftwaffe's most influential figures from 1942 to 1944, General der Jagdflieger Adolf Galland was relieved of his post early in 1945. Shortly thereafter, he was allowed to form his own jet fighter squadron, Jagdverband 44. It was with this unit that he would fly his last mission…

T he failure of Operation Baseplate had put the leadership of the Jagdwaffe, the fighter wing of the Luftwaffe, in a difficult position in January 1945. Reichsmarschall Hermann Göring himself had become dissatisfied with what he saw as the failures of General der Jagdflieger 'General of Fighters' Adolf Galland.

The fact that Galland's rebuilt fighter force had been whittled away by Operation Watch on the Rhine was of little concern to him. Galland himself had been ground down by the constant struggle to keep his forces going in the face of overwhelming enemy opposition and the belligerence of his own High Command.

In late December 1944, Galland visited fighter units across the Western Front and was shocked by the lack of leadership being displayed by unit commanders, the poor training being given and the general bitterness of personnel towards their leaders.

He compiled a report and sent it to Göring, who then sacked him. His dismissal was officially announced less than four weeks later on January 23, 1945, and his replacement was a former member of his staff, Oberst Gordon Gollob – a man who had sworn revenge on him after a previous disagreement.

Galland requested that he be allowed to return to a front line unit flying the Messerschmitt Me 262, a type he had supported ever since first flying the Me 262 V4 prototype on May 22, 1943. Instead, Gollob set about arranging his transfer to take command of 4./JG 54 in the northern sector of the Eastern Front, flying missions against the Russians over the Kurland Pocket.

Defeated and under effective house arrest in Berlin, Galland's car was seized, his telephone was wire tapped and he was placed under round the clock surveillance. He then received a phone call out of the blue summoning him to the Reich Chancellery for a meeting with Adolf Hitler.

When he arrived he was surprised to be told that Hitler was unavailable but that the Führer had now put a stop to the security forces' investigation into his affairs and would allow him to establish a new unit flying the Me 262. He was told to report to Göring for the details.

The meeting began with the truculent Reichsmarschall reiterating how Galland had failed him but then Göring outlined his plan for Galland. In his autobiography, The First and the Last, Galland wrote: "I was to set up a small unit to demonstrate that the Me 262 was the superior fighter that I had always claimed it was. A small unit only in Staffel strength was to be organised – any more than that would not be possible.

"I would have to find the aircraft myself. He told me that Oberst Johannes Steinhoff, whom he had dismissed, and whom he had considered to be a 'sad case' could be made available to me, and that Obserst Lützow would be available immediately, if I wanted him. I was to submit my proposals.

"The unit was not to be under the command of any division, corps or air fleet – I was to be totally independent. However, there was to be no contact between the new unit and any other fighter or jet unit."

He was able to give the unit any name he chose as long as it did not include the name 'Galland', so he came up with Jagdverband 44 or JV 44. The name, loosely translated, means Fighter Association, with the '44' apparently chosen to commemorate the year of his dismissal as General der Jagdflieger.

Next, he had to decide on a base for JV 44 so he picked Brandenburg-Briest about 30 miles west of Berlin. This was close to a Me 262 aircraft acceptance park, had strong anti-aircraft defence and perhaps most importantly was already home to III./JG 7, which operated the Me 262.

JG 7 had been formed by Steinhoff on January 1, 1944 and III./JG 7 had originally been Kommando Nowotny – a unit personally established by Galland under the command of Austrian ace Major Walter Nowotny to evaluate the Me 262.

Once this was approved, he set about gathering the necessary resources and personnel. Allocation of the former – 16 Me 262s, munitions, fuel, spares, tools, flight equipment, trucks, personnel carriers, tractors, trailers, cars and bicycles – was approved by Luftwaffe Chief of General Staff, General der Flieger Karl Koller.

Mechanics and ground crew were allocated from 16./JG 54 and the first pilot Galland called was Steinhoff, who quickly agreed to sign up. After drawing up a list of the other pilots he wanted, some of the Luftwaffe's very finest, Galland attempted to recruit them. Gollob, however, stood in his way though not entirely out of malice.

He recalled later: "At exactly the moment when Galland and everyone else in the Luftwaffe knew that there was a shortage of experienced formation leaders, this gentleman in no way held back from requesting for himself – without

ABOVE: Six Me 262s of JV 44 are lined up ready for takeoff at Munich-Riem. The unit's aircraft are seldom seem together in the same frame, since they were usually dispersed beyond the edges of the airfield to hide them from marauding fighter-bombers and to prevent them from being damaged if the airfield itself was bombed.

BELOW: Several JV 44 pilots flew Me 262 WNr. 111745 'White 5'. Though it is unreadable in this view, the legend on the nosewheel hatch door reads 'ACHTUNG – Nicht am Bugrad Schleppen' or 'ATTENTION – do not tow by nosewheel'. The weakness of its nosewheel was one of several Achilles heels present in the Me 262 design. In practice, the aircraft had to be towed by its mainwheels.

BOTTOM: Schallmoser, right, and another pilot at Munich-Riem with JV 44's best known aircraft Me 262 'White 5'.

exception – our aces. But he only got those I let him have, and a few that he 'organised' for himself by roundabout methods."

Among the new recruits were Steinhoff's former wingman and adjutant Leutnant Gottfried Fährmann, 500 mission veteran Major Karl-Heinz 'Bubi' Schnell, the similarly experienced Major Erich Hohagen, who was recovering from a serious head injury, veteran ground-attack pilot Unteroffizier Johann-Karl 'Jonny' Müller, twin-engined aircraft specialist and flying school instructor Feldwebel Otto Kammerdiener, Oberfeldwebel Leopold Knier, who it was rumoured had been paid a large sum of money to deliver a Bf 109 intact to the Soviets for inspection, another flying instructor Oberfeldwebel Josef Dobnig, who had been about to join an 'infantry' unit using Panzerfausts against Soviet tanks, and former night flying instructor Unteroffizier Eduard Schallmoser.

Schallmoser was one of the few JV 44 pilots who had actually been fully trained to fly the Me 262. His conversion training had just been completed when he was posted to JV 44 on March 2, 1945, arriving at Brandenburg-Briest the following day. Many of the others had never flown the jet fighter before so Galland secured a number of twin-engined Siebel Si 204s for a crash course of training between March 4 and March 18.

FIGHTER TACTICS

The first Me 262s arrived on March 14 and once training had been completed Galland set about developing his unit's tactics – setting out with a Kette, a formation of three jets, rather

than the usual four-aircraft Schwarm – on March 22. The Kette had the advantage of enabling all three aircraft to take off side-by-side on a standard 60m wide German runway, allowing them to maintain formation right from the start of the mission rather than wasting time forming up once airborne.

Combat operations began at the end of March when Steinhoff reported shooting down an Ilyushin Il-2 Sturmovik that had been attacking a German column on the ground.

With JV 44 now fully operational, Koller ordered Galland to transfer it south so that its fighters could be used to defend fuel, arms and aircraft production facilities. After scouting out the area in his BMW sports car, Galland decided on the large civil airport of Munich-Riem as his unit's new home.

It had 35 off-field blast pens to protect aircraft from bombing raids, a large underground fuel store, three heavy and 12 light flak emplacements and a runway that was ample for the 1850m takeoff run required by the Me 262. By March 29, all of JV 44's equipment had been loaded onto a train at Berlin and was ready to be transported down to Munich.

The unit had nine Me 262s at this point, all factory fresh from Messerschmitt's production lines, but six were unserviceable and one was being repaired. The aerial transfer, with all the jets now ready to fly, took place on March 31.

More training was carried out as more pilots were recruited who had no prior experience of flying the Me 262. On April 4, at 11am, Fährmann and Schallmoser set off together to attack a formation of 12 P-38 Lightnings from the USAAF's Fifteenth Air Force near Munich.

After sighting the formation and flying in to attack, Schallmoser attempted to open fire with his quartet of 30mm MK 108 cannon, only to find that nothing happened. He looked down and realised that he had failed to fully disengage the safety. When he looked up, he realised that the Me 262's incredible speed had carried him far too close to one of the Lightnings.

He tried to turn but it was too late and he collided with it. The impact jarred him but he span away with only minor damage. Quickly finding Fährmann and preparing to return to base, he looked back and saw that the Lightning had not been so lucky – it was heading towards the ground and the pilot was bailing out.

The P-38 was 44-25761 flown by Lt William Randle of the 49th Fighter Squadron, 14th Fighter Group. One of his comrades, 2nd Lt Robert Slatter recalled: "At 11.20am at an altitude of 15,000ft I saw the Me 262 which came past our leader and towards Randle. The jet was approaching very quickly and after the leader went to the left, I saw that the tail of Lt Randle's aircraft had been completely torn off. His plane fell into a flat spin and began to fall. I watched the jet and saw Lt Randle jump out. About three minutes later, I saw the parachute, floating at a height of 1000ft. I also saw a flash of fire as his plane hit the ground."

On April 5, Steinhoff, Fährmann and three others flew out to intercept B-17s of the 379th Bomb Group and shot one of them down. Fährmann, however, suffered engine trouble and was forced to bail out near the Danube after he was attacked by the bombers' escort. He landed safely but could not return to Riem until the following day.

PRIORITY TARGET

By now the Allies had identified Riem as a priority target – any airfield where jet types were seen to operate was immediately pushed to the front of the queue – and on April 8 it was hit by a force of 228 B-17s.

JV 44 still only had 18 Me 262s and the attack resulted in six of them receiving damage from bomb fragments. Only seven had been serviceable to begin with. This was not the only effect on the unit however. Riem's control tower, main hangar and administration buildings were wrecked and six men were killed. Fifty personnel were wounded including two members of JV 44's ground crew.

Damage to the main runway was quickly repaired, however, and that afternoon Müller took off in Me 262 WNr. 111745 'White 5' to go after the B-17s. He returned to base without success.

The next attack on Riem came on April 10 when P-51 Mustangs of the 353rd Fighter Group strafed the airfield. They succeeded in destroying a trio of Me 262s and causing damage to another three. Thirteen new aircraft had just been delivered to JV 44 but by the end of the day just two were left undamaged.

Again, Müller took off after them but he encountered P-47s instead, probably of the 36th Fighter Group, and this time he was able to shoot one down.

In mid-April, JV 44 was joined by Major Wilhelm Herget, who brought with him the experimental Me 262A-1a/U4 WNr. 111899. This aircraft was fitted with a 50mm Mauser MK 214 cannon, the barrel of which protruded from the nose by around 2m. This is believed to have been used with JV 44 on only two occasions and it was unsuccessful on both.

April 16 saw around 14 of JV 44's Me 262s attacking a formation of 322nd Bomb Group Martin B-26 Marauders. Galland himself led the assault and shot down two of the medium bombers. Some of the Me 262s had been equipped with the new 55mm R4M air-to-air rockets – 12 under each wing – and these were used during the attack.

Two days later, a force of six Me 262s from JV 44 was sent up against a formation of 760 B-17s that was hitting targets across southern Germany. During takeoff, Steinhoff's Me 262 hit some debris left on the runway from a bombing raid the previous day and his port wing dipped, sending him swerving to the left.

As per Galland's 'Kette' idea, Steinhoff had been flying one of three jets taking off at the same time and his sudden

change in direction almost caused him to crash into Krupinski's machine, which was rolling alongside. Krupinski just managed to pull up in time but Steinhoff wasn't so lucky. He hit an embankment at the end of the runway and, loaded with fuel, his Me 262 began to burn furiously.

In his book The Final Hours, Steinhoff wrote: "Catapulted high into the air, the stricken bird dragged itself through several more seconds of existence. Shortly before the impact, my hands flew instinctively to the shoulder belts. I tugged so violently on the straps that my body slammed back against the seat.

"Then, all of a sudden, everything seemed to grow still. There was only the hissing of the huge flames. As if in slow motion, I saw a wheel go soaring through the air. Metal fragments and bits of undercarriage flew after it, spinning very slowly. Wherever I looked was red, deep red. Grasping the sides of the cockpit, I pulled myself up until I was standing on the parachute. I had got my feet over the cockpit rim when the rockets started exploding under the wings.

"They skittered over the field and went off with a hellish bang. Taking great leaping strides, I ran out along the wing to escape from the inferno, and my straining lungs filled with fresh air, I sank to my knees as if under the impact of a mighty blow.

"I managed to get to my feet, and as I stumbled a few steps farther everything went black – my eyes had swollen shut. I became aware of piercing pain in my wrists where

ABOVE: Four pilots of JV 44's Fw 190D-flying Platzschutzschwarm – Leutnant Karl-Heinz Hofmann, Leutnant Heinz Sachsenberg (seated on the muddy mainwheel of Fw 190D-9 'Red 3'), Hauptmann Waldemar Wübke and Oberleutnant Klaus Faber. **RIGHT:** Two of the pilots who gave JV 44 its reputation as a 'squadron of aces' – Oberfeldwebel Klaus Neumann, who had previously served with IV.(Sturm)/JG 3 and had 37 victories, and Major Erich Hohagen, who had scored 55 victories but was now supposed to be recovering from a serious head injury.

ABOVE LEFT: Pilots had to pitch in with ground crew at Munich-Riem to dig foxholes and shallow trenches where personnel could take cover in the event of an attack. The huge airport had a great runway for jets but was also characterised by huge wide open spaces with little in the way of cover.

ABOVE: Just two Me 262A-1a/U4s, fitted with the enormous 50mm Mauser MK 214 cannon, were built and one of them was brought to JV 44 for active use by Major Willi Herget. WNr. 111899 was used on at least two occasions, its nose remaining unpainted, but without result – except for worrying American aircrew with the sheer size of its armament.

BELOW: Oberst Günther Lützow seated with Galland at Munich-Riem.

TOP: The other side of 'Red 1', the aircraft of Platzschutzschwarm leader Leutnant Heinz Sachsenberg, bears the slogan 'Verkaaft's mei Gwand I foahr in himmel!' or 'Sell my clothes, I'm going to heaven!'

ABOVE: Parked alongside one of JV 44's transport aircraft, Siebel Si 204 'White 63' is Fw 190D-9 WNr. 600424 'Red 1'. The pair are pictured at the unit's heavily damaged one-time base Munich-Riem airport.

ABOVE RIGHT: Another view of 'Red 13', this time with a second JV 44 Fw 190D-9.

the flames shooting through the cockpit floor had burned off the skin between my gloves and the sleeves of my leather jacket."

Badly wounded, Steinhoff was taken to hospital and remained there for the rest of the war.

WARMING UP
That same day, III./KG(J) 54, which was being dissolved, attempted to transfer its aircraft over to JV 44 to replace its losses, only for most of them to be destroyed by American B-26 bombers after they were left at the transit field at Erding.

A trio of JV 44 fighters downed a B-26 on April 19 but perhaps the unit's greatest success of the war came on April 20 when it attacked another formation of Marauders of the 323rd Bomb Group at around 11am near Memmingen.

One Me 262 shot out the port engine of 1st Lt Dale E Sanders' B-26B-30-MA 41-31918 Can't Get Started aka Texas Tiff then another fired an R4M rocket into its fuselage, blowing a huge chunk out of it.

A waist gunner in a nearby B-26, Technical Sergeant Robert M Radlein, later remembered: "Our top turret gunner, Staff Sergeant Edmundo Estrada, started firing. He had raised his guns straight up and was shooting at a Me 262 passing overhead. He yelled: 'I got him! I got him!' because he had seen all kinds of metal and debris come flying past our airplane. He was convinced he had hit it but unfortunately the pieces of metal had not come from the German fighter but from our No. 3 airplane, piloted by 1st Lt Sanders.

"I looked out of my left waist window at Sanders' airplane as it started to drop away from the main formation, and I was able to see the entire radio compartment. The fighter attack had stripped away all the metal from the top of the wing, as well as the compartment for the radio man and navigator – I guess from just aft of the windows in the pilot's compartment. And, of course, one engine was also gone. As I watched the bomber falling out of formation, I reached over to snap on my chest pack parachute. Things were warming up pretty fast."

Müller, who was one of the attackers, flying 'White 15', fired an R4M rocket into B-26F-1-MA 42-96256 Ugly Duckling, flown by 1st Lt James L Vining.

He later recalled: "In a fast glance over my shoulder, I saw a jet rapidly approaching us in a slight turn, with muzzle flashes around the four 30mm cannon in the nose. I turned my attention back to my position, tucking my wing closer to

"He had raised his guns straight up and was shooting at a Me 262 passing overhead. He yelled: 'I got him! I got him!'"

No. 4, and at that instant a terrific blast went off below my knees and the airplane rolled to the right.

"Sensing that my right leg was gone, I looked toward my co-pilot and while ordering him to take his controls, I noted that the right engine was at idle speed. So, in one swift arcing motion of my right hand, I hit the feathering button, moved to the overhead rudder trim crank and trimmed the airplane for single engine operation and – just as rapidly – pressed the intercom button to order the bombardier to jettison the two tons of bombs.

"We were losing altitude at 2000ft per minute, which slowed to 1000ft per minute with the load gone."

Incredibly, Vining managed to keep his aircraft aloft long enough, despite repeated attempts by JV 44's fighters to bring it down, to crash-land it behind Allied lines.

Schallmoser was also involved in the attack but again he struggled to get his four MK 108s to fire. He looked down again, to check the safety, but in that split second his jet took him too close to one of the B-26s. His 'White 11' was sliced open by the propeller blades of the bomber's starboard engine.

Gushing black smoke, its right wing shedding debris, Schallmoser's Me 262 rolled over and plunged through the bomber formation. The pilot managed to bail out and floated down on his parachute – only to land in the garden of his mother's home in Lenzfried-im-Allgäu. Stunned, he packed up his parachute as best he could before staggering inside.

As he sat down at the kitchen table, nursing his leg, which had been struck a glancing blow by the aircraft as he fell away from it, his mother set about making him pancakes.

The leg injury turned out to be more serious that he had thought, however, and he ended up in the same hospital as Steinhoff for five days.

JV 44 had brought down three B-26s and seriously damaged another seven. The only German aircraft lost was Schallmoser's Me 262.

DARK HUMOUR
Around this time there was another unusual addition to JV 44 – five Fw 190D-9s. These 'long noses' were brought in to defend the Me 262s when they were at their most vulnerable – as they landed and took off. Their pilots formed a separate unit, a Platzschutzschwarm, within JV 44 led by Leutnant Heinz Sachsenberg. Each had its underside painted

bright red with unevenly spaced white stripes to provide easy recognition for flak gunners on the ground who might otherwise be tempted to open fire on them.

The Focke-Wulfs also had darkly humorous individual slogans painted on their fuselage sides. The words on Sachsenberg's own aircraft, Red 1, were 'Verkaafts mei Gwand I foahr in Himmel' or 'Sell my clothes, I'm going to heaven', Red 3's slogan read 'Im Auftrage der Reichsbahn' or 'By Order of the State Railway', Red 4's was 'Der nachste Herr, deselbe Dame!' or 'The next man, the same woman!' and Red 13's was 'Rein muss er wen wir beide weinen' or 'In he goes and then we both cry'.

The pilots of these aircraft were ordered to keep a watchful eye out for enemy fighters but only to defend the Me 262s, rather than to go on the offensive and pursue any attackers. They were also barred from attempting to fly their Fw 190s alongside the Me 262s for any reason. No radio contact was made between the pilots of the Fw 190s and those of the jets either.

April 24 saw 11 of JV 44's now growing number of Me 262s set off at 9.50am to combat yet another formation of B-26s, this time from the 17th Bomb Group. Most of them were equipped with R4M rockets.

As the jets approached the bomber formation, they began to launch salvos of rockets and one of the B-26s, 42-107729 Stud Duck, was hit in the rear. Its tailplane was torn off, a wing and the side of the fuselage were damaged and the bomb bay doors were blown open.

It peeled away to the right and plummeted to the ground. Only one crewman survived – gunner Staff Sergeant Edward F Truver, who had been thrown clear by the force of the blast and was able to open his parachute.

Also shot down by an R4M was B-26B 42-95991 Skipper, flown by 1st Lt Leigh Slates.

JV 44 flew another sortie in the afternoon but this time the Americans suffered no casualties and Oberst Günther Lützow failed to return.

On April 25, the experimental Me 262A-1a/U4 was taken into action against B-26s of the 323rd Bomb Group. It was alone and despite making an attack run on a bomber formation it failed to fire – probably due to one of the regular mechanical failures that afflicted its massive 50mm Mauser cannon.

BRAKE! BRAKE!

The following day Galland himself led another sortie, this time against the B-26 Marauders of the 17th Bomb Group. He set off with his men at 11.30am.

In The First and The Last, he wrote: "On April 26, I set out on my last mission of the war. I led six jet fighters of the JV 44 against a formation of Marauders. Our own little directing post brought us well into contact with the enemy. The weather: varying, clouds at different altitudes, with gaps, ground visible in about only three tenths of the operational area.

"I sighted the enemy formation in the district of Neuburg on the Danube. Once again I noticed how difficult it was, with such great difference of speed and with clouds over the landmarks, to find the relative flying direction between one's own plane, and that of the enemy, and how difficult it was to judge the approach.

"This difficulty had already driven Lützow to despair. He had discussed it repeatedly with me, and every time he missed his run-in, this most successful fighter commodore blamed his own inefficiency as a fighter pilot. Had there been any need for more confirmation as to the hopelessness of operations with the Me 262 by bomber pilots, our experiences would have sufficed.

"But now there was no time for such considerations. We were flying in an almost opposite direction to the Marauder formation. Each second meant that we were 300 yards nearer. I will not say that I fought this action ideally, but I led my formation to a fairly favourable firing position.

"Safety catch off the gun and rocket switch. Already at a great distance we met with considerable defensive fire.

TOP: JV 44's 'Red 3' pictured at Ainring.

ABOVE LEFT: Heavy exhaust staining is visible on the side of 'Red 13'.

ABOVE: Another of JV 44's Fw 190D-9s, 'Red 13' had the slogan '"Rein muss er" und wenn wir beide weinen!' or '"In he goes" and then we both cry!'

BELOW: A wide view of 'Red 13' as it was abandoned at Ainring, surrounded by Messerschmitt Bf 109Gs of II./JG 52.

ABOVE: Galland walks beside Oberst Günther Lützow at Munich-Riem.

RIGHT: Flown by 1st Lt Dale E Sanders, B-26B-30-MA 41-31918 Can't Get Started aka Texas Tiff was shot down by JV 44 fighters on April 20 near Memmingen.

BELOW: The burned out shell of Oberst Johannes Steinhoff's Me 262 after it crashed on takeoff on April 18, 1945. Steinhoff, effectively JV 44's second in command, survived but was badly burned and spent the rest of the war in hospital.

BELOW RIGHT: An American GI poses with a JV 44 Fw 190D-9 – the unevenly placed white stripes on the underside of the aircraft are clearly visible.

As usual in a dogfight, I was tense and excited. I forgot to release the second safety catch for the rockets. They did not go off. I was in the best firing position, I had aimed accurately and pressed my thumb flat on the release button – with no result. Maddening for any fighter pilot.

"Anyhow, my four 30mm cannon were working. They had much more firing power than we had been used to so far. At that moment, close below me, Schallmoser, the jet-rammer, whizzed past. In ramming he made no distinction between friend or foe."

Schallmoser, flying 'White 14', fired off his R4M rockets and blew up one of the B-26s.

Galland wrote: "This engagement had lasted only a fraction of a second – a very important second to be sure. One Marauder of the last string was on fire and exploded. Now I attacked another bomber in the van of the formation. It was heavily hit as I passed very close above it.

"During this breakthrough I got a few minor hits from the defensive fire. But now I wanted to know definitely what was happening to the second bomber I had hit. I was not quite clear if it had crashed. So far I had not noticed any fighter escort. Above the formation I had attacked last, I banked steeply to the left, and at this moment it happened: a hail of fire enveloped me. A Mustang had caught me napping."

In fact, Galland had been hit by defensive fire from one of the B-26s – Technical Sergeant Henry Dietz, a former weapons instructor, had targeted him as he tried to assess the damage he had caused to his most recent victim.

Dietz remembered: "Probably the most important thing I remembered from gunnery school was to fire short bursts and forget about the tracer bullets – just use your sights.

"That day, we were flying as flight leader, and we were about 10 minutes from the target. I flew in the waist position from where I could see all the mechanical parts of the aircraft.

"A sharp rap hit my right knee. The instrument panel with its indispensable instruments was shattered."

I had never seen a jet before. Galland slowed down to the speed of the B-26 so that he could observe and take score. I thought 'dummy'. He was flying low, right into the sights of my machine gun. I shot a burst. Nothing happened. A little higher, a little lower, I just kept shooting."

As Dietz poured fire into Galland's machine, the pilot of a Republic P-47 Thunderbolt escort fighter, 1st Lt James Finnegan of the 10th Fighter Squadron, 50th Fighter Group, had also spotted him.

Finnegan later recalled: "I was leading the top-cover of P-47s that was escorting the B-26s to their target. As I gazed down I saw two objects come zipping through the formation, and two bombers blew up immediately.

"I watched the two objects go through the bomber formation, and thought 'That can't be a prop job, it's got to be one of the 262 jets'. I was at about 13,000ft and estimated them to be at about 9000-10,000. They were climbing, and I pulled a split-S toward the one that turned left, and almost ended up right on top of him – about 75 yards away.

"I gave a three second burst and saw strikes on the right hand engine and wing root. I was going so fast, I went right through everything, and guessed my speed at about 500mph. I recorded it as a probable. I was flying a D model Thunderbolt with a bubble canopy, a natural metal finish and a black nose. The 262 had green and brown mottled camouflage with some specks of yellow. That turned out to be my last flight in a P-47."

Galland wrote: "A sharp rap hit my right knee. The instrument panel with its indispensable instruments was shattered. The right engine was also hit. Its metal covering worked loose in the wind and was partly carried away. Now the left engine was hit too. I could hardly hold her in the air.

"In this embarrassing situation I had only one wish: to get out of this crate, which now apparently was only good for dying in. But then I was paralysed with terror of being

ABOVE: At the end of the war there was no paint available for new aircraft and this one, Me 262 WNr. 111712 entered service with JV 44 in bare metal finish with lines of panel gap filler paste giving it a very distinctive look.
BELOW: The nose art of Martin B-26 Marauder 42-107729 Stud Duck. The aircraft was shot down by JV 44 jets on April 24, 1945, with only one crew member surviving.

shot while parachuting down. Experience had taught us that we jet fighter pilots had to reckon on this. I soon discovered that my battered Me 262 could be steered again after some adjustments.

"After a dive through the layer of cloud I saw the Autobahn below me. Ahead of me lay Munich and to the left Riem. In a few seconds I was over the airfield. It was remarkably quiet and dead below. Having regained my self-confidence, I gave the customary wing wobble and started banking to come in.

"One engine did not react at all to the throttle. I could not reduce it. Just before the edge of the airfield I therefore had to cut out both engines. A long trail of smoke drifted behind me. Only at this moment I noticed that Thunderbolts in a low-level attack were giving our airfield the works.

"Now I had no choice. I had not heard the warnings of our ground post because my wireless had faded out when I was hit. There remained only one thing to do: straight down into the fireworks. Touching down, I realised that the tyre of my nosewheel was flat. It rattled horribly as the earth again received me at a speed of 150mph on the small landing strip.

"Brake! Brake! The kite would not stop. But at last I was out of the kite and into the nearest bomb crater. There were plenty of them on our runways. Bombs and rockets exploded all around; bursts of shells from the Thunderbolts whistled and banged.

"A new low-level attack. Out of the fastest fighter in the world and into a bomb crater, that was an unutterably wretched feeling. Through all the fireworks an armoured tractor came rushing across to me. It pulled up sharply close

by. One of our mechanics. Quickly I got in behind him. He turned and raced off on the shortest route away from the airfield. In silence I slapped him on the shoulder.

"He understood better what I wanted to say than any words about the unity between flying and ground personnel could have expressed.

"The other pilots who took part in this operation were directed to neighbouring airfields or came into Riem after the attack. We reported five certain kills without loss to ourselves. I had to go to Munich to a hospital for treatment of my scratched knee. The X-ray showed two splinters in the kneecap. It was put in plaster. A fine business."

With Galland now out of action and Steinhoff still in hospital, Oberstleutnant Heinz Bär assumed operational command of JV 44. On April 28, the unit received orders to relocate to Salzburg-Maxglan, where it was to operate from woodland positions along the sides of the Munich-Salzburg Autobahn. This proved to be JV 44's final move.

On May 4, with the Americans closing in, the unit destroyed its Me 262s by placing grenades in their engine intakes. The surviving pilots were taken prisoner and taken in for interrogation. Galland surrendered to American forces the following day and JV 44 was no more. ●

TOP: Seated atop his Republic P-47 Thunderbolt 'The Irish Shillalah' is 1st Lt James J Finnegan, left. The 10th Fighter Squadron, 50th Fighter Group, pilot shot up Adolf Galland's Me 262 and forced him to make a hasty landing. The German general met Finnegan after the war and the pair became friends.

ABOVE: The broken-backed wreck of B-26F-1-MA 42-96256 Ugly Duckling, flown by 1st Lt James L Vining. Vining was badly injured when his aircraft was hit by an R4M rocket fired by one of JV 44's Me 262s but he still managed to pilot it all the way down to crash-land behind Allied lines.

BELOW: Another postwar shot of a JV 44 Me 262, this time WNr. 500490, which was captured relatively intact.

VOLKSJÄGER VICTORY

MAY 4, 1945: HEINKEL HE 162 PILOT LEUTNANT RUDOLF SCHMITT CLAIMS A TYPHOON

The last German fighter to enter service during the war was Heinkel's He 162. It went from drawing board to front line combat in just six months but at terrible cost – from the slave labourers who died building it to the pilots who died trying to fly it. But did it achieve any success at all?

BELOW: The sorry remains of Flying Officer Tom Austin's Hawker Tempest JN877 SA-Y being recovered on the back of a lorry. Was this the only aircraft ever shot down in combat by a Heinkel He 162?

The Heinkel He 162 was an aircraft born out of urgent requirements, innovative design under pressure and pure desperation.

During the summer of 1944 it was considered that while the twin-engine Me 262 was well suited to combat against bombers and their escorts at medium to high altitude, it was incapable of tackling the large number of fighter-bombers now ranging over the battlefield at low level.

Even with reduced armament and lower performance requirements, the Me 262's insurmountable Achilles heel was the sheer cost and time taken to produce it. Managing two engines also required a degree of skill and expertise that few newly qualified fighter pilots possessed.

A single engine jet was needed that could be rapidly and cheaply produced in large numbers using basic materials where possible. It was even decided, initially, that the aircraft in question should be so simple and easy to fly that even 15-year-old Hitler Youth members whose only training was on gliders could pilot it into combat.

The RLM specification of September 1944 called for a BMW 003 jet engine powered fighter that could be built as a flying prototype within five months and on the production lines in six. Heinkel had already spent two months working on a jet fighter design study it called P.1073. This had two engines, one mounted under the nose and another on its back.

It was a relatively simple matter to take this design and scale it down so that only one engine, the one on its back, would be required. Other firms tendered designs to meet the specification – Arado's E.580, Blohm & Voss's P.211 and Junkers' EF 123 or 124, and two from Focke-Wulf – but in the end the Blohm & Voss P.211 emerged as the front runner.

Heinkel complained that it had been given a different formula with which to work out the P.1073's performance so the following day all the other companies were forced to recalculate their figures based on the same formula.

This only served to demonstrate that the P.1073 was lacking in range and was capable of carrying only a relatively light weapons load. Heinkel's representatives, however, pointed out that with aircraft such as the He 177 bomber no longer in production, there was now spare capacity available at its capacious and well-equipped factories.

At the same time, concerns arose about the length and position of the P.211's intake duct. It was close to the ground, which would mean any debris lying around on a less-than-perfect airstrip was likely to be sucked into it. Its shape could also induce unwanted drag.

Finally, on September 23, Hitler ordered the P.1073 into mass production as the He 162. Because it was intended to be so easy to fly, even civilian glider pilots could step into the cockpit and pilot it straight into combat, the project was also given the name Volksjäger, or 'People's fighter'.

In his autobiography The First And The Last, Adolf Galland wrote: "From the beginning I had strongly opposed the Volksjäger project. In contrast to the creators of this idea, my objections were based on factual reasons such as insufficient performance, range, armament, bad conditions of sight, and dubious airworthiness.

"Furthermore I was convinced that this aircraft could not be brought into worthwhile operation before the end of the war. The terrific expenditure of labour and material was bound to be at the expense of the Me 262.

"To my mind all forces ought to be concentrated on this well-tested jet fighter in order to make the best of the possibilities remaining to us. If we scattered our strength once more in this last phase of the war, then all efforts would be in vain."

He went on: "My suggestion was to increase mass production of the Me 262 by having it built under licence by all aircraft factories that were not working to capacity, and further to use all these planes only for the air defence of the Reich. This earned me a sharp rebuke from Göring which ran something like this: 'This is unheard of! Now the general of the fighter arm refuses a jet fighter plane which the armament production is offering him by the thousands within a few months.'

"The Volksjäger was to represent a sort of levee en masse in the air. Incredibly schedules were fixed, astronomical production figures were planned. Göring himself became a victim of the national frenzy with which the planning of the Volksjäger had infested almost everyone connected with air defence.

'Hundreds! Thousands! Umpteen thousands!' he cried. 'Until the enemy has been chased back beyond the borders of Germany'."

BUILDING THE PEOPLE'S FIGHTER

Work on building the first prototypes began on October 25, 1944 – 10 days before the last of the detailed construction drawings had even been completed. The He 162 was to be tested with both 30mm MK 108 and MG 151/20 cannon, projected as the A-1 and A-2 versions respectively.

It was also to be fitted with a BMW 003 jet engine, an undercarriage derived from that of the Bf 109 to cut production time and cost, and a Heinkel device first seen on the He 219 night fighter – the world's first operational military ejection seat.

The He 162 M1 (V1) was finished and ready to fly on December 1, 1944. Its maiden flight came on December 6. Four days later, during another test, it was destroyed when instability combined with poor glue bonding led to the leading edge of the starboard wing coming off mid-flight. Test pilot Gotthold Peter was killed.

The second prototype, He 162 M2 WNr. 200002, first flew on December 22. Another eight prototype and pre-production machines followed in quick success and were soon being used to test everything from landing gear and armament to vibration and directional snaking. Meanwhile, Heinkel's factories were gearing up for full production – a quota of 30 He 162A-1s was expected by the end of January 1945.

There were five facilities involved: EHAG (Ernst Heinkel AG) Nord Rostock-Marienehe, EHAG Süd Wien-Schwechat, Junkers' Bernburg factory and the underground facilities at Hinterbrühl, codenamed 'Languste', and Mittelwerk Nordhausen.

All of them employed slave labourers – some 22,500 in total, including 8000 at Rostock alone, accounting for 55% of the work force.

During an inspection of the production lines on January 27 it was determined that so far, two production machines had been flown, 12 had had engine tests

ABOVE: A large wind tunnel model of the He 162 being tested in early 1945 at Berlin-Adlershof.

LEFT: A drawing of the Heinkel P.1073 design from a report dated September 23, 1944. Work on the project had begun two months earlier, envisioning a larger aircraft with a second jet engine beneath the cockpit. This drawing shows the P.1073 close to its final form as the He 162.

completed, 58 fuselages were complete and another 71 were nearing completion.

A second test pilot was killed on February 4, 1945. Oberleutnant Georg Weydemeyer crashed the sixth prototype during its 11th test flight. It was found later that there appeared to have been insufficient glue used on the plywood skin covering the ribs of the tail unit.

TOP: A row of rear fuselages awaiting components. Manufacturing delays were commonplace as essential parts took days to arrive where they were needed and regular powercuts caused blackouts underground.

ABOVE: Fuselages under construction at the underground 'Languste' facility near Hinterbrühl. This was one of five sites involved in He 162 production.

ABOVE RIGHT: Workers fit the wiring connections inside a He 162 fuselage at 'Languste'.

The first five production machines were ready to go by February 9 – work at Heinkel's factories having been slowed by blackouts resulting from the damage caused to Germany's electrical power infrastructure during heavy bombing.

It was decided in January that rather than form a new Luftwaffe unit to operate the He 162, an established unit should be converted to it, and JG 1 was chosen. I./JG 1 was pulled back from the front line on February 6 for this purpose and its 23 surviving Fw 190A-8s and A-9s given to II./JG 1 to replace losses it had suffered.

The Gruppe, now minus its aircraft, transferred to Parchim, 50 miles south of Rostock, on February 9. No He 162s were immediately available, so I./JG 1's pilots and crew began familiarisation training with EHAG personnel on February 12.

An Auffangsstaffel or 'collection squadron' from 2./JG 1 was sent to Heidfeld – the airfield at Heinkel's Rostock headquarters – on February 27 to pick up a single aircraft brought over from Junkers at Bernburg. This was He 162 M19 WNr. 220002.

A second group of pilots, from I./JG 1, arrived at Rostock on March 4 to collect more aircraft but none were available

A third pilot was killed in a He 162 on March 14, when Unteroffizier Tautz of 2./JG 1 hit a stack of barrels while attempting to land M19. The aircraft span into the ground and Tautz, thrown clear of the cockpit, suffered fatal injuries.

Now there were no He 162s available for conversion training. On March 26, it was announced that JG 1 would relocate in readiness to receive completed aircraft leaving the Junkers production line. A group of 15 pilots from 3./JG 1 moved to Lechfeld but there was still nothing available to fly.

On the 27th, Hermann Steckham attempted to take off on a test flight at Bernburg in production He 162 WNr. 310001 but suffered engine failure which resulted in the aircraft coming down hard. It was a total write-off and Steckham was badly injured.

I./JG 1 was told on March 31 that it would have to move to Leck at the northernmost extreme of Germany. On the same day, with JG 1 personnel now scattered across Germany, He 162 deliveries finally began.

Simultaneously, as the enemy advanced from east and west, evacuation of He 162 production facilities was begun. EHAG Süd at Wien began shutting down on April 1.

He 162 'White 1' was flown by 2./JG 1's Leutnant Rudolf Schmitt for 20 minutes at Parchim on April 3. Having joined the Luftwaffe as an 18-year-old in August 1943, he initially trained at Luftkriegschule 2 in Berlin before moving to Flugzeugführerschule C6 in Kolberg. In May 1944 he was transferred to 2./JG 107, which was stationed in Hungary, and then 5. and 6./JG 108, based at Wiener-Neustadt. Finally, on February 16, 1945, he joined 1./JG 1, switching to 2./JG 2 shortly thereafter.

Unteroffizier Helmut Rechenbach of 2./JG 1 crashed and was killed while ferrying a He 162 from the factory on April 6, bringing the aircraft's death toll to four.

By April 12, 1945, I./JG 1 had 16 He 162s at Parchim, of which 10-12 were serviceable. Two days later, one of the unit's most experienced pilots, Feldwebel Friedrich Enderle, was killed when his He 162 came down shortly after take-off at Ludwigslust and exploded.

RIGHT: The sixth He 162 prototype, M6, rolls down the runway at the beginning of a test flight in early 1945.

The following day, April 15, I./JG 1 began its delayed move to Leck. Flying He 162 'White 7' from Ludwigslust to Husum, a fuel stop along the way, Leutnant Schmitt encountered a Spitfire at 3.40pm but used his aircraft's speed to avoid an engagement, as he had been ordered.

On April 17, Unteroffizier Josef Rieder had a problem with his He 162's flaps on take-off and crashed, suffering serious spinal injuries but the following day Unteroffizier Wolfgang Hartung of 2./JG 1 came down during another transfer flight and was killed in the crash – the sixth He 162 fatality.

LAST STAND AT LECK

With I./JG 1 now settling in at Leck, it wasn't long before they were called into action. A report of enemy aircraft in the vicinity at 12.20pm resulted in a pair of He 162, piloted by Feldwebel Günther Kirchner and Leutnant Gerhard Stiemer, being sent up.

Stiemer reported that just as they left the runway, two enemy fighters flew right over them. Within seconds, Kirchner had activated his ejection seat – but he was still barely off the ground and although the device performed correctly, there wasn't enough time for his parachute to open and he fell to his death.

All Stiemer could do was to evade the fighters, which he believed to be American P-47 Thunderbolts. When he came in to land, his undercarriage failed to deploy and he was forced to make a belly landing.

These enemies were, in fact, Hawker Tempests of 222 (Natal) Squadron.

Flying Officer Geoffrey Walkington later reported: "I was flying as Blue 1 strafing Husum airfield when I sighted an aircraft flying in a northerly direction away from the aerodrome. I immediately broke off my attack on the airfield and chased this aircraft which was camouflaged mottled green with a yellow underside and appeared to have twin fins and rudders and one engine.

"The nose of the aircraft had a drooping appearance and the wings (plan view) resembled those of an Me 109. Due to my loss of speed on turning the enemy aircraft pulled away to about 1500 yards. Having recognised this aircraft as hostile by its camouflage, I gave chase, but was unable to close, my IAS being 360mph.

"The enemy aircraft did a 360° turn to starboard which I followed, turning inside. During my turn I managed to close to 1000 yards. Being unable to gain further I trimmed my aircraft carefully and, allowing about three quarters of a ring above the enemy aircraft, I fired short bursts.

"The enemy aircraft then pulled up through cloud which was eight tenths at 3000ft. I followed through a gap and passed the enemy aircraft spinning down out of control from about 3500ft. I then watched the enemy aircraft explode on the ground near Husum aerodrome."

The accounts of the action differ significantly, but the date, time and location matches. It was the first combat loss of a He 162. It would not be the last.

April 20 saw four He 162s despatched to intercept RAF Typhoons strafing targets in the Leck area. 'Yellow 7' and 'Yellow 11' took off first, followed by 'Yellow 1'. 'Yellow 3', piloted by Oberleutnant Wolfgang Wollenweber, was delayed by 10 minutes due to engine problems.

Once he was in the air, he heard that the other three had been unable to locate the Typhoons but when he spotted a burning bus below he realised he must be on their trail. Pressing on, he found the British attacking Husum.

Having already released the safety switch on his cannon, Wollenweber lined up the last Typhoon and pressed the trigger but nothing happened. He lined up the second

machine and tried again but still nothing. In frustration, he shot over the Typhoon barely 5m from its canopy and climbed steeply away.

Spotting him at last, the Typhoons broke off their attack and tried to follow but were rapidly outpaced. Wollenweber flew home.

That afternoon, Leutnant Schmitt had cause to use his machine's ejection seat after suffering a malfunction during a familiarisation flight and yet another pilot, Unteroffizier Gerhard Fendler, was killed during a ferry flight. This brought the total number of non-combat related He 162 deaths to seven.

Another pilot, Feldwebel Erwin Steeb, was forced to eject due to a mechanical failure on April 21. Feldwebel Rolf Ackermann of 3./JG 1 was killed while attempting his land another new He 162 after a ferry flight on April 23 and the following day the commander of II./JG 1, Hauptmann Paul-Heinrich Dähne, was also killed.

Dähne, new to the He 162, encountered a common problem – when accelerating into a turn, the jet wash from the engine forced the rudder to jam. This made the aircraft uncontrollable and at low level the only thing to do was eject.

It is believed that Dähne did attempt to eject but neglected to jettison the canopy of his machine first – not an automatic process. This resulted in him smashing his head against the inside of the canopy, probably killing him before his He 162 hit the ground.

On April 25, Leutnant Schmitt took off in 'White 5' to intercept a low-flying British de Havilland Mosquito at 11.20am but there was no engagement. Two pilots, Unteroffizier Helmut Rechenbach and Fähnrich Emil Halmel,

> *"Having already released the safety switch on his cannon, Wollenweber lined up the last Typhoon and pressed the trigger but nothing happened. He lined up the second machine and tried again but still nothing. In frustration, he shot over the Typhoon barely 5m from its canopy and climbed steeply away."*

BELOW: The first He 162A-1 off the production line, WNr. 120001, is readied for its first flight on January 14, 1945.

BELOW: A row of He 162s lined up at Leck and ready to be surrendered to the British. In the foreground is 'White 1' WNr. 120013 – the aircraft flown by Leutnant Rudolf Schmitt on May 4, 1945, when he claimed to have shot down an RAF Typhoon.

ABOVE: One of the pilots who flew the He 162 with JG 1 – Oberleutnant Wolfgang Wollenweber. He came close to shooting down an RAF Typhoon in the aircraft but his guns jammed at the critical moment.

ABOVE RIGHT: After Germany's capitulation, the Allies were amazed to discover the extent of facilities dedicated to production of the Luftwaffe's single-jet fighter. This is the Junkers facility in a former salt mine at Tarthun, near Egeln.

RIGHT: One of the He 162s at Leck as seen from the rear.

BELOW: The He 162s of JG 1 at Leck. They were lined up in two neat rows ready to greet the arrival of British forces. After they were 'captured' in this way, the jets were divided up between the victors.

were injured when their He 162s both crashed during ferry flights on April 26. Three more pilots crashed their He 162s during ferry flights on April 30. One of these, flown by Leutnant Hans Rechenberg of II./JG 1, was shot at by a Spitfire before it went down near Wismar.

On May 1, Oberleutnant Wollenweber and his men had to detach the final two He 162s from their construction jigs at Rostock before they could be ferried to Leck. After attempting and failing to get them to work, Wollenweber, two other pilots and an engineer were forced to escape the airfield in a Fieseler Storch as the advancing Russians threatened to overrun the facility.

JG 1 now had around 45 He 162s stationed at Leck but since the airfield was one of the few places left in Germany where aircraft could operate relatively freely, it was now becoming crowded with a variety of other units and aircraft.

On May 4, the war diary of JG 4 recorded: "Orders arrive at 0200 – the serviceable aircraft must fly on, either to Norway or the Protectorate, to avoid being captured by British troops. Take-offs should be completed by 0600. The three Bf 109s of the former III./JG 4 are to remain at Leck. German forces in north Germany have signed a surrender, capitulating to Montgomery.

"It is forbidden to fire at any low-flying aircraft. At the same time no further take-offs are authorised. A lone Spitfire circled the airfield. The war is over! The Helferinnen Dobner and Augsen arrived on the airfield after an incredible journey. They are the only two service-women from their convoy that have been able to reach us here at Leck."

Seemingly undaunted by all this, Leutnant Rudolf Schmitt took off in He 162A-2 'White 1' at 11.38am and flew south. He was attempting to intercept RAF Typhoons that had been reported in the area and it wasn't long before, at 11.45am, he found an Allied aircraft south-east of the airfield at Husum.

ABOVE: Heinkel He 162A-2 WNr. 120230 'White 23' is believed to have been the personal aircraft of JG 1's commander, Oberst Herbert Ihlefeld. It was captured at Leck by the British but then turned over to the Americans.

During a brief encounter, Schmitt opened fire and later recorded in his logbook: "Typhoon wirksam besschossen" or 'Typhoon fired on with effect'. This would seem to indicate that Schmitt believed he had fatally damaged a Typhoon fighter-bomber, though had not necessarily witnessed its final destruction.

The only corresponding Allied loss in about the right area and at anything like the right time was that of Flying Officer Tom M Austin's Hawker Tempest JN877 SA-Y. Austin, of 486 Squadron, crash-landed after suffering what he described as engine trouble in the Satrup area – though the 'trouble' did cause it to blow up.

Satrup was a good 20 miles east from Husum and perhaps seven or eight miles north of it. In addition,

Austin is believed to have gone down at around 7.10am. Nevertheless, in the confusion of those final days of the war, the possibility remains that Austin was indeed the one and only combat victim of a He 162.

It is believed that, in the end, some 171 He 162s were built, with 116 actually being delivered. The Luftwaffe received 56 of these before production finally collapsed at the end of April. At least nine men had been killed in flying accidents involving the He 162 – whether due to a failed airframe, a failed engine, inherent design flaws or simply the sheer trickiness of piloting the delicate little aircraft.

Whether Rudolf Schmitt actually managed to shoot down an Allied aircraft with a He 162 may never be known for certain. ●

ABOVE AND LEFT:
After its transfer to the US, 'White 23' was given Foreign Equipment number FE-504 and an erroneous new tail number, 120222, and after undergoing a few tests was shown as a static display at air shows across America. It is now in storage at the National Air and Space Museum in Washington DC.

ABOVE: A rare view of the He 162 in flight – in this case captured He 162A-2 WNr. 120098, which was given the serial VH513 in British service. It is pictured here at RAF Farnborough in mid to late 1945.

FINAL DOGFIGHT

MAY 8, 1945: WHO SCORED THE LAST AERIAL VICTORY OF THE AIR WAR IN EUROPE?

While most of the Luftwaffe facing the western Allies had officially surrendered by May 8, some units, particularly those on the Eastern Front, continued a desperate resistance right until the end of the day. But who fired the final shots in aerial combat?

TOP: The last Luftwaffe aircraft to be shot down by an RAF fighter during the war was a Siebel Si 204. Three days later, another Si 204 became the last German victim of a USAAF fighter.

With Adolf Hitler having committed suicide on April 30, 1945, the Third Reich staggered on for another week with Reichspräsident Karl Dönitz, formerly Grand Admiral of the Naval High Command, at the helm as his chosen successor.

From May 1, his first day in office, until the end of the war, Dönitz did everything he could to ensure as many German servicemen as possible could surrender to the British and Americans while simultaneously continuing the war against the Soviets by whatever means remained available.

He first surrendered his forces in the Netherlands, Denmark and north-western Germany to Field Marshal Bernard Law Montgomery on May 4 – the terms including a complete ban on flights by Luftwaffe aircraft. With Luftwaffe opposition ended, this effectively brought hostilities to a close for the RAF.

The only known exception was at around 6.30am on May 5 when a patrol of three 130 Squadron Spitfire XIVs came across a Siebel Si 204 twin-engined transport/trainer flying over the sea west of Hamburg. After it began evasive manoeuvres, it was shot down and jointly claimed by Flight Lieutenant Dudley Guy Gibbins and Warrant Officer Vic J Seymour – the last British victory of the air war.

The fighting carried on elsewhere however. Dönitz had Admiral Hans-Georg von Friedeburg begin negotiations with US commander General Dwight D Eisenhower at Reims in France on May 5 and the German Chief of Staff Generaloberst Alfred Jodl arrived on May 6. Dönitz had told him to hold off

on agreeing to a full surrender for as long as possible so that more German forces could escape the Soviets.

He managed less than 24 hours, signing the instrument of unconditional surrender at 2.30am on May 7 with Dönitz's permission. The critical phrase in the instrument was "all forces under German control to cease offensive operations at 23.01 hours, central European time, on May 8, 1945".

In the west, May 8 began with American airmen stationed in England preparing for two very different missions. Mission 986 was the Eighth Air Force's last operational mission over Europe during the war and it involved 12 B-17s of the 306th Bomb Group dropping leaflets over key locations.

Aircraft of the 369th Bomb Squadron set off at 7.45am to fly over Dunkirk. The fortified town was still in German hands, having been surrounded and then bypassed by the British during the drive into occupied Europe. The leaflets told the garrison that they had been ordered to surrender – which they eventually did the following day.

The day before, the 369th had been dropping leaflets over Buchenwald concentration camp, telling inmates in six different languages to stay put and that help was on the way.

The Americans' other major air operation of May 8 was Trolley Mission 2. The Eighth Air Force had actually ceased combat operations on April 25 but its mission planners had not been idle. They came up with Operation Trolley to "provide all ground (non-rated) personnel with an opportunity of seeing the results of their contribution in the strategic air war against Germany".

Effectively, ground crews would be flown over areas bombed by the Eighth to show them what they had helped to achieve.

Both B-17s and B-24s were used, but with crews pared back to five – pilot, co-pilot, navigator, engineer and radio operator – plus 10 passengers. The passengers each got a parachute and a life jacket plus candy and a pack of sandwiches for the six to seven hour trip.

Every effort was made to avoid accidents with pilots being instructed on "the deplorability of needless loss of life to carelessness, particularly now that hostilities in Europe are at an end". They were required to maintain an altitude of at least 1000ft over terrain for the whole flight with no buzzing or circling.

An escort aircraft, known less than affectionately as the 'Gestapo a/c', accompanied each group to make sure the rules were followed. Even so, the day before, during Trolley Mission 1, a 389th BG B-24 had crashed into the remains of a railway bridge over the Rhine, killing 19 men.

On the opposite side of Europe however, combat was still raging. The highest scoring fighter ace of all time, 23-year-old Major Erich Hartmann of I./JG 52, took off with his wingman in their Bf 109s from his unit's base in Czechoslovakia at 8am to intercept Soviet fighters over Brno.

Recalling the events later in life, he said: "My wingman and I saw eight Yaks below us. I shot one down and that was my last victory. I decided not to attack the others once I saw that there were 12 Mustangs on the scene above me.

"My wingman and I headed for the deck where the smoke of the bombing could hide us. We pulled through the smoke and saw once again the two allies fighting each other above us. Incredible! Well, we landed at the field and were told that the war was over."

Hartmann, who ended the war with 352 victories, and his men fired off all their remaining munitions into the woods, destroyed their 25 remaining aircraft and set off in search of some British or American forces to surrender to. He succeeded in finding Americans but was then turned over to the Soviets anyway.

Also stationed in Czechoslovakia was Fw 190-equipped ground attack unit III./SG 77. Pilot Unteroffizier Bernhard Ellwanger recalled: "On May 8 all aircraft, with the exception of four, were drained of fuel. Why my crate was one of those four, I don't know to this day.

"Led by Hauptmann Günther Ludigkeit, Kapitän of 7. Staffel, we took off in the direction of Prague. Our mission was to destroy Prague radio station which was in the hands of Czech partisans. When we were at 4000m Prague came in sight.

"Then I saw something I couldn't take my eyes off: hundreds of American fighters filled the sky like some gigantic flypast at an air show. The whole mass flashed silver

in the sun. The sight almost made me miss our attack. Our Schwarm dived away to port with me following.

"With the target centred in my Revi, I released my bomb at 1500m. A direct hit. Then we got out of there, eastward back to base. So ended my last sortie on the very day of the capitulation, and with it my last chance of landing in the American zone."

Oberleutnant Fritz Stehle, Staffelkapitän of 2./JG 7, is believed to have scored the final Luftwaffe victory of the Second World War over Czechoslovakia at 4pm on May 8. He had taken off in Me 262A-1a WNr. 111690 'White 5' at 3.20pm to intercept Soviet Yak-9 fighters and succeeded in destroying one of them.

He then flew 'White 5' to Fassberg, where it was captured by the British.

The final American victory, and possibly the last Luftwaffe aircraft to be shot down during the war, was another Siebel Si 204. At 8pm, just three hours before the official cessation of hostilities, 2nd Lieutenant Kenneth L Swift, of the 429th Fighter Squadron, 474th Fighter Group, USAAF Ninth Air Force, was flying his Lockheed P-38 Lightning 'Beauty Juny' three miles southeast of Bad Rodach, Bavaria, when he encountered the German aircraft.

He fired warning shots, which were enough to prompt its pilot to crash land it. While most other USAAF units were stood down by this point, the 474th continued to provide tactical air support for the US First Army until May 9 from its base, R-2 at Bad Langensalza. It was the only group in Northern Europe flying the P-38 by the end of the war.

The Siebel was Swift's first and only victory of the war – although he would go on to fly North American F-86 Sabres during the Korean War, adding a further 'kill'. Promoted to major, he later became an instructor in the German Air Force.

Overall, it is believed that nine German aircraft were shot down on May 8, 1945. How many Allied aircraft were shot down by Luftwaffe machines is unknown. Similarly, there are numerous reports of American and Soviet aircraft attacking one another on May 8, but how many machines, if any, were shot down is unknown.

Finally, the last RAF pilot to die before the war's official end was killed on May 8. Flight Lieutenant Donald James Hunter, 22, of Upminster, Essex, a member of 322 (Dutch) Squadron, was killed after his Spitfire LF XVI, TB383 3W-A, suffered engine failure during a victory flypast near the unit's base at Varrelbusch, Germany, and he made an unsuccessful emergency landing. ●

ABOVE: Just days after joining 130 Squadron on the front line, Flight Lieutenant Dudley Guy Gibbins, flying a Spitfire XIV, shot down a Si 204 – a victory shared with Warrant Officer Vic Seymour – as the final RAF 'kill' of the war.

BELOW: The last known wartime photo of the highest scoring fighter ace of all time, Major Erich Hartmann of I./JG 52, was taken shortly after his 350th kill on April 17, 1945, beside his Bf 109G-10. On May 8, he shot down a Yak-9 for his 352nd.

ABOVE: One of 474th Fighter Group's used and abused P-38 Lightnings, pictured in Belgium in February 1945. The final aerial victory of the Second World War, three hours before the official capitulation of all German forces on May 8, 1945, was achieved by 2nd Lieutenant Kenneth L Swift of the 474th's 429th Fighter Squadron, flying his Lightning 'Beauty Juny'.

AFTERMATH

AFTERMATH

MAY 9, 1945, AND BEYOND

With Germany defeated the remaining world powers focused their attention on the war still ongoing elsewhere and on dismantling the German war machine.

The process of German weapons and equipment being handed over to the victorious Allies had begun long before May 9 but from this point on it took place in earnest.

Britain had already built up quite a collection of German aircraft by this point. Some had fallen into Allied hands when their pilots accidentally landed in Britain due to a navigational error or had been forced to land there due to mechanical failure.

A unit had even been set up in 1941 to operate these – 1426 (Enemy Aircraft) Flight, otherwise known as the 'RAFwaffe' – though this was disbanded on January 31, 1945, and its surviving machines handed over to the Central Flying Establishment.

The first German jet to be captured intact had fallen into American hands, however. An Arado Ar 234 suffered engine failure west of Cologne in February 1945 and made a belly landing. Having been seized by the US Army, it was taken back to the Royal Aircraft Establishment (RAE) at Farnborough for examination.

As the end of the war drew near, Air Technical Intelligence teams were given the task of locating and securing the most advanced German aircraft while a team led by test pilot Captain Eric 'Winkle' Brown, who could speak German, was given the job of getting them back to the RAE.

The Americans combined their numerous efforts to gather German technology under the heading of Operation Lusty. Leading the effort to find and extract completed aircraft was test pilot Colonel Harold 'Hal' E Watson.

The first fruits of the British effort were two-seater Messerschmitt Me 262B-1a/U1 night fighter 'Red 8' and

an Arado Ar 234B, captured at Schleswig in April. Later, at Farnborough, the former was given the Air Ministry number AM 50 while the latter became AM 54.

A single Me 163B Komet was also captured during April, though the circumstances are unknown. It was given the RAF serial VF241. Also in April, the Americans found an intact Me 262 at Giebelstadt airfield, dismantled it, and had it flown to Bovington in England by Curtiss C-46 Commando for examination.

Focke-Wulf's Bremen works was overrun by the British on April 8, which effectively ended any further development of the Ta 152 and also put an end to efforts directed towards building the next generation German single jet fighter – the Ta 183.

When the Gotha facilities near Leipzig were captured in mid-April, the US Third Army found the almost complete, but outer-wingless, Horten 8-229 V3 flying wing jet fighter prototype plus the skinless centre sections of the V4 and the steel frame centre section of the V5. Elsewhere they found a set of completed wings which were later attached to the V3.

Advancing French forces captured the first Dornier Do 335s at the company's Friedrichshafen-Löwenthal airfield on April 27 but these had been blown up by retreating German forces and were little more than wrecks. The Americans found a number of complete examples when they captured Dornier's München-Oberpfaffenhofen factory on April 29. Since this was to have been the main Do 335 assembly plant, they found a large number of partially completed ones too.

Two examples, including a two-seat Do 335A-10 trainer (WNr. 240112 – later AM 223) and a single-seater (later AM

BELOW: The Americans found a number of complete examples of the Dornier Do 335 when they captured the company's München-Oberpfaffenhofen factory on April 29. The aircraft pictured here is parked beside the burned-out remnants of a Heinkel He 162, left, and a Messerschmitt Me 262 on the right.

225) were gifted to the British and the French captured the prototype single-seat Do 335 M14 at Mengen and the two-seat M17, which had not yet flown and needed substantial work to make it airworthy.

Also on April 29, the Americans discovered the Messerschmitt facility at Oberammergau, and captured the only prototype of a new single jet engine design, the P.1101.

British forces occupied the Blohm & Voss aircraft factory at Hamburg on May 3 and captured the three prototypes for the Bv 155B high-altitude fighter. An extreme development of the Bf 109, the project had been handed to Blohm & Voss due to Messerschmitt's preoccupation with other projects. The V1 crashed during transfer to Britain and was destroyed, V2 was crated up and taken back to Britain and V3 was incomplete. The V2, WNr. 360052, was eventually handed over to the Americans.

That same day, the Americans took over the Prien am Chiemsee airfield in the south east of Germany and found a highly unusual aircraft still under construction there – the Darmstadt Munich DM-1, a glider designed by Alexander Lippisch to test the aerodynamics of his planned Lippisch P.13a ramjet fighter.

On May 4, the USAAF's 54th Air Disarmament Squadron (54th ADS), the 'Feudin' 54th' took over the Messerschmitt company's main headquarters airfield at Lager-Lechfeld, near Augsburg. There they found some 50 Me 262s, most of them shot up and ruined by "rampaging GIs" who had reportedly driven tanks into some of them or crushed them with bulldozers.

Also found at Lechfeld were several Heinkel He 219 Uhu night fighters, Focke-Wulf Fw 190s and Heinkel He 177s. Over the next few days, more aircraft arrived from all over the region as German forces attempted to surrender to the Americans rather than risk capture by the advancing Soviets.

Lechfeld became the base of Colonel Watson as he attempted to gather 15 flyable Me 262s for delivery back to the United States – his unit eventually becoming known as 'Watson's Whizzers'.

Five intact Me 262s were captured by the British at Fassberg on May 5: Me 262A-2a fighter-bomber 'Yellow 7', from Fassberg, became AM 51 and a second example, 'Yellow 17', was AM 52. Me 262A-1a 'White 5' was AM 80 and Me 262A-2a 'Black X' was AM 81. The number and fate of the fifth is unknown.

On the same day, at Stravanger in Norway, four more Arado Ar 234s were captured by Allied forces. While this was going on, the Allies were also in the process of capturing scores of conventional Luftwaffe machines, accepting the surrender of Luftwaffe personnel across the Western Front, disarming them, and sending them to holding camps or home to their families.

> **"Perhaps the greatest coup of the British mission came on May 6-8 when the airfield at Leck was captured along with between 22 and 26 of JG 1's Heinkel He 162s."**

Perhaps the greatest coup of the British mission came on May 6-8 when the airfield at Leck was captured along with between 22 and 26 of JG 1's Heinkel He 162s. At least 10 of these were shipped, rather than flown, back to Britain and kept by the RAE while at least three more were handed over to the Americans.

On May 8, the British captured the nearby aerodrome at Husum where II./JG 400 had ended up and captured at least 23 Me 163 Komets. Again, some were given to the Americans.

The next day, General George S Patton arrived at Prien am Chiemsee airfield to view the DM-1 glider, on which work was now to continue under American supervision.

At Lechfeld, meanwhile, Watson had managed to assembled 10 airworthy Me 262s and a selection of other types. The jets had initially been 'named' by the 54th ADS but Watson and his pilots decided to give them colourful new names such as Happy Hunter II, Jabo Bait and Screamin' Meemie.

While the British continued to ferry their prizes the relatively short distance home, during early to mid-July, the Americans' selected test aircraft were gathered at Cherbourg in France and loaded onto a Royal Navy aircraft carrier, the *HMS Reaper*, for transfer to the United States.

The *Reaper* set off on July 20, bound for New York. On board were 41 airframes – 10 Me 262s, four Ar 234s, two Do 335s, one Ta 152H, four Fw 190Ds, five Fw 190Fs, three He 219s, three Bf 109s, two Bücker Bü 181s, one WNF 342 helicopter, two Fl 282 helicopters, one Ju 88G, one Ju 388, one Bf 108 and a single American P-51.

Numerous other types were transferred individually on other vessels – the Horten 8-229 was loaded onto the *SS Richard J Gatling* before loading of the *Reaper* had been completed and was dispatched for the US on July 12.

TOP LEFT: When the 54th Air Disarmament Squadron got their hands on 50mm cannon test-bed Me 262A-1a/U4 WNr. 170083, they painted their own unit number on one side and 'Wilma Jeanne' on the other. The Me 262 held a particular fascination for the Americans and they tried to acquire as many working examples as they could.

TOP: One of the most sought-after German jets at the beginning of 1945 was the Arado Ar 234. However, soon after the first example was captured and examined in February, the Allies managed to acquire many more in various states of repair ranging from factory fresh to worn and damaged, and finally to absolute wrecks.

ABOVE: WNr. 170083 with the 54th ADS's artwork as seen from the other side.

ABOVE: Captured by British forces from IV./NJG 11, Messerschmitt Me 262B-1a/U1 WNr. 110306 'Red 6' was earmarked for the Americans, who took possession of it and allocated it the serial FE-610.

ABOVE RIGHT: Also from NJG 11 was Messerschmitt Me 262B-1a/U1 WNr. 110305 'Red 8', given the serial AM 50 by the British.

RIGHT: The name given to WNr. 170083 by Watson's Whizzer-in-chief Colonel Hal Watson himself was Happy Hunter II, the second aircraft he had named after his son, Hunter. The captured aircraft was ferried from Lager-Lechfeld to Melun near Paris on June 10. Then, on June 30, ex-Messerschmitt test pilot Ludwig Hofmann was flying it to Cherbourg when it suffered engine failure, crashed and was destroyed.

FAR RIGHT: The full history of Messerschmitt Me 163B WNr. 191190, later FE-500 and then T-2-500, is unknown but it was most likely given to the Americans by the British.

BELOW: Lend-lease American-built Royal Navy aircraft carrier HMS *Reaper* was used to ferry a 'treasure trove' of captured Luftwaffe aircraft to the US two and a half months after the war's end. Some survive, many were scrapped.

The DM-1, meanwhile, was not packed into its crate for the journey to the US until November 9, 1945. It finally arrived at Boston on January 19, 1946.

It is interesting to note that for all the fanfare and acknowledgement given to the American effort in capturing German war gear, the British managed to capture more than three times as many machines and ended up giving many of them to the Americans to make up for gaps in the US 'collection' of types.

There was no British 'Watson's Whizzers' yet the British undoubtedly captured more German jets intact and Watson needed machines from America's ally to make up his numbers.

A selection of the British held machines were displayed to the public in Hyde Park from September 16-22, 1945, including a Heinkel He 162 and Messerschmitt Me 163. A larger and longer lasting exhibition was staged at RAE Farnborough from October 29 to November 9, 1945. In

addition to the other jets, this one featured a pair of Arado Ar 234s and a Messerschmitt Me 262.

Also on show were a Ta 152, Dornier Do 335, Fw 190/Ju 88 Mistel, Fi 103 V-1, Fa 330, Horten Ho IV glider and the Fw 190D-9 of Leutnant Theo Nibel, 'Black 12', mentioned in the 'January 1' section of this publication. Conventional types abounded too, including a Bü 181, Bf 108, Bf 109G, Bf 110, Me 410, Do 217, Fi 156, Fw 189, Fw 190A, Ju 52, Ju 352, Ju 88G-6, Ju 188, Ju 290A and Si 204D. There was even a flying display involving 10 of the captured types on Sunday, November 4.

ADVANCED TECHNOLOGY

Meanwhile, the Allies also sought out technical data and information both on the aircraft they had captured and on design projects still in progress when the war ended. The intelligence effort was led by the British, under the umbrella of the British Intelligence Objectives Sub-committee (BIOS)

and usually included personnel from MAP – the Ministry of Aircraft Production.

The British also worked in co-operation with their American counterparts as the Combined Intelligence Objectives Sub-committee (CIOS) and as the Field Information Agency Technical (FIAT).

Headquartered at the seemingly innocuous London address of 32 Bryanston Square, BIOS had teams travelling all over Germany, following in the wake of the Allied advance during 1945, working through a list of key 'targets' drawn up in 1944.

These were primarily sites of scientific, technical and engineering importance. High on the list were the offices, design studios and manufacturing facilities of Germany's aircraft manufacturers and their vast armies of sub-contractors.

By the time BIOS and CIOS personnel arrived at their target sites, however, they often found them already looted or sabotaged, with many important documents burned or missing. Nevertheless, they were usually able to track down the people who worked at these facilities and encourage them to revisit or reconstruct their most recent work.

For example, the investigation of airborne gun sights involved visits to Zeiss in Jena, Leitz in Wetzler, Steinheil in Munich, Görtz in Vienna and the Berlin-based facilities of Siemens, Blaupunkt, Telefunken, Lorenz and Askania. Key personnel were interviewed, made to write monologues about their work and, if necessary, taken back to Britain for further interrogation.

It is stated time and again that German technology at this time was far in advance of anything the British or Americans were working on but this proved not to be the case in many instances. The report on airborne gun sights concludes: "As regards technical development it appears that the Germans were in general behind us." Though it concedes: "The main projects of interest being the stabilised fighter armament scheme, the automatic triggering project, the television scanning and the work on infrared radiation, all of which seem worth following up."

Much valuable information was also gleaned from sites such as the Luftfahrtforschungsanstalt Hermann Göring weapons institute at Volkenrode, Brunswick – which worked on stabilisation to aid fighter gun aiming, research on automatic guns, theoretical ballistic work and fire control systems.

Interrogation of Telefunken staff in Hamburg and Berlin gave an insight into work on coaxial ceramic radio valves – the British and Americans used more problematic glass ones.

A visit to the Focke-Wulf structural research facility at Bad Eilsen yielded valuable information about stressed-skin structures for aircraft, methods of bonding metal with wood and the use of high tensile steel.

The list was long and interrogations of hundreds of German engineers, scientists and designers went on

throughout the remainder of 1945. Some ended up working for the British, some for the Americans, but in time many of those that had chosen to work for the British ended up in America due to the availability of much larger research budgets.

But as thoughts turned towards the development of new technology, particularly the development of rockets and missiles, the captured German aircraft were left to rot and most were scrapped during the two or three years that followed.

Many German aviation personnel started new lives as civilians and many pilots, such as Johannes Steinhoff, formerly of JV 44, and Erich Hartmann joined the postwar Luftwaffe in West Germany. Heinz Bär became a test pilot for sports aircraft, Hajo Herrmann became a lawyer, Galland went to Argentina and flew with the Argentine Air Force before returning to Germany to set up an aviation consultancy firm.

Similarly, Allied airmen found themselves beginning new lives beyond those dark days at the beginning of 1945 when it seemed as though the air war in Europe could only end in a welter of death and destruction. ●

ABOVE: Typical of the Watson's Whizzers aircraft, this Me 262A-1a, its only known German marking being the letter 'L', went through a series of paint jobs after being captured. Starting out in its original markings it was then painted up as 'Doris' by the 54th ADS, before being renamed 'Jabo Bait' by Messerschmitt test pilot Karl Baur. In the US, it was repainted again in plain black with its serial, T-2-110, more prominently displayed.

BELOW: One of the more unusual German aircraft captured by the Allies was the Flettner Fl 282 V23. The Fl 282 Kolibri or 'Hummingbird' was the world's first series production helicopter. After the war, its creator, Anton Flettner, went to work in the US. After his own company failed he then joined Kaman Aircraft as its chief designer.

WATSON'S WHIZZERS

Most of Colonel Watson's Me 262s were first named by the 54th ADS but then renamed by their pilots.

000 Wilma Jeanne/Happy Hunter II (Me 262A-1a/U4 WNr. 170083. Renamed by Col Watson after his son, Hunter. Hunter I had been a P-47 Watson used as a runabout)

111 Beverly Anne/Screamin' Meemie (Possibly 'White 5' JG 54. Renamed by Bill Strobell as in some thing that gives you the jitters, although his original choice was The Blowtorch)

222 Marge/Lady Jess IV (Me 262A-1a/U3. Renamed by Ken Dahlstrom)

333 Pauline/Delovely (Me 262A-1a. Renamed by Bob Anspach after the lyrics to Cole Porter's 1936 hit It's Delovely)

444 Connie the Sharp Article/Pick II (Me 262A-1a/U3 WNr. 500453, later FE-4012. Renamed by P-47 pilot Roy Brown, his first aircraft having been Pick)

555 Vera/Willie (Me 262B-1a WNr. 110639 'White 35'. Renamed in honour of Messerschmitt test pilot Ludwig Hoffmann, who worked with the Americans and earned their trust)

666 Joanne/Cookie VII (Me 262A-1a/U3 WNr. 500098. Renamed by P-47 pilot Fred Hillis. Cookie was his daughter's nickname and it was his seventh aircraft)

777 Doris/Jabo Bait (Me 262A-1a 'L', later FE-110. Renamed by Messerschmitt test pilot Karl Baur)

888 Dennis/Ginny H (Me 262A-1a WNr. 500491 'Yellow 7' of 11./JG 7, later FE-111, then T2-111. Renamed after Jim Holt's then-girlfriend)

999 Ole Fruit Cake (Me 262B-1a/U1 WNr. 110305 'Red 6' of IV./NJG 11. USA 2, later FE-610)

CAPTURED AIRCRAFT LISTS

Large numbers of German aircraft were either flown or shipped out of Europe by the British and Americans. This index is intended to serve as a guide to what was captured, rather than what ultimately became of these war prizes, since that is documented, where known, elsewhere.

GERMAN AIRCRAFT GIVEN BRITISH AIR MINISTRY NUMBERS

AM 1 – Junkers Ju 88G-6 WNr. 622983 4R+RB of NJG 2
AM 2 – Junkers Ju 88G-6 WNr. 620560 4R+CB of NJG 2
AM 3 – Junkers Ju 88G-6 WNr. 622838 3C+AN of II./NJG 4
AM 4 – Siebel Si 204D-1 WNr. 322127 BU+PP
AM 5 – Siebel Si 204D-1 WNr. 321523
AM 6 – Junkers Ju 290A-1 WNr. 110186 A3+OB of III./KG 200
AM 7 – Dornier Do 217M-9 WNr. 0040 KF+JN
AM 8 – Junkers Ju 352A-0 WNr. 100010 KT+VJ also VP550
AM 9 – Junkers Ju 88G-6 WNr. 621965 4R+DR of III./NJG 2
AM 10 – Focke-Wulf Fw190A-6/R6 WNr. 550214 PN+LU of III./NJG 11
AM 11 – Focke-Wulf Ta 152H-1 WNr. 150004 6+ of JG 301
Second AM 11 – Focke-Wulf Ta 152H-1 WNr. 150168 9+ of Stab/JG 301
AM 12 – Siebel Si 204D-3 WNr. 351547
AM 13 – Siebel Si 204D-1 WNr. 251922
AM 14 – Junkers Ju 88G-6 WNr. 620788 C9+AA of NJG 5
AM 15 – Messerschmitt Bf 110G-4/R8 WNr. 180560 3C+BA of NJG 4
AM 16 – Junkers Ju 88G-6 WNr. 622311 3C+DA of NJG 4
AM 17 – Arado Ar 232B-0 WNr. 305002 A3+RB of III./KG 200
AM 18 – Junkers Ju 352A-1 WNr. 100015 G6+WX of V./TG 4
AM 19 – Junkers Ju 252A WNr. unknown G6+YX of V./TG 4
AM 20 – Heinkel He 219A-3 WNr. 290126 D5+BL of I./NJG 3
AM 21 – Heinkel He 219A-2 WNr. 310109
AM 22 – Heinkel He 219A-5/R2 WNr. 310108 D5+CL of I./NJG 3
AM 23 – Heinkel He 219A WNr. 310200 D5+DL of I./NJG 3
AM 24 – Arado Ar 234B-2 WNr. 140466 8H+HH of AufklGr.33
AM 25 – Arado Ar 234B WNr. 140608 T9+GL of 3./Versuchsverband.d.OKL – also coded VK880
AM 26 – Arado Ar 234B-1 WNr. 140476 8H+DH of AufklGr.33
AM 27 – Focke-Wulf Fw 189A-3 WNr. 0173 3X+AA
AM 28 – Siebel Si 204D-1 WNr. 221558 BJ+90
AM 29 – Focke-Wulf Fw 190F-8/U1 WNr. 584219 'Black 38'
AM 30 – Messerschmitt Bf 110G-4/R3 WNr. 730037 D5+DK of I./NJG 3
AM 31 – Junkers Ju 88G-6 WNr. 623193 C9+HB of NJG 5
AM 32 – Junkers Ju 88G-6 WNr. 622960 +VH
AM 33 – Junkers Ju 88G-6 WNr. 622186
AM 34 – Messerschmitt Bf 110G-4/R6 WNr. 730301 D5+RL of I./NJG 3
AM 35 – Junkers Ju 188D-2 WNr. 150245 shipped to the US and became FE-1597/T2-1597
AM 36 – Focke-Wulf Fw 190F-8/U1 WNr. 580058 '55'
AM 37 – Focke-Wulf Fw 190S-1 WNr. 582044 '54'
AM 38 – Messerschmitt Bf 110G-4/R8 WNr. 180551 D5+DM of II./NJG 3
AM 39 – Messerschmitt Me 410A-1/U2 WNr. 420439
AM 40 – Focke-Wulf Fw 190F-8/U1 WNr. 580392 '51'
AM 41 – Junkers Ju 88G-6 WNr. 622054 7J+OV of NJG 102
Second AM 41 – Junkers Ju 88G-6 WNr. 622461 7J+CV of NJG 102
AM 42 – Siebel Si 204D-1 WNr. 251147 7J+XL of NJG 102
AM 43 – Heinkel He 219A-2 WNr. unknown
AM 44 – Heinkel He 219A-2 WNr. 310106
AM 45 – Junkers Ju 388L-1 WNr. 180485
AM 46 – Siebel Si 204D-1 WNr. unknown
AM 47 – Junkers Ju 88G-6 WNr. 620968
AM 48 – Junkers Ju 88G-6 WNr. 622811 3C+MN of II./NJG 4
AM 49 – Siebel Si 204D-1 WNr. 251104 D5+OM of II./NJG 3
AM 50 – Messerschmitt Me 262B-1a/U1 WNr. 110305 'Red 8' of IV./NJG 11
AM 51 – Messerschmitt Me 262A-2a WNr. 112372 'Yellow 7' of I./JG 7
AM 52 – Messerschmitt Me 262A-2a WNr. 500210 'Yellow 17' of I./JG 7
AM 53 – Bücker Bü 180 WNr. unknown
AM 54 – Arado Ar 234B WNr. 140113 F1+AA of KG 76
AM 55 – Siebel Si 204D-1 WNr. 321288
AM 56 – Siebel Si 204D WNr. 251190
AM 57 – Junkers Ju 290A-2 WNr. 110157 9V+BK of 2./***r.5
AM 58 – Heinkel He 162A-2 WNr. 120221 of JG 1
AM 59 – Heinkel He 162A-2 WNr. 120076 'Yellow 4' of JG 1
AM 60 – Heinkel He 162A-2 WNr. 120074 'White 11' of JG 1
AM 61 – Heinkel He 162A-2 WNr. 120072 of JG 1
AM 62 – Heinkel He 162A-2 WNr. 120086 of JG 1
AM 63 – Heinkel He 162A-2 WNr. 120095 of JG 1
AM 64 – Heinkel He 162A-2 WNr. 120097 of JG 1
AM 65 – Heinkel He 162A-2 WNr. 120227 of JG 1
AM 66 – Heinkel He 162A-2 WNr. 120091 of JG 1
AM 67 – Heinkel He 162A-2 WNr. 120098 of JG 1
AM 68 – Heinkel He 162A-2 WNr. unknown of JG 1
AM 69 – Blohm & Voss Bv 138 WNr. unknown
AM 70 – Blohm & Voss Bv 138C-1 WNr. 0310081 of FA 125
AM S-2 – Blohm & Voss Bv 138B-1 WNr. unknown
AM 71 – Blohm & Voss Bv 138 WNr. unknown
AM 72 – Messerschmitt Me 410A-1/U2 WNr. 420430
AM 73 – Messerschmitt Me 410A-1 WNr. 130360
AM 74 – Messerschmitt Me 410B-6 WNr. 410208
AM 75 – Junkers Ju 88H-1 WNr. unknown/Focke-Wulf Fw 190A-8/R6 WNr. 733682 Mistel S 3B of IV./KG 200
AM 76 – Junkers Ju 88H-1/Focke-Wulf Fw 190A-8 Mistel S 3B of IV./KG 200
AM 77 – Junkers Ju 88 WNr. 2492/Focke-Wulf Fw 190A WNr. 733759 Mistel S 3A of IV./KG 200
AM 78 – Unknown
AM 79 – Messerschmitt Me 262A WNr. unknown
AM 80 – Messerschmitt Me 262A-1 WNr. 111690 'White 5' of I./JG 7

AM 81 – Messerschmitt Me 262A-2a WNr. 500200 9K+XK 'Black X' of II./KG 51
AM 82 – Junkers Ju 86P WNr. 5132 T5+PM of Aufkl.Gr.100
AM 83 – Junkers Ju 388L-1/V6 WNr. 500006 PE+IF
AM 84 – Messerschmitt Bf 108B WNr. 1547 GJ+AU
AM 85 – Messerschmitt Bf 110G-5/R1 WNr. 420031
AM 86 – Messerschmitt Bf 110G WNr. unknown
AM 87 – Messerschmitt Bf 108D-1 WNr. 3059 VE+LI
AM 88 – Messerschmitt Bf 110 WNr. unknown
AM 89 – Messerschmitt Bf 108B-1 WNr. unknown
AM 90 – Arado Ar 196A WNr. unknown
AM 91 – Arado Ar 196A-5 WNr. 127
AM 92 – Arado Ar 196A-5 WNr. 514
AM 93 – Arado Ar 199 WNr. unknown
AM 94 – Focke-Wulf Fw 200C-4/U1 WNr. 176 Himmler's personal aircraft GC+AE
AM 95 – Focke-Wulf Fw 200C WNr. unknown possibly Fw 200C-4/U1, WNr. 0240 TK+CV Hitler's personal transport
AM 96 – Focke-Wulf Fw 200C WNr. 0111
AM 97 – Focke-Wulf Fw 200C WNr. 0181 GC+SJ
AM 98 – Unknown
AM 99 – Fieseler Fi 156C-7 WNr. 475099 VD+TD
AM 100 – Fieseler Fi 156C WNr. 2008 CV+KB
AM 101 – Fieseler Fi 156C-7 WNr. 475081 RR+KE
AM 102 – Junkers Ju 52/3m WNr. 6840
AM 103 – Junkers Ju 52/3m WNr. 6567
AM 104 – Junkers Ju 52/3m WNr. 641038
AM 105 – Dornier Do 217M WNr. unknown
AM 106 – Dornier Do 217M-1 WNr. 56527 U5+HK of I./KG 2
AM 107 – Dornier Do 217M-1 WNr. 56158 U5+?? of KG 2
AM 108 – Junkers Ju 188A-1 WNr. 230776
AM 109 – Junkers Ju 352A WNr. unknown G6+RX of V./TG4
AM 110 – Junkers Ju 352A WNr. unknown G6+SX of V./TG4
AM 111 – Focke-Wulf Fw 190F-8/R15 WNr. unknown
AM 112 – Junkers Ju 88A-6/U WNr. 0660 1H+MN of II./KG 26
AM 113 – Junkers Ju 188A-2 WNr. 190327 1H+GT of III./KG 26
AM 114 – Dornier Do 24T WNr. 1135 of SNG 81
AM 115 – Dornier Do 24T-3 WNr. unknown of KG 200
AM 116 – Dornier Do 24T WNr. 3435 VH+JM of SNG 81
AM 117 – Focke-Wulf Fw 58C-2/U6 WNr. 2093 TE+BK of Ekdo.40
AM 118 – Unknown
AM 119 – Siebel Si 104A WNr. unknown
AM 120 – Arado Ar 96B WNr. unknown
AM 121 – Bücker Bü 181 WNr. unknown
AM 122 – Bücker Bü 181C-3 WNr. 120417
AM 123 – Arado Ar 96B WNr. unknown
AM 124 – Messerschmitt Bf 108 WNr. unknown
AM GD1 – Junkers Ju 52/3m WNr. 5375
AM GD – Siebel Si 204D WNr. unknown
AM 200 – Messerschmitt Me 163B WNr. 191329of JG 400
AM 201 – Messerschmitt Me 163B WNr. 191330 of JG 400
AM 202 – Messerschmitt Me 163B WNr. 191915 of JG 400
AM 203 – Messerschmitt Me 163B WNr. 310061 'Yellow 13' of JG 400
AM 204 – Messerschmitt Me 163B WNr. 191454 'Yellow 11' of JG 400
AM 205 – Messerschmitt Me 163B WNr. 191905 of JG 400
AM 206 – Messerschmitt Me 163B WNr. 191902 of JG 400
AM 207 – Messerschmitt Me 163B WNr. 191461 of JG 400
AM 208 – Messerschmitt Me 163B WNr. 191912 of JG 400
AM 209 – Messerschmitt Me 163B WNr. 191315 of JG 400
AM 210 – Messerschmitt Me 163B WNr. 191316 'Yellow 6' of JG 400
AM 211 – Messerschmitt Me 163B WNr. 191095 of JG 400
AM 212 – Messerschmitt Me 163B WNr. 191965 of JG 400
AM 213 – Messerschmitt Me 163B WNr. 191954 of JG 400
AM 214 – Messerschmitt Me 163B WNr. 191660 of JG 400
AM 215 – Messerschmitt Me 163B WNr. 191659 'Yellow 15' of JG 400
AM 216 – Messerschmitt Me 163B WNr. 191309 of JG400 - fate unrecorded
AM 217 – Messerschmitt Me 163B WNr. 191917 of JG400 - fate unrecorded
AM 218 – Messerschmitt Me 163B WNr. 191654
AM 219 – Messerschmitt Me 163B WNr. 191904 '25' of JG 400
AM 220 – Messerschmitt Me 163B WNr. 191914? of JG 400
AM 221 – Messerschmitt Me 163B WNr. 191961 of JG 400
AM 222 – Messerschmitt Me 163B WNr. 191907 of JG 400
AM 223 – Dornier Do 335A-12 WNr. 240112
AM 225 – Dornier Do 335A-1 WNr. unknown
AM 226 – Arado Ar 234B WNr. 140336 of II./KG 76
AM 227 to AM 229 – Arado Ar 234s but AM numbers to WNr. unknown
AM ??? – Arado Ar 234B WNr. 140141 of 1(F)/Aufkl.Gr.123
AM ??? – Arado Ar 234B WNr. 140493 of 1./***r.1
AM ??? – Arado Ar 234B WNr. 140581 of 1(F)/Aufkl.Gr.123
AM 229 – Messerschmitt Bf 109G-14 WNr. 413601 'Black 7'
AM 230 – Focke-Wulf Fw 190A-8D/NL WNr. 171747 '13'
AM 231 – Junkers Ju 88G-1 WNr. 712273 4R+UR of III./NJG 2
AM 232 – Unknown
AM 233 – Focke-Achgelis Fa 223E WNr. V14 DM+SR

GERMAN AIRCRAFT CAPTURED BY THE BRITISH BUT SET ASIDE FOR THE AMERICANS

USA 1 – Messerschmitt Me 262A WNr. 500443 'Yellow 5'
USA 2 – Messerschmitt Me 262B-1a/U1 WNr. 110306 'Red 6' of IV./NJG 11 allocated FE-610
USA 3 – Messerschmitt Me 262B-1b WNr. 110165 allocated BuNo. 121441
USA 4 – Messerschmitt Me 262B-1/U1 WNr. 110635 'Red 10' of IV./NJG 11
USA 5 – Arado Ar 234B WNr. 140489 allocated either FE-202 or FE-303
USA 6 – Arado Ar 234B WNr. unknown
USA 7 – Arado Ar 234B WNr. unknown
USA 8 – Heinkel He 219A-0 WNr. 210903 SP+CR allocated FE-612
USA 9 – Heinkel He 219A-2 WNr. 290060 CS+QG allocated FE-613
USA 10 – Heinkel He 219A WNr. 290202 allocated FE-614
USA 11 – Focke-Wulf Ta 152H-0 WNr. 150003 allocated FE-112
USA 12 – Focke-Wulf Fw 190D-9 WNr. unknown allocated either FE-119 or FE-120
USA 13 – Focke-Wulf Fw 190D-9 WNr. 401392 'Black 5' of JG 26 allocated FE-121
USA 14 – Focke-Wulf Fw 190D-13 WNr. 836017 'Yellow 10' of JG 26 allocated FE-118
USA 15 – Focke-Wulf Fw 190D-9 WNr. 500618 allocated either FE-119 or FE-120
USA 16, USA 17, USA 18, USA 19 – possibly allocated to Me410s
USA 20 – Unknown
USA 21 – Junkers Ju 88G-6 WNr. unknown allocated FE-611
USA 022 – Junkers Ju 290A-4 WNr. 110196 PI+PS allocated FE-3400
USA 23 to USA 39 – untraced
USA 40 – Arado Ar 234B-2 WNr. 140311 of II./KG 76 allocated FE-1011
USA 41 to USA 49 – Unknown
USA 50 – Arado Ar 234B-2 WNr. 140312 of II./KG 76 allocated FE-1010

AIRCRAFT GIVEN FOREIGN EQUIPMENT NUMBERS BY THE AMERICANS

FE-107 – see FE 711
FE-110 – Messerschmitt Me 262A-1a 'L' WNr. unknown
FE-111 – Messerschmitt Me 262A-1a WNr. 500491 'Yellow 7' of 11./JG 7
FE-112 – Focke-Wulf Ta 152H WNr. 110003 of JG 301
FE-113, FE-114, FE-115 – All apparently Fw 190As
FE-116 – Focke-Wulf Fw 190F-8 WNr. unknown
FE-117 – Focke-Wulf Fw 190F-8/R1 WNr. 931884 'Yellow 10'
FE-118 – Focke-Wulf Fw 190D-13 WNr. 836017 'Yellow 10' of 3./JG 26
FE-119 – Focke-Wulf Fw 190D-9 WNr. 210010 'White 14' 5./JG 26
FE-120 – Focke-Wulf Fw 190D-9 WNr. 601088 of IV./JG 3
FE-121 – Focke-Wulf Fw 190D-9 WNr. 401392 'White 5-+-' of JG 26
FE-122 – Messerschmitt Me 109G-10/U4 WNr. 611943 'Yellow 13'
FE-123 – Messerschmitt Me 109G-10 '7' WNr. unknown
FE-124 – Messerschmitt Me 109G-10/U4 WNr. unknown
FE-489 – Heinkel He 162A WNr. 120077, 'Red 1' of 2./JG 1
FE-490 – Horten Ho 229 V3 WNr. unknown
FE-494 – Heinkel He 162A WNr. 120017, 'Yellow 6' of 3./JG 1
FE-495 – Messerschmitt Me 163B WNr. unknown
FE-496 – Messerschmitt Me 109G-6 WNr. unknown
FE-499 – Messerschmitt Me 410A-3 WNr. 018 F6+WK of 2.(F)/FAG 122
FE-500 – Messerschmitt Me 163B WNr. 191190
FE-501, -502, -503 – Messerschmitt Me 163Bs
FE-504 Heinkel He 162A WNr. 120230 'White 23' of 1./JG 1
FE-505 Blohm & Voss Bv 155B V3 WNr. unknown
FE-610 Messerschmitt Me 262B-1a/U1 WNr. 110306 'Red 6' of 10./NJG 11
FE-611 Junkers Ju 88G possibly W7+IH of 1./NJG 100
FE-612 Heinkel He 219A-2 WNr. unknown
FE-613 Heinkel He 219A-7 WNr. 290060
FE-614 Heinkel He 219A WNr. unknown
FE-711 Messerschmitt Me 262A WNr. 111711
FE-1010 Arado Ar 234B WNr. 140312 of KG 76
FE-1011 Bachem Ba 349B-1 WNr. unknown
FE-1012 Dornier Do 335 WNr. unknown
FE-1597 Junkers Ju 188 possibly WNr. 150245, British serial AM 35
FE-1598 Junkers Ju 88D-1/Trop WNr. 430650 British serial HK959
FE-1599 Junkers Ju 88A WNr. unknown
FE-1600 Heinkel He 111H-16 WNr. 8433 +DC
FE-2000 Dornier Do 217 WNr. unknown
FE-2100 Heinkel He 177A-7 WNr. unknown of KG 40
FE-2600 Schneider Grunau Baby LZNC
FE-2700 Gotha Go 242B-1 WNr. unknown
FE-3400 Junkers Ju 290A-7 WNr. 196, PJ+PS
FE-4010 Junkers Ju 388L-1 WNr. 560049
FE-4012 Messerschmitt Me 262A-1a/U3 'White 25' WNr. unknown
FE-4600 Henschel Hs 129B WNr. unknown
FE-4610 Messerschmitt Me 108B WNr. 8378
FE-4611 Bücker Bü 181 WNr. unknown
FE-4612 Bücker Bü 131 WNr. unknown
FE-4613 Flettner Fl 282 V23 Possibly CI+TW WNr. unknown
FE-4614 Flettner Fl 282 WNr. 28368
FE-4615 Doblhoff/WNF 342 V4 WNr. unknown
FE-4617 Focke-Achgelis Fa 330 WNr. unknown
FE-4618 Focke-Achgelis Fa 330 WNr. unknown
FE-? He 162A WNr. 120067 'White 7' 1./JG 1
FE-? Me 163B WNr. 191301
FE-? Messerschmitt P.1101 V1 WNr. unknown
FE-? Lippisch DM-1 WNr. unknown